Polarized Cities

Portraits of Rich and Poor in Urban China

Edited by
Dorothy J. Solinger
University of California, Irvine

ROWMAN & LITTLEFIELD
Lanham • Boulder • New York • London

Published by Rowman & Littlefield
An imprint of The Rowman & Littlefield Publishing Group, Inc.
4501 Forbes Boulevard, Suite 200, Lanham, Maryland 20706
https://rowman.com

Unit A, Whitacre Mews, 26-34 Stannary Street, London SE11 4AB,
United Kingdom

British Library Cataloguing in Publication Information Available

Library of Congress Cataloging-in-Publication Data
Names: Solinger, Dorothy J., editor.
Title: Polarized cities : portraits of rich and poor in urban China / edited by Dorothy J. Solinger, University of California, Irvine.
Description: Lanham : Rowman & Littlefield, [2018] | Includes bibliographical references and index.
Identifiers: LCCN 2018016765 (print) | LCCN 2018032253 (ebook) | ISBN 9781538116494 (electronic) | ISBN 9781538116470 (cloth : alk. paper) | ISBN 9781538116487 (pbk. : alk. paper)
Subjects: LCSH: Urban poor—China. | Poverty—China. | Rich people—China. | Wealth—China. | Social classes—China.
Classification: LCC HV4150.A5 (ebook) | LCC HV4150.A5 P65 2018 (print) | DDC 305.5/2340951091732—dc23
LC record available at https://lccn.loc.gov/2018016765

™ The paper used in this publication meets the minimum requirements of American National Standard for Information Sciences Permanence of Paper for Printed Library Materials, ANSI/NISO Z39.48-1992.

Printed in the United States of America

Contents

Acknowledgments

The papers by Goldstein, Osburg, Solinger, Wang, and Zhang were originally presented at a workshop held at the University of California, Irvine under the auspices of the UC Irvine John S. and Marilyn Long US-China Institute on May 13, 2016. Entitled "Poor China, Rich China: Poverty, Wealth and Inequality," the symposium included several other papers dealing with the rural areas. In the end we judged that those on the cities constituted the most coherent package.

We extend much gratitude to Professor Benjamin Van Rooij, then of the University of California Irvine School of Law and Director of the Long Institute, for suggesting that we convene this meeting. We are also so grateful to John Long for his very generous financial support that made this meeting possible and for his constant engagement. Members of the audience should be thanked as well, since their enthusiasm that day helped us decide to move forward to recrafting those pieces, and soliciting other ones, in order to compile a volume.

Throughout the process of creating this book, from its very first days, Susan McEachern at Rowman & Littlefield was encouraging, cooperative, and uniformly helpful. As the editor, I especially appreciated her detailed attention to every kind of matter connected to producing this study. With her assistant, Katelyn Turner, we always received most efficient and informed assistance with each aspect of the entire work. Jehanne Schweitzer also contributed advice and facilitated the final stages of the operation. It was truly a pleasure to work with all of these people.

Dorothy J. Solinger
Irvine, CA

Introduction

State Policies, Castes, and Agency

Dorothy J. Solinger

Two new castes have emerged in China in the wake of the nation's urban economic reforms, one super-wealthy and the other abjectly indigent. As Martin Whyte expressed the situation, "The rising incomes of the nouveaux riches have resulted in very conspicuous consumption . . . The gaps between the rich and the poor are not only much larger today but strikingly visible."[1] Meanwhile, according to two researchers who have written on the Minimum Livelihood Guarantee (*zuidi shenghua baozhang*, *dibao* for short), the government's program for the urban-registered destitute, "The *dibao* merely prevents recipients from starving."[2]

Much has been made in both the academic literature and in the press—whether foreign or in China—of the rise in incomes in the country, across the board, over almost forty years of spectacular economic growth, along with an accompanying social transformation. The media has also showered attention on an emerging and expanding middle class. But, counterintuitively, in this era of rapid economic rise, it is not just the nouveaux riches, among whom billionaires multiply monthly,[3] or the members of the mushrooming middle class who now populate the municipalities. The poverty-stricken, if often hidden around the edges of the cities, are also present.[4]

These several collectivities—wealthy, middle class, and indigent—it could be argued, have each become inbred, nearly as if they were members of distinct lineages. In the earlier phases of the reform process, there was a window for significant upward social mobility, and the middle class does continue to expand. But the fact still stands that both the very poor and the ultra-prosperous are increasingly members of caste-like formations, closed social structures from which exit is prohibitive for the former, and entry into the latter of which is unlikely for those outside it, as this volume will detail.[5]

Along with these bounded structures a hierarchy of *agency* has emerged in Chinese cities. Here I imagine a pyramid of progressively wealthier people who, compared to those less and less endowed with resources as that pyramid widens below, have increasingly more power over their lives as their riches expand (as one moves up the structure). In the terminology of Anthony Giddens, "agency" refers to "be[ing] able to deploy (chronically, in the flow of daily life) a range of causal powers."[6] I use this notion of variable ranges in agency (or of differential degrees of command over one's life) to represent the great discrepancies in room for choice and maneuver among those in these two castes in today's Chinese cities, respectively.

How can this bifurcation (and this remarkable coproduction of flashy affluence and dire penury) be accounted for, even as China's extraordinary productivity and profits fill the news? In this introduction, I will argue that it has been state policies and their consequences that are the culprit,[7] even if this outcome has not necessarily been intentional on the part of state leaders. Accordingly, I review here the many ways in which a range of state strategies and decisions over four decades has contributed to this effect.

In what follows I first offer an explanation for my adoption of the concept of "caste"; then I take a look at the role of the state in forging this framework. Finally, I fit the book's chapters into this interpretative model.

CASTE IN CONTEMPORARY CHINESE CITIES

There are a multitude of definitions for the term "caste," and scholars disagree even about its most critical features.[8] But commentators do concur that its boundaries are fixed and set by endogamy (marriage within a given social unit), coresidence, and kinship.[9] In India, where caste is pervasive, there are rigid barriers against mobility out of the caste of one's birth;[10] in the words of Ekta Singh, "Ascriptive rather than achieved characteristics are the basis of exclusion . . . [these characteristics] are not amenable to alteration as a consequence of individual agency."[11] So, admittedly, core components of the caste system in its pure form are incompatible with the room for agency or movement that I see in the groupings featured in this book.

Other characteristics of castes would also appear to frustrate an effort to compare them to China's urban wealthy and poor: for one, they situate their members hierarchically into *occupationally and ritually ranked* groupings, which is not the case in China. Additionally, unlike Chinese social formations, castes are primarily distinguished by religiously based notions of purity and pollution, with those at the bottom being subject to violence, social ostracism, and economic penalties, none of which typically befall China's indigent in the cities.[12]

And yet, in a number of critical ways, what the Chinese state has wrought *does* amount to a caste system of sorts. This is so perhaps above all in the unshakeable power and wealth that mark those at the pinnacle of the social pyramid in both countries.[13] But the analogy applies best with regard to the lowliest in the two societies. For members of the Dalit (or "untouchable") community[14] are "hidden" and "forgotten," "shunned from society," and face "widespread discrimination,"[15] much like the recipients of the Minimum Livelihood Guarantee (*dibaohu*), those urban-registered city residents assessed as sufficiently below the poverty line to qualify for a monthly compensatory allowance. Indeed, many who are in severe need eschew applying for the grant precisely because of the shame they would feel in living on it. These humbled subjects, like Dalits, bear a social identity that matches the societal neglect and disparagement their Indian counterparts also receive.

Such social rejection (as well as approbation for the occupants of the highest rungs) is justified officially in both societies. The position of both conglomerations is legitimated in China with reference to "reform," the country's quest for "modernity" and its glorious future generally, of which the poor are not to be a part (as spelled out in chapter 3).[16] Instead, in the words of Chinese past-president Jiang Zemin, it is especially those with "advanced culture" and those managing "advanced productive forces" who can make a valuable contribution to the nation. And as a laid-off worker, perhaps convinced by the state's propaganda, is quoted as having said: "Our generation is just the sacrificial victims of reform and opening! The leaders said so."[17] In India, contrastingly, justification occurs as well, but it is Hindu religious doctrine and accompanying indoctrination that validate distinction.[18]

And while in India those viewed and treated as belonging at the base are forbidden to marry outside their station,[19] surely in China no one capable of self-support would want his or her child to wed a *dibao* dependent. It is true that Indian "untouchables" have formally been denied proper education.[20] But the inferior neighborhood schools to which the impoverished children in urban China are assigned by the state and the costs of school fees, tutors, trips, uniforms, computer use, and senior high school may not forbid but surely undercut opportunity for learning by the poor.

Another issue is employment: in both countries the job market is fixed. In India this occurs by custom and sanction; in China exclusion happens on the basis of education, skill, ageism, social background, and money. Dalits are explicitly forbidden from taking positions that could entail any physical contact with their social betters, and also are explicitly appointed to such menial posts as cleaning toilets and collecting garbage (jobs which are, interestingly, also allocated to *dibaohu*). And for those at the bottom in both countries there is great difficulty acquiring a steady income and also much involuntary unemployment. In both places, personal connections make much difference, whether for those of means who possess them or for those with none.[21] How, exactly, has this sort of structure come about in China in recent decades?

THE STATE'S CONSTRUCTION OF SOCIAL DISPARITY

Conventionally commentators have pointed to *markets* and market reforms as the origin of change. The truth, though, is that the program that set the process of social polarization into gear was in fact the leadership's move to modernize the economy in late 1978. Politicians aimed to do so by providing firms and farmers with incentives to produce more, and by gradually diminishing state planning (which, over time, did lead to the emergence of markets). Thus markets can be conceived as a proximate (but not a fundamental) root of the nation's subsequent developmental social trajectory.

It was this initial project of top politicians to revamp the economy so it squarely faced modernization (and not a choice for markets per se) that led on to an unfolding of political and social reversals. And these events, ultimately, spawned this split-at-the-extremities in what was once a relatively equal society. To illustrate: China's billionaires as of 2015 held $1.4 trillion in known net worth,[22] close to the gross domestic product of all of Australia.[23] At the same time, according to one account, the number of individuals with a net worth over 10 million yuan has been increasing yearly. But as of the mid-2010s the number of such individuals amounted to under 0.1 percent of the total population.[24] At the other end, just in the cities alone, roughly twenty million residents who are legally urbanites are known officially to live below their cities' poverty lines; uncounted others exist as well.

This volume presents five cases that represent these two urban Chinese castes. It begins with a chapter that sets up the sociological background in which these caste-like formations exist and an ethnographic chapter that contrasts the lifestyles of the social segments at each end of China's urban polarization. Here I preface these analyses and portraits by pointing to specific state policies that produced this extreme divergence in incomes. I then review a number of recent studies, both quantitative and qualitative, to account for my use of the concept of "caste." Finally, I summarize the ways in which each chapter presents its picture of polarization. As I do so, I will use the studies to defend my image of a hierarchy of "agency."

In the early 1980s, when chief strategist and top leader Deng Xiaoping took over the helm of state from Mao-appointed Hua Guofeng he allegedly publicized an aphorism allowing—or even encouraging—"some [to] get rich first." This maxim served to glorify the pursuit of wealth for those positioned to participate in it.[25] In so announcing, Deng legitimized at the popular level practices that had been anathema, even criminal, for nearly three decades under Mao Zedong and his followers.

In addition to that adage, there was another origin of the plunge from the early 1980s onward into profit-seeking in the commercial and industrial sectors. This was the Communist Party Politburo members' consensual assessment that the economy was seriously stagnating, and they attributed this outcome to two sets of factors. The first of these were the longer-term rigidities that were part and parcel of the state planning system borrowed from the Soviet Union; the obsolete machinery long used in that system contributed mightily, too. And second were the more recent assaults the economy had endured in the destruction, the battles, and the work stoppages of the just-concluded Cultural Revolution.[26]

These problems became starkly salient as the country began, at Deng's and his colleagues' instigation, to engage with the world economy and its threatening force of competition. Though this involvement had begun, if hesitantly, in the early 1970s, it took on growing intensity as the years passed. Another crucial factor was the Communist Party's urgent need to justify its rule among a populace that had sustained a yearning for commodities for decades. As I noted many years ago:

> Politicians taking stock of the state of the national economy in early 1979 identified two separate strands of the crisis it faced. One of these was new: the recently greatly intensified "opening to the world" which China had launched in 1978 posed novel challenges, both developmental and budgetary. The other one was older: a systemic crisis that could be traced back to the installation of the Soviet-style growth model in the 1950s, combined with troubles from the ten-year Cultural Revolution, which exaggerated features of that Soviet model . . . a backward and imbalanced industrial structure.[27]

As noted above, the decisions the leadership initially made were not meant specifically to induce market practices. They were aimed instead at less abstract, totalistic goals. First, they sought to shift the weight of state investment from heavy to light industry (that is, from big machinery, chemicals, metals, and the like to items of daily use) in order to meet domestic consumers' desires and the world market's demands. The second objective was to stimulate the output in industrial firms. The political elite understood that by allowing enterprises to retain a small portion of their earnings, and by permitting them to take responsibility for their own profits and losses, productivity would increase.

In agriculture, too, it was not really an adoption of markets that spurred reforms. Rather, local cadres, in conjunction with daring peasants, of their own volition returned to practices authorized by the Party nearly twenty years earlier but which the leadership had then soon afterward rescinded. The critical behavior, now authorized, was to contract production quotas to teams instead of to their higher-level commune brigades (though some farmers in desperate straits stealthily contracted directly to households).[28] In both cases—in industry and in agriculture—the idea was to incentivize and thereby enhance production. Firms were empowered to sell surpluses above their quotas and rural market fairs were sanctioned for the first time since the early 1960s, all in the interest of improving economic achievement.

As the 1980s wore on, however, bit by bit these steps did lead to markets. A critical mechanism in this process was "dual-track pricing." This mechanism encouraged officials who managed scarce resources and goods to use market prices to sell items in short supply even as state-plan-dictated prices remained in effect for business with those without this power.[29] By the late 1980s, farmers, along with enterprise managers, were willy-nilly deeply involved in markets and "collectively" (not state-owned) firms were proliferating. These developments happened more or less spontaneously, outside of specific official orders.

It was not until 1992 that central-level political elites were prepared to endorse the notion of a "socialist market economy," thus signaling their rhetorical support for the markets that had already appeared in practice. By then, the number of "collective" firms operating outside the rules of the state-led economy (that is, they were free to dispense with allocating benefits to their workers and tended to set low wages, not dictated by the state) mounted[30] while more and more foreign-invested companies also entered the country (many of which also treated employees in accordance with rules of their own[31]). Old state-sectoral factories suffered perilously in the ensuing competition. And it became ever-more apparent that state planning could not keep up with markets; it also seemed that continuing to order state enterprises to dispense welfare to their staff and workers was putting them at a comparative disadvantage.

Quantitative Studies of the Impact of State Policies

In response, state policies were eventually rewritten to let state enterprises better match up with their competitors. Welfare outlays gradually fell away as net subsidies and transfers to state-affiliated workers declined from 39 percent of a worker's income in 1988 to only 11 percent by 1995.[32] Meanwhile, the free education and medical care of the state planning days gradually disappeared for state workers. Even the advent of medical insurance did not afford much solace, as the premiums could surpass the ability of the new poor to pay.[33] Besides, beginning in the early 1980s and continuing throughout the 1990s, China's leaders edged the nation further and further into global markets, especially in preparation for acceptance and entry into the World Trade Organization. This process entailed drastically lowering tariffs, adding yet one more dimension to the problems that the inferior goods manufactured in state factories faced in domestic markets. So not only did internal competition become considerably more severe but there was now, for the first time, a need to attract foreign buyers and external investment.[34]

Property rights reform got underway in the early 1990s with experiments with the share-holding system,[35] yet another governmental decision to stir up incentives to generate superior output. But as Wu and Huang assert, despite the rapid economic growth of these years stimulated by economic reforms, such success spawned not only great wealth but also new poverty.[36] Finally in the fall of 1997, the Fifteenth Congress of the Communist Party announced that factories must "cut their personnel [to] raise their efficiency" (*jianyuan zengxiao*), a momentous decision that set untold numbers of layoffs into motion.

Other changes in the domestic political economy spurred inequality as well. Privatization of housing assets and educational-cost-cutting reforms were two of these. Another, fundamental issue that underlay many of the other transformations was officials' ability to play off the power, access to resources, and inclusion in networks with businesspeople they had acquired over many years.[37] Such partnerships sped up the emergence of the highly moneyed and the very poor, two castes whose presence in the cities had already become evident by the late 1990s. All of these changes were the product of state policies (as highlighted in chapter 1).

By the latter part of the 1990s, China's acceptance into the World Trade Organization (for which it had applied more than a decade earlier) seemed soon to be on the horizon. This prospect appeared to spell the denouement of central policymakers' long-standing coddling of loss-making enterprises. It presaged a huge-scale prod to such plants to throw off their less-productive workers and led local officials to push these firms toward bankruptcies, shutdowns, mergers, and takeovers. These various measures ultimately supplied the fuel that propelled a spree of bloodletting; according to at least one source, some sixty million workers who had been employed in state and collective firms were dismissed almost at one shot.[38]

Even though inequality had been mounting in the country before this showdown,[39] the huge number of layoffs had momentous consequences for the emergence of extremes in urban riches and destitution. On the one hand, enterprise sellouts and purchases and the privatization of housing, both at the heart of the property rights reforms, made it possible for officials and managers to gain excessive wealth through the sale of assets. At the same time, entrepreneurs collected rents and—heavily dependent on political figures for capital, credit, favorable policies, and connections—handed over bribes on an extensive scale. Surveying the period from 2002 to 2007, economists found that asset ownership had by then become the number-one factor responsible for inequality.[40]

On the other hand, many analysts concur that the massive unemployment that arose in the aftermath of the 1997 Party Congress was the most potent cause of a new form of poverty that quickly manifested.[41] Even before 1997, as joblessness rose, poverty had already accelerated and deepened: in the seven years leading up to 1995, the most grinding level of poverty in the cities increased as a percentage of the urban population by more than 145 percent over what it had been in 1988.[42]

Meng Xin has shown that in the short period from 1995 to 1999, China's unemployment rate rose from 8 to 17 percent. She concluded that, by 1999, "The most important factor in income inequality" had become "economic restructuring," as those in the lowest 5th percentile in income distribution fell victim to further income reduction while those at the top enjoyed significant income gains.[43] Similarly, Jinjun Xue and Wei Zhong found that in 1999 the poverty rate was 13.2 percent for families in which at least one member was jobless versus just 2.8 percent in families where everyone was employed.[44]

Shi Li also reported a 56 percent decrease in a worker's income if the person lost his or her job compared with that individual's income before losing the job.[45] An additional aggravating factor was that, with the collapse of the low-grade manufacturing sector, a disabled person or a person in poor health had a 74 percent higher probability of falling into poverty than a healthy person did as of the early 2000s. And yet even those quite capable of laboring were also unable to find stable work.[46]

In short, scholars concur that it was first the state's ultimatum on forced unemployment and later government-generated shifts in asset ownership (including housing) that were the root causes of enormous income shifts and accompanying surges in poverty and wealth. There is also agreement that both of these phenomena, the by-products of state-structural "readjustment" and privatization, were the fruits not simply of market forces in motion but of specific and explicit state policies. This is not to claim that the leadership willed this social cleft, only that its intentional goals and programs brought it about.

Others have written of yet more explanations for the new and growing chasm between social classes. The first of these was a decentralization of costs and responsibilities which saddled lower-level administrations with the payment of welfare assistance. But despite the localities' new obligations, the "reform" did not extend to these authorities the funds necessary to meet the relevant expenses. This decision hurt the less well-off while providing the connected with even more opportunities for graft.[47] Another factor was the demographic composition of the poor. That is, those who were dismissed—being older, less educated, and less skilled as a result of Cultural Revolution school closures—were people who found it difficult to find new positions.[48]

One additional and significant issue was the state policy offering preferences and priorities for places with regional or geographic advantages, thus boosting the fortunes of those living there while putting those residing in areas that lacked such governmental privileges at an even further disadvantage.[49] And finally, undergirding it all was an opening to entrepreneurship, along with the increasing role of technology in production. These factors meant cuts in jobs for the lower-skilled while affording those who were more intelligent or more educated or otherwise in possession of greater human capital the chance to do well in business or to make good on their property.[50]

Qualitative Studies on the State, the Poor, and the Wealthy

Granted, China has no formal structure that explicitly creates a caste system like that in India. Yet qualitative studies highlight how the processes of economic transition and transformation, combined with remnants of the institutions and conventions inherited from the previous, planned-era economy, have engendered polar entities that perform in practice as castes do in a number of ways. A telling statement made by a wealthy businessman contemplating emigrating to the United States from China (which requires making a business investment in the States worth at least 500,000 USD) epitomizes this observation: "People like us are all emigrating," he remarked to explain his decision to leave his country. "If staying in China, my children will have to marry the children of my drivers and employees."[51] The man implies here that he fears if he were to remain in China and if his business should fail, his offspring might sink into a largely endogamous social group of poor people.

Anthropologists, sociologists, political scientists, cultural studies scholars, historians, and geographers who work on China have contributed in-depth treatments of the impoverished and the wealthy and the impact of the state on these new formations; several studies of the habits and practices of the middle class are also instructive. Such ethnographies showcase the informal prohibitions in urban China that in recent decades have limited entry into the world of great wealth, or else they delineate the hopelessness of exit from the holes into which the indigent have sunk.[52] What has resulted, their studies reveal, is an aura of entrenchment-cum-exclusiveness on one side and inescapability-cum-exclusion on the other. This presence of two sets of enclosed collectivities in the cities suggests that the concept of caste is apposite.

Social scientists have attributed this rise of what I am calling castes to one of two broad categories of events: change or continuity. Pointing to change, some scholars maintain that the rich acquired their wealth chiefly as beneficiaries of state-led economic liberalization and accompanying economic growth.[53] The evidence here is that the most advantaged have been Communist Party (and often state) officials. These people, along with their accomplices, have been in a position to milk their proximity to power to "hoard [the] income-generating opportunities and extract [the] major rents"[54] that their grip on power, resources, and regulations affords them. For the poor, crucial shifts in state policy, especially the end of assured employment and the withdrawal of free medicine and cheap secondary education, have shut the gate on advancement, promising an unending stasis in a base status for these people and their descendants.[55]

Still another critical change that scholars highlight has to do with the state's granting of home ownership to most urban residents, either outright or at far-below-market prices. This handout has given new proprietors the ability to amass vast rents, as Luigi Tomba shows in his book, *The Government Next Door*. Tomba also demonstrates the boost in status that new homeowners, especially those residing in high-class gated communities, have acquired. This is in obvious contrast to what often amount to hovels inhabited by citizens subsisting in "dilapidated working class areas."[56] Li Zhang's portrait of the new middle class in Kunming, *In Search of Paradise,* makes a similar point. She narrates how differently the members of this class are treated by officialdom and developers, particularly how the poor—frequently forced, even violently, from their soon-to-be-demolished homes—fare in this regard.[57] Those who have made it good warrant a shot at self-governance, in the eyes of officials, while the rest become the acted-upon.[58]

But other scholars look to continuity, not change, as the cause of caste formation, despite the fact that pre-1978 China was remarkably egalitarian. Glancing backward, they argue that the rewards and the losses brought on by reform have accrued to their recipients on the basis of legacies from the state's policies and programs from the socialist era. That explanation refers to old inequality-producing institutions that have persisted across the border of economic systems. The result is that persons who stood in positions of state-sponsored privilege and priority before 1978—not only in political offices but also because of various state-decreed policies—have managed to continue to stay atop the social hierarchy.

These policies include people's household registration, past employment in the stronger state-owned enterprises, and even, within cities, residence in the relatively more affluent neighborhoods or favored sites under the planned economy.[59] Those on the fortunate end of the spectrum got a significant head start once structural transformation got underway, while those unfavorably situated in earlier years went on being at a disadvantage. That disadvantage was only magnified by the policies of the transition and also by these people's long-term lack of the human capital that market success calls for. In his book *Boundaries and Categories,* Wang Feng takes a somewhat different tack. He does not exclude the role of either the new market system nor of prior institutions. His main focus, however, is to illuminate how socioeconomically disparate categories of groups have arisen as a function of social processes of differentiation and realignment, processes that were set into motion by both old and changing state policies.[60] Another related sort of interpretation that explicitly links the two themes of change and continuity centers on ties between party officials and businesspeople. These bonds enable individuals who have found ways to succeed financially to do so on the strength of befriending the powerful, thereby acquiring potent political capital themselves which, in turn, assists them mightily in acquiring their wealth. John Osburg's book, *Anxious Wealth,* explicates in great depth the workings of such "elite networks," as it portrays these connections and graphically conveys the clout they lend.[61]

Those not enjoying such liaisons have no way to attain entrée to the channels of upward social mobility. By the same token, a poverty-stricken interview subject, holder of a diploma from a third-rate college, was spending his post-graduation time loitering in his family's tiny one-room apartment when I spoke with him. Urged to look for a job, he was defended by his mother, who excused him by bemoaning, "We have no connections (*guanxi*), how can he find any work?"[62]

The recitals of the sagas and the fine-grained analyses of the urban middle class by Luigi Tomba, Li Zhang, and Deborah Davis; of the ultra-rich by John Osburg and David Goodman; of the ultra-poor—whether jobless past-workers or displaced migrants—by Jie Yang, Mun Young Cho, and Fulong Wu et al.; and of the disparate shopping habits of each of the urban classes by Amy Hanser all outline vast discrepancies in how the members of urban society's respective social sections live their lives.[63] Through its manifold manipulations, it is the state that has fabricated this diversity of situations among those who populate the municipalities. This, again, is a disparity that has manufactured a virtual, emblematic caste system whose upper tiers are tough to dislodge and whose base is bolted into a groove from which escape is virtually impossible. In what follows I review the chapters in this volume and use the material in them to assess the degrees of agency open to those perched at each of these two social poles. The discrepancies displayed form a pattern that constitutes a hierarchy of agency.

The Volume: A Hierarchy of Agency

In the framework outlined by Anthony Giddens, "structure" forms the fields in which each caste functions and experiences its daily pleasures or sufferings. But in Giddens' words, "Structure is not to be equated with constraint but is always both constraining and enabling."[64] This is a judgment that, at least for some, can allow for agency, or individual choice and maneuver, within structure. But how much space does each social segment really have? That is, what space is accessible to "make a difference to a preexisting state of affairs or the course of events?" For, in Giddens' perspective, "action [and, obviously, agency] depends upon the capability of the individual" to do just that.[65]

My argument is that the chapters share a prominent message: their stories display not just the caste-like containers in which rich and poor persist, they also reveal the grossly dissimilar bounds within which the urban wealthy and poor do or do not have "agency" that allows them to rearrange or transcend their roles and their behaviors.

The volume begins with two macroanalyses that provide overviews; they graphically depict the respective shapes of, and the contrasts that separate, these castes. The first of these is sociological; the other is ethnographic. In chapter 1, Wang Feng presents a sociological study of the formidable situation facing the political elite in confronting rapidly rising inequality, even if its members wished to alleviate it. He makes a strong argument that housing and education policies, along with an individual's political power, have pushed the already-advantaged into positions where "economic inequality that began in income . . . evolv[ed] into a form of more durable and consequential inequality, namely inequality in wealth." This has occurred as the privileged have worked in firms that heavily subsidized their acquisition of property (which has inflated in value over time), through their access to resources and power that enabled further accumulation, or via their ability to afford and enter costlier, better-equipped institutions of learning. Regressive public transfers also play a role in Wang's account. Absence of access to these assets has had the reverse effect.

Wang also details how wealth has increasingly been turned into a commodity that is passed along to the next generation, feeding an intergenerational stasis as to where occupants stand on the rungs of the social ladder, or an "intergenerational transfer in social status." "A society of unequal starting lines for the next generation has been formed," he contends. Wang's chapter bolsters my claim that we have not just two separate castes in the present but a case of an ever-more-inexorable caste-like system under construction. And given his account of state structures and benefits impossible for the poor to penetrate and secure, it seems reasonable to hold that where the rich have nearly unlimited agency (should they not be caught at corruption), those lacking means are essentially without any.

Chapter 2 by Li Zhang serves as an ethnographic companion piece to Wang Feng's, as she compellingly offers snapshots of three arenas of daily urban life—worsening air pollution, psychological stress, and fights for space and land. She elucidates how each of these pressures impacts disparate segments of the urban populace respectively. Thus, for each of these spheres of ordinary existence, Zhang draws upon vivid examples to illustrate how vastly dissimilar the means and the tools for coping with these issues are for the members of the two social groupings at the extreme poles of the social hierarchy. For example, whereas the wealthy can afford expensive air filters, country homes, vacation trips, and even emigration abroad to escape the befouled air, the poor are often consigned to their contaminated abodes and to work (if they can find any) out in the streets.

She argues that "a new form of environmental injustice that reinforces class inequality is emerging." This is a sort of inequality that creates different "chambers" in the city, the best of which can be accessed only by advantaged people. "This form of exclusivity regarding the very basic necessity of living is unprecedented and troubling," she maintains. Once again one obtains a sense of social spaces as closed to entrée as castes are, on the one hand, and as difficult to escape, on the other. Indeed, her story delineates cities as polarized places in which quite disparate occupants reside, in groupings whose members are able, respectively, to exercise vastly discrepant degrees of agency.

Following these two introductory pieces, the volume presents five case studies. Moving from those with the very least agency to those whose situations grant them much greater degrees of it, the chapters by Dorothy Solinger (chapter 3) on the Minimum Livelihood Guarantee, Mun Young Cho (chapter 4) on migrant factory workers, and Joshua Goldstein (chapter 5) on garbage collectors showcase portraits of the very poor, noting that the range of agency to which each group is privy ascends in that order. The other two pieces—Andrew David Field and James Farrer's on the nightlife of the opulent populace of Shanghai (chapter 6) and John Osburg's on networks that more and more exclude the nonpolitical elite (chapter 7)—also depict groups whose agency escalates along an upward trending scale.

Solinger's account of the Minimum Livelihood Guarantee (*dibao*) emphasizes the unwillingness of the Chinese government to take measures that would bolster the chances of the children of the urban-registered poor. The analysis underlines the trap that holds these people latched in place. A diminishing portion of officially urban indigent parents are accorded what amount to relatively decreasing allowances.

But a critical feature is that these grants are given without conditions—that is, recipients are not required to tend to their children's nutrition, education, or health care—as is mandated in other countries that give "conditional cash transfers." Moreover, the funds the families receive are too paltry to enable the parents to see to these needs. These arrangements thereby reduce the hopes of the impoverished for departure from destitution. Besides, the chapter argues, opportunities for work are limited to the young and the hale. Policies and attitudes that block the very poor from bettering the lot of their offspring or from finding employment would seem to cut the agency of the needy down nearly to nil.

Cho's chapter, on the "passionate poor," is a picture of factory workers who gain a sense of "ethical citizenship" by volunteering in social work centers, while they themselves are mistreated in their factories and denied genuine "social membership" (with its political and social rights and economic entitlements) in the larger society. Her analysis presents a mixed case of agency: these workers do have a chance to choose to reinvent themselves as volunteers outside the factory, even as they have no agency whatsoever while laboring. She also suggests that the spectacle of volunteering activities as part of "social governance" (a concept the regime has heralded) converts class-based relationships into moral ones, obscuring the grim fact that these workers are increasingly marginalized from government schemes.

This then is a group whose members are further along the spectrum of agency—or, alternatively, situated differently within what she terms the "multi-layered dimensions of poverty"—than either Solinger's *dibao* recipients or the great mass of Goldstein's subjects, the trash gatherers. Cho speaks of "structural, institutional barriers both in the city and in the workplace which, however, fail to stop the protagonists from taking up 'immaterial labor.'" Even while being "stuck in precarious life conditions," these workers somehow manage to "pursue individual strategies for self-development."

Goldstein's contribution plots out the trajectory that urban migrant trash recyclers have pursued over some twenty-five years. He depicts how "a substantial minority" of these garbage workers have found economic success. But this has occurred even as thousands of other roving refuse pickers scramble at the lowest reaches of a network of refuse collectors who market rubbish. In the past, he notes, some of those whom he terms "entrepreneurial trash barons," people who made "large and risky investments and gray market deals with Beijing local governments and industrial buyers," rose to the apex of the business by reinvesting profits and luring co-provincials to become their underlings.

Despite the opportunities the trade has offered for the bosses, however, stratification persists, with those at the ground level subsisting in unhealthy, impermanent, crowded shanties. Goldstein also comments that, as of the mid-2010s, "The alluring dynamism of economic mobility of the 1990s has all but disappeared from the sector." Here it is clear that at least in the past there was a path up and out for the venturesome, a sign that people in this sector have had some room to rely on their own agency and to rise.

Flipping the focus to the opposite point in the spectrum of classes, Field and Farrer introduce readers to those near the very peak of the prosperous. These are members of the tiny segment of society they term "the big-spending *fuerdai*," that is, the children of the urban ultra-wealthy, whose fortunes were accrued chiefly in the real estate markets. Field and Farrer recount how dance halls, sites for equitably priced enjoyment as recently as the 1980s, were overtaken in the 2000s by nightclubs, scenes of spectacular display for those prepared to put out tens of thousands of yuan on an evening's spree, sometimes nearly nightly.

The authors' purpose is to set down "how social class distinction is now expressed, performed, and exulted over in contemporary China." By the mid-2010s, a VIP arena held aloft on hydraulic pumps lifted the moneyed above the other patrons in the most exclusive of the clubs. Seated there they could lay out 9,000 yuan to ride a train to the table and be waited upon by the most beautiful showgirls. These outfits serve as barriers to entry into the world (or, one might say, the caste) of the extreme elite. The barriers are set not just by dint of what could be viewed as the "dues" their customers are equipped to expend to partake of their pleasures but also by the restricted access that gatekeepers of various sorts permit. In this case, agency among the clients is almost unlimited, as revealed in their choice for unbounded exorbitant consumption.

Last, the subjects who populate the chapter by Osburg arguably do Field and Farrer's wealthy folks' offspring one better. Osburg writes of businesspeople and state officials whose networks are blocked to those without bonds of kinship to top politicians. By investigating the practices of bribery, entertaining, and gift-giving that coalesce into forming elite spheres of extraordinary power and influence, Osburg demonstrates how this virtual nobility is encasing a new class at the ultimate summit of society. He is able to document the impact these private and secretive connections have upon entrepreneurs' businesses, their ethics, and their leisure activities. For these people, outlays can reach as much as three million yuan of spending yearly in just one nightclub. Where actual blood ties are not the bond that undergirds the relationships, "idioms of kinship" take their place, as "big brothers" must meet familial-type obligations that seal the circles against outsiders.

But most arresting in what Osburg found is a shift he documents from "brothers" to "aristocrats." He discovered that this change has occurred as the old *guanxi* connections have been replaced by close friendships and linkages founded on kinship. The upshot is that *beijing,* literally "background" of a most specific sort, especially strong family affiliations, overrides more mundane connections. As inherited *guanxi* has substituted for earned cultivation, Osburg sees a novel form of class consolidation in the making. Only those with the most durable class of bond, that of blood, a blood type that flows just through the veins of the "princelings" (also known in China as the "nobility" or *guizu*), were set to prosper in the mid-2010s. This, then, is the paramount form of caste, a form that, like the castes of India, is hereditary; this too is agency in its most expansive style.

CONCLUSION

This volume aims to accomplish two ends: first, to narrate the situations of members of two collectivities in China's cities who maintain monumentally disparate lifestyles; and second, to demonstrate that the divergence is largely the outcome of policies and practices devised and enforced over forty years by the regime's political elite. As we write in 2018, it would appear that there has come to be a kind of finality to the barriers to entry at the top, as well as an absence of an exit door at the bottom. Though there may have been some space for independent action and choice before these formations congealed, the authors detail a kind of looming closure taking hold for those lower down, along with totally unbounded opportunity at the top.

NOTES

We extend much gratitude to Benjamin van Rooij, formerly chair in US-China Business and Law at the University of California, Irvine (UCI), School of Law, and director of the Long US-China Institute at UCI, for suggesting that we convene a meeting on the topic of rich and poor China; and to John Long, benefactor of the Long Institute, for his very generous financial support, which made it possible to hold this workshop, where Dorothy Solinger, Wang Feng, Li Zhang, Joshua Goldstein, and John Osburg launched the initial project.

1. Martin King Whyte, "China's Dormant and Active Social Volcanoes," *The China Journal* 75 (January 2016): 12, 13. The best and most thorough book on class in China is David S. G. Goodman, *Class in Contemporary China* (Cambridge: Polity Press, 2014).

2. Fulong Wu and Chris Webster, "What Has Been Marginalized?," in *Marginalization in Urban China*, eds. Fulong Wu and Chris Webster (London: Palgrave/Macmillan, 2010), 303; Qin Gao, *Welfare, Work and Poverty: Social Assistance in China* (New York: Oxford University Press, 2017).

3. BBC News, "China Tops US in Numbers of Billionaires," dated October 13, 2016, accessed December 15, 2016, states that as of late 2016 China had 594 billionaires, according to Shanghai publisher Hurun's annual list, http://www.bbc.com/news/business-37640156. Two hundred forty-two of these had been added that year, accessed December 15, 2016, http://money.cnn.com/2015/10/15/investing/china-us-billionaires/.

4. Using data from China's National Statistical Yearbook, Jacob Shapiro, "China Is Still Really Poor," *RealClear World*, September 16, 2016, notes that urban households in many of China's interior provinces are earning far less than the per capita average, accessed December 15, 2016, https://www.realclearworld.com/articles/2016/09/16/china_is_still_really_poor_112050.html.

5. The term "caste" has been used to characterize the *hukou* (household registration) system in China. Fei-Ling Wang, "Conflict, Resistance and the Transformation of the *Hukou* System," in *Chinese Society: Change, Conflict and Resistance*, ed. Elizabeth J. Perry and Mark Selden (London and NY: Routledge, 2010), 90, reports that in 2008 and 2009 essays on the Chinese internet characterized the hukou system as China's "caste system"; Wenfang Tang and Qing Yang, "The Chinese Urban Caste System in Transition," *China Quarterly* 196 (December 2008): 2, 10, also refer to "the traditional socialist urban caste system"; and see Mun Young Cho, *The Specter of "The People"* (Ithaca: Cornell University Press, 2013). But that usage is flawed as it obscures the vast disparities that exist among urban residents.

6. Anthony Giddens, *The Constitution of Society: Outline of the Theory of Structuration* (Berkeley and London: University of California Press, 1984), 14.

7. Azizur Rahman Khan and Carl Riskin, *Inequality and Poverty in China in the Age of Globalization* (Oxford: Oxford University Press, 2001), 120; Shi Li, Hiroshi Sato, and Terry Sicular, "Rising Inequality in China: Key Issues and Findings," in *Rising Inequality in China: Challenges to a Harmonious Society*, ed. Shi Li, Hiroshi Sato, and Terry Sicular (New York: Cambridge University Press, 2013), 37.

8. Richard G. Fox, "Resiliency and Change in the Indian Caste System: The Umar of U.P.," *Journal of Asian Studies* 26, no. 4 (August 1967): 575; Charles Lindholm, "Caste in Islam and the Problem of Deviant Systems: A Critique of Recent Theory," *Journal of Anthropological Research* 42 (1986): 1–13.

9. Fox, "Resiliency," 586.

10. Ekta Singh, "Caste System in India: A Historical Perspective" (PhD diss., Bundelkhand University, 2003), 1.

11. Sukhadeo Thorat and Katherine S. Newman, "Caste and Economic Discrimination: Causes, Consequences and Remedies," *Economic and Political Weekly* (Mumbai) 42, no. 41 (October 13, 2007): 4121. See also Dipankar Gupta, "Caste and Politics: Identity Over System," *Annual Review of Anthropology* 34 (October 21, 2005): 410.

12. Fox, "Resiliency," 577, drawing on the work of E. R. Leach; Gupta, "Caste and Politics," 411. Also, Nicholas B. Dirks, "The Original Caste: Power, History and Hierarchy in South Asia," *TRANSFORMATIONS: Comparative Study of Social Transformations* (CSST Working Paper #10, CRSO Working Paper #367, University of Michigan, Ann Arbor, November 1988), 23; Thorat and Newman, "Caste," 4122; and McKim Marriott, "Caste Ranking and Food Transactions: A Matrix Analysis," in *Structure and Change in Indian Society*, ed. Milton B. Singer and Bernard S. Cohn (Chicago: Aldine, 1968).

13. On India, see Gupta, "Caste and Politics," 412. (Of course, wealth *did* become shakeable in party chairman Xi Jinping's anti-corruption campaign after 2013.)

14. Dalits are technically outside the caste system, but they are also sometimes referred to as the lowest caste.

15. Jasmine Rao, "The Caste System: Effects on Poverty in India, Nepal and Sri Lanka," *Global Majority E-Journal* 1, no. 2 (December 2010): 100, 101; Thorat and Newman, "Caste," 4121.

16. Dorothy J. Solinger, "Temporality as Trope in Delineating Inequality: Progress for the Prosperous, Time Warp for the Poor," in *Unequal China : The Political Economy and Cultural Politics of Inequality* , ed. Wanning Sun and Yingjie Guo (London and New York: Routledge, 2013), 59–76.

17. Han Keqing, ed., *Zhongguo chengshi dibao fangtanlu* [Interviews with Minimum Livelihood Guarantee Recipients in Urban China] (Jinan: Shandong renmin chubanshe, 2012), 95.

18. Nirmal Kumar Bose, "Class and Caste," *Economic Weekly* (Bombay) (July 28, 1965): 1339; Singh, "Caste System," 12; Thorat and Newman, "Caste," 4122.

19. Rao, "The Caste System," 101.

20. Rao, 101.

21. Rao, 101, 105; Singh, "Caste System"; Thorat and Newman, "Caste," 4122, 4123. For China, see Lisa M. Hoffman, *Patriotic Professionalism in Urban China: Fostering Talent* (Philadelphia: Temple University Press, 2010).

22. Melanie Manion, "The Challenge of Corruption," in *China's Challenges*, ed. Jacques deLisle and Avery Goldstein (Philadelphia: University of Pennsylvania Press, 2015), 128, states that total hidden income is equivalent to 30 percent of gross domestic product; Rupert Hoogewerf, chairman and chief researcher of Hurun Report, has reported that investigators were able to identify only about half of the country's billionaires since so many manage to find ways to conceal their wealth, accessed January 1, 2017, http://money.cnn.com/2015/10/15/investing/china-us-billionaires/.

23. Accessed January 1, 2017, http://www.bbc.com/news/world-asia-china-35657107.

24. Gracia Liu-Farrer, "Migration as Class-based Consumption: The Emigration of the Rich in Contemporary China," *China Quarterly* 226 (June 2016): 504.

25. Ezra F. Vogel, *Deng Xiaoping and the Transformation of China* (Cambridge, MA: Belknap Press of Harvard University Press, 2011), 391. Deng Xiaoping did use this phrase with a visiting American delegation in 1985 and again with the Prime Minister of New Zealand in 1986. "邓小平: 让一部分人先富起来" (Deng Xiaoping: First allow one group of people to get rich), 中国共产党新闻网 (News of the Communist Party of China), http://cpc.people.com.cn/GB/34136/2569304.html, accessed June 25, 2016. Thanks to Karl Gerth for this data.

26. Barry Naughton, *Growing Out of the Plan: Chinese Economic Reform, 1978–1995* (New York: Cambridge University Press, 1995); Dorothy J. Solinger, *From Lathes to Looms: China's Industrial Policy in Comparative Perspective, 1979–1982* (Stanford: Stanford University Press, 1991), chapters 3 and 4.

27. Solinger, *From Lathes*, 47.

28. Dali L. Yang, *Calamity and Reform in China: State, Rural Society, and Institutional Change Since the Great Leap Forward* (Stanford: Stanford University Press, 1996), chapters 5 and 6. According to Thomas P. Bernstein, "Ideology and Rural Reform: The Paradox of Contingent Stability," in *State and Society in China: The Consequences of Reform,* ed. Arthur Lewis Rosenbaum (Boulder, CO: Westview, 1992), 143, "The reshaping of agricultural institutions and policies . . . culminated in the virtually universal adoption of household contracting by 1983."

29. Naughton, *Growing Out,* 181ff.

30. Barry Naughton, "Implications of the State Monopoly Over Industry and its Relaxation." *Modern China* 18, no. 1 (1992): 14–41.

31. Dorothy J. Solinger, "The Chinese Work Unit and Transient Labor in the Transition from Socialism," *Modern China* 21, no. 2 (April 1995): 155–83.

32. Khan and Riskin, *Inequality and Poverty,* 105.

33. Fulong Wu and Ningying Huang, "New Urban Poverty in China: Economic Restructuring and Transformation of Welfare Provision," *Asia Pacific Viewpoint* 48, no. 2 (2007): 178, 180.

34. Khan and Riskin, *Inequality and Poverty,* 8, 112. See also Qin Zhou, Gordon G. Liu, Yankun Sun, and Sam A. Vortherms, "The Impact of Health Insurance Cost-Sharing Method on Healthcare Utilization in China," *China Journal of Social Work* 9, no. 1 (2016): 38–61.

35. Shu Y. Ma, "The Chinese Route to Privatization: The Evolution of the Shareholding System Option," *Asian Survey* XXXVIII, no. 4 (1998): 379–97; and *Property Rights and Economic Reform in China,* ed. Jean C. Oi and Andrew G. Walder (Stanford: Stanford University Press, 1999), especially chapters 1, 6, and 7.

36. Wu and Huang, "New Urban Poverty"; Li, Luo and Sicular's analysis of income data from 2002 to 2007 uncovered the significance of the impact of the reform of property rights on expanding inequality (Shi Li, Chuliang Luo, and Terry Sicular, "Overview: Income Inequality and Poverty in China, 2002–2007," in Li, Sato, and Sicular, *Rising Inequality,* 77).

37. This is also discussed in Manion, "The Challenge."

38. Deng Quheng and Bjorn Gustafsson, "A New Episode of Increased Urban Income Inequality in China," in Li, Sato, and Sicular, *Rising Inequality,* 257. The bulk of the layoffs took place between 1997 and 2002.

39. There have been a number of studies on the topics of inequality, the wealthy, and poverty in the years since 1978. Among them are: *Paying for Progress in China: Public Finance, Human Welfare and Changing Patterns of Inequality,* ed. Vivienne Shue and Christine Wong (London and New York: Routledge, 2007); *Unemployment, Inequality and Poverty in Urban China,* ed. Shi Li and Hiroshi Sato (London and New York: Routledge, 2006); Li, Sato, and Sicular, *Rising Inequality;* Khan and Riskin, *Inequality and Poverty; Creating Wealth and Poverty in Postsocialist China,* ed. Deborah S. Davis and Wang Feng (Stanford: Stanford University Press, 2009); *The New Rich in China: Future Rulers, Present Lives,* ed. David S. G. Goodman (Abingdon, Oxon: Routledge, 2008); John Osburg, *Anxious Wealth: Money and Morality Among China's New Rich* (Stanford: Stanford University Press, 2013); Sun and Guo, *Unequal China;* Wang Feng, *Boundaries and Categories: Rising Inequality in Post-Socialist Urban China* (Stanford: Stanford University Press, 2008); and Fulong Wu, Chris Webster, Shenjing He, and Yuting Liu, *Urban Poverty in China* (Cheltenham, UK: Edward Elgar, 2010).

40. Shi, Sato, and Sicular, "Rising Inequality," 37; Deng and Gustafsson, "A New Episode," 256, note the heightened significance of business income (from both self-employment and from owning a private business) in the early 2000s and the rapid growth of imputed rent from owner-occupied housing, which, again, they attribute to state policies. Deborah Davis and Wang Feng, "Poverty and Wealth in Postsocialist China: An Overview," in Davis and Wang, *Creating Wealth,* 13, also attribute inequality to the sale of previously publicly owned industrial assets.

41. Jinjun Xue and Wei Zhong, "Unemployment, Poverty and Income Disparity in Urban China," in Li and Sato, *Unemployment*, 44, note that "inequality worsened because of asset income and rise in the unemployment rate" between 1988 and 1996.
42. Khan and Riskin, *Inequality and Poverty*, 147.
43. Xin Meng, "Economic Restructuring and Income Inequality in Urban China," in Li and Sato, *Unemployment*, 15–16.
44. Xue and Zhong, "Unemployment, Poverty," 13–14.
45. Shi Li, "Rising Poverty and Its Causes in Urban China," in Li and Sato, *Unemployment*, 136. The only citation to Appleton in the bibliography of this Li and Sato book is to a publication dated 2002; this is S. Appleton, J. Knight, L. Song, and Q. Xia, "Labour Retrenchment in China: Determinants and Consequences," *China Economic Review* 13 (2002): 252–75.
46. Li, "Rising Poverty," 137, and Wu and Huang, "New Urban Poverty," 171.
47. Carl Riskin, "Has China Reached the Top of the Kuznets Curve?," in Shue and Wong, *Paying*, 42; Manion, "The Challenge," 43; Christine Wong, "Can the Retreat from Equality Be Reversed? An Assessment of Redistributive Fiscal Policies from Deng Xiaoping to Wen Jiabao," in Shue and Wong, *Paying*, 12–28; and Christine P. W. Wong, "Central-Local Relations in an Era of Fiscal Decline: The Paradox of Fiscal Decentralization in Post-Mao China, *China Quarterly* 128 (December 1991): 691–715.
48. Wu and Huang, "New Urban Poverty," 176.
49. Khan and Riskin, *Inequality and Poverty*, 116.
50. Wu and Huang, "New Urban Poverty," 176; Khan and Riskin, *Inequality and Poverty*, 111.
51. Liu-Farrer, "Migration," 513.
52. The works I have in mind here are Cho, *The Specter*; Goodman, *Class;* Goodman, *The New Rich;* Deborah S. Davis, ed., *The Consumer Revolution in Urban China* (Berkeley: University of California Press, 2000); Davis and Wang, *Creating Wealth;* Amy Hanser, *Service Encounters: Class, Gender, and the Market for Social Distinction in Urban China* (Stanford: Stanford University Press, 2008); Osburg, *Anxious Wealth*; Sun and Guo, *Unequal China*; Luigi Tomba, *The Government Next Door: Neighborhood Politics in Urban China* (Ithaca and London: Cornell University Press, 2014); Tiantian Zheng, *Red Lights: The Lives of Sex Workers in Postsocialist China* (Minneapolis: University of Minnesota Press, 2009); Wang, *Boundaries*; Wu and Webster, *Marginalization*; Jie Yang, *Unknotting the Heart: Unemployment and Therapeutic Governance in China* (Ithaca and London: ILR Press, 2015); T. E. Woronov, *Class Work: Vocational Schools and China's Urban Youth* (Stanford: Stanford University Press, 2016); and Li Zhang, *In Search of Paradise: Middle-Class Living in a Chinese Metropolis* (Ithaca and London: Cornell University Press, 2010).
53. This is the case for Zhang, *In Search*, 11, and Goodman, *The New Rich*, 2, 3, 5. Deborah S. Davis, "Introduction: A Revolution in Consumption," in Davis, *The Consumer*, 1, refers to "financial gains from the post-Mao economic reform" that have been "rapid and impressive." Hanser, *Service Encounters*, 4, mentions new socioeconomic conditions that have "reconfigured social relations."
54. Davis and Wang, "Poverty and Wealth," 3.
55. Wu and Huang, "New Urban Poverty," 178, explain that these newly poor "might not be able to afford the increasing education costs and thus have to reduce human capital investment. Consequently, the next generation of impoverished households will still be in a poverty situation." See also Davis and Wang, "Poverty and Wealth," 10–11, and Dorothy J. Solinger, "The Creation of a New Underclass in China and Its Implications," *Environment and Urbanization* 18, no. 1 (April 2006): 177–93.
56. Tomba, *The Government*, 10.
57. Zhang, *In Search*, 16–19, chapter 5.
58. Cho, *The Specter*, and Yang, *Unknotting*, also limn the tools and styles of domination that signal to the poor that they are best subdued, handled in ways that subtract them from the mainstream populace.
59. Wu et al., *Urban Poverty*; Davis and Wang, "Poverty and Wealth," 3–5; Fulong Wu and Chris Webster, "Introduction: China's Urban Marginalization," in Wu and

Webster, *Marginalization*, 11, and Wang, *Boundaries*, 13, emphasize the combination of reforms and legacies.

60. Wang, *Boundaries*, especially chapter 1.

61. Osburg, *Anxious Wealth.* Similarly, David Wank, *Commodifying Communism: Business, Trust, and Politics in a Chinese City* (New York: Cambridge University Press, 1999), wrote of the same phenomenon a decade-and-a-half earlier, calling them social networks and clientelist networks. I also wrote on this subject, as long ago as 1990, published two years later as Dorothy J. Solinger, "Urban Entrepreneurs and the State: The Merger of State and Society," in Rosenbaum, *State and Society*, 121–41. See also David S. G. Goodman, "Why China Has No New Middle Class: Cadres, Managers and Entrepreneurs," in Goodman, *The New Rich* ("networks of mutual obligation"), 12; and Davis and Wang, "Poverty and Wealth," 3.

62. Conversation, Wuhan, June 2012. The young man was able to attend college because of two benefactors.

63. Tomba, *The Government*; Zhang, *In Search*; Davis, *The Consumer*; Osburg, *Anxious Wealth*; Goodman, *The New Rich*; Yang, *Unknotting*; Cho, *The Specter*; Wu et al., *Urban Poverty*.

64. Giddens, *The Constitution*, 25.

65. Giddens, 14.

Part I

Polarization: Scope, Causes, Manifestations

ONE

China's Uphill Battle Against Inequality

Wang Feng

In the closing decades of the twentieth century, China's economic boom and rising inequality reshaped the global landscape of inequality. The "China effect" is twofold: reducing global inequality between countries and, at the same time, increasing inequality within the world's largest country. On a global scale, China's economic boom narrowed the income gap between China and the richer parts of the world, hence reducing global inequality between countries.[1] At the national level, economic growth of historical proportions in China lifted hundreds of millions of people out of poverty and raised the standards of living for one-fifth of humanity. Yet at the same time that China has become a country with an extremely rapid pace of wealth accumulation, it has also become one of the most economically unequal countries in the world, with a rate of increase in income inequality over the last three decades that is virtually unparalleled elsewhere globally.[2]

Nearly four decades after its postsocialist turn, China is today a society that has punctured predictions repeatedly, both about its rise and in projections of its demise. China's economic growth has far exceeded the wildest imaginations of both its planners and participants, and its demise has been repeatedly eluded. Whatever bad turns China has taken did not follow the commonly prescribed routes either. China today is a society that defies easy categorization and description,[3] one where the majority of the workforce is employed outside the state-controlled sector. Yet in the course of market-oriented reforms, the state has regained prominence in the economy. It is also a society where the officials of the Communist

Party are the best bedfellows of the capitalists, domestic or overseas. And it is a society that is increasingly unequal, yet governed by a political party whose legitimacy continues to be based on Marxist ideology, for which equality is an essential element. Finally, it is a society in which rising inequality has been a pressing social concern, but where a so-called social volcano has not erupted.[4]

To be sure, departing from the socialist era of "engineered equality" was in the design of the post-Mao leadership; there was an explicit intention to remake Chinese society. Yet, once out of the Pandora's box, rising inequality and deepening social division have taken their own course. The dichotomous contrast of state versus market—or political redistributive power versus distribution based on market abilities—has proven to be too simplistic and facile to describe what has occurred in China, as the state has not only learned to embrace but also to utilize the market.[5] The long-wished-for Kuznets turning point, by which income inequality rises but then falls, has yet to appear on the horizon.[6] What China faces today, instead, is not just a markedly high level of inequality permeating society but a complex set of powerful forces, old and new, that drive and structure the deepening inequality. These forces make the leadership's efforts to reduce inequality an uphill battle.

In this chapter, I focus on three aspects of this uphill battle. First, I will look at new features of economic inequality, primarily how economic inequality that began in income has now evolved into a form of more durable and consequential inequality, namely inequality in wealth. This new feature of inequality is resetting the starting lines of the next generation and beyond, resulting in inequalities that for the first time in recent Chinese history can be passed on from one generation to the next.

Second, and partly resulting from the first feature of China's new landscape of inequality, are the shrinking opportunities for social and economic mobility, here seen most readily in low or even nonexistent educational mobility and occupational mobility. This feature is generating long-term, entrenched social poles where groupings akin to castes are congealing at either end of the societal formation, the ultra-rich at the top and the impoverished at the base. Third, I look at the efforts made by the Chinese government to reduce inequality and examine their effectiveness and fairness.

RESETTING THE STARTING LINE: FROM INCOME TO WEALTH INEQUALITY

Rising economic inequality began with a simple increase in income disparities, in itself striking as they emerged within a social context of a general income equality (though one disguised by many forms of inequality in a society that was in fact more segmented than was always obvious). Indeed, during China's socialist years up to the early 1980s, the promised equality was never universal. Rather, it was equality within segmented strata, with large inequalities that grew with time between different social categories: urban versus rural China, among geographic regions, and across work organizations of different ownership types.[7] Equality existed in monetary terms but not in welfare provision. Besides, this form of economic equality came with a heavy price in political freedom and social mobility.[8]

Economic reforms beginning after 1978 allowed the population to move across some of these categories and ushered in measures that permitted people to make money. "To get rich is glorious," went the popular saying of that time. In the early years of the postsocialist era, the notion (and possibility) of "getting rich" for the majority was based on seizing the new economic opportunities that came with market freedom. Such opportunity, even if not available to everyone, depended chiefly upon labor input and, therefore, certainly upon agency for those with the resources and ability to utilize it: working for a multinational company; moving from the inland rural areas to the coastal cities that the regime designated as "special economic zones" in 1980; migrating from rural to urban areas as manual laborers; starting a township and village enterprise in the countryside; or creating a small business in the cities.

Income inequality increased hand in hand with rising income levels. As shown in figure 1.1, in the first decade after 1980 per capita income level, measured by purchasing power parity (PPP), tripled and it did so at roughly the same pace for two-and-a-half decades thereafter. Income inequality, measured by the Gini index, rose from 0.30 in 1980 to nearly 0.35 by the end of the 1980s, marking the first of two periods of rapid increase. The second phase of rapid increase in inequality took place during the decade after the mid 1990s, when its degree rose to above 0.45 on this index. By then China had joined the ranks of societies with the highest levels of income inequality in the world. While more recent numbers differ, ranging from 0.462 from the Chinese government to 0.55 based on an analysis of household surveys,[9] there is no ambiguity about the income inequality in China today being among the highest in the world.

Decades of rising income inequality have made Chinese society into one that once again is separated into different social strata, if not classes, and into social groups with enormously different resources, consumption patterns, lifestyles, and now, vastly disparate life chances. A society of unequal starting lines for the next generation has been formed. The basis for these distinct starting lines goes far beyond simply discrepant income levels. What we see instead is a rapid accumulation and redistribution of wealth during one of the greatest economic booms in human history.

A wealth boom soon followed income increase, yielding a far more ferocious pace of increase and concentration of resources than income

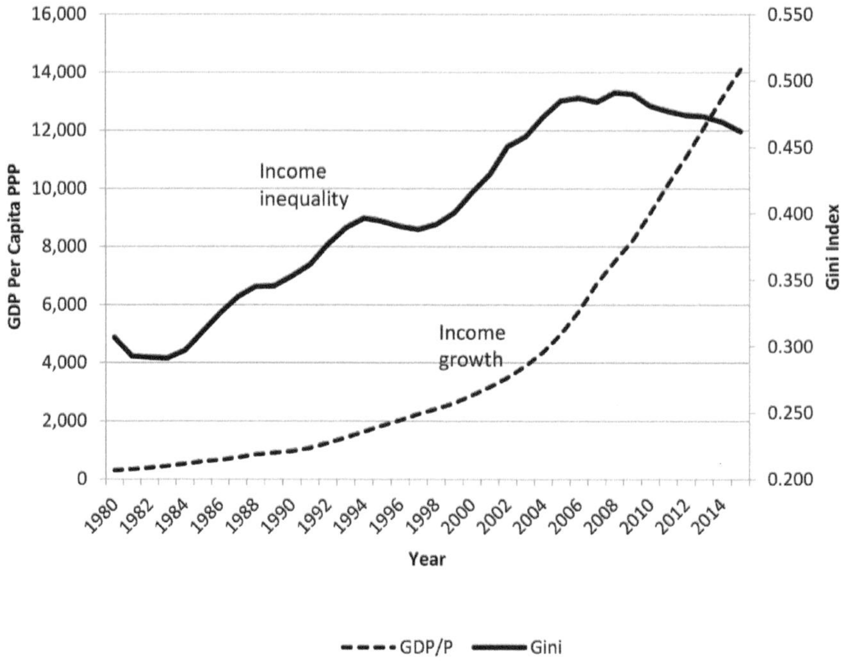

Figure 1.1. Growth with Inequality, China, 1980–2015
***Sources:* Income: IMF World Economic Outlook, 2016; Gini Index: National Bureau of Statistics, China**

alone would provide. Unlike increases in income growth and income inequality, wealth growth developed from what was almost a blank slate. At the end of the socialist days, the notions of wealth, capital, and private property belonged only to dictionaries and political studies materials. Under socialism, all means of production, from factories, mines, railways to rivers, land and draft animals, were in the hands of the state or what was known as the "collective" in the form of the People's Communes. Though families in rural areas owned their homes, private ownership of housing virtually disappeared in urban China in the early 1950s. In state-owned public housing, even furniture was publicly owned and stingily provided. In the late 1970s, the four most-prized consumption items were the sewing machine, the bicycle, the watch, and the radio—all of which were well beyond the financial capacity of the majority of the population to purchase. In 1980, for instance, even in Chinese cities, only 11.7 out of 100 persons owned a sewing machine, 27.9 had a bicycle, 44.4 had a watch, and 29.6 a radio. As for television sets (mostly black and white and small-sized), 3.5 per 100 persons possessed them.[10] Nationwide, when the 80 percent rural population was included, these numbers were even more dismal.

Once economic reforms got underway in the 1980s, rising income soon translated into rising consumption and increasing wealth for many. The four big-ticket items in demand in the early 1980s were quickly replaced by new consumer durables: color TVs, washing machines, and refrigerators. By the end of the 1990s, in urban China almost every household had these items. The first decade of the twenty-first century saw a quick saturation of in-house air conditioners, and by the mid-2000s there appeared a very rapid rise in the ownership of private automobiles. By 2014, a quarter of all urban Chinese households owned a car, up from only 0.5 percent in the year 2000 and close to 3.5 percent in 2005 (table 1.1). The most important source of private wealth is no doubt in housing. Back in 1978, only about 50 percent of the national housing stock was in the hands of private individuals, or more accurately, households, and almost all of these were in rural areas. It has been estimated that by 2015, 95 percent of all national housing stock was in the hands of private individuals or households.[11]

Reliable and accurate data on personal wealth are much harder (and perhaps impossible) to obtain as compared with data on the ownership of commodities. But abundant data from varying sources all portray an unmistakable picture, which is one of explosive growth and concentration of wealth that has accompanied China's economic boom. One recent systematic estimate puts China's national wealth-to-income ratio as rising from 3.5 to 1 in 1978 to 7 to 1 in 2015.[12] And following China's transition away from socialism, rising wealth changed the nature of wealth distribution between the state and society: whereas public property has been estimated to have accounted for 70 percent of all wealth in China back in 1978, by 2015 the ratio between public and private ownership flipped, with private property accounting for a full 70 percent of all

Table 1.1. Ownership of Consumer Durables and Private Automobiles, Urban China (per 100 households)

	TV (Color)	*Washing Machine*	*Refrigerator*	*Air Conditioner*	*Automobile*
1981	0.59	6.31	0.22		
1985	17.21	48.29	6.58		
1990	59.04	78.41	42.33	0.34	
1995	89.79	88.97	66.22	8.09	
2000	116.56	90.52	80.13	30.8	0.5
2005	134.8	95.5	90.72	80.67	3.37
2010	137.47	96.92	96.91	112.07	13.07
2014	122	90.7	91.7	107.4	25.7

Sources: China Statistical Yearbooks, various years.

national wealth. Despite this huge increase, the share belonging to the public in China is still far above that in Western countries.[13]

China is now a land filled with millionaires and billionaires. In 2005, according to *Forbes*, there were fewer than a quarter million Chinese (236,000) counted as dollar millionaires. As a comparison, the United States in 2005 had over ten times as many such individuals, about 2.7 million. But less than a mere decade later, the number of millionaires in China is widely believed to have at least quadrupled, to well over one million. A report in 2017 puts the number of millionaires in China at 1.7 million, the sixth largest in the world.[14] A study by Bain & Company reports that the number of high net worth individuals (those with 10 million RMB or 1.6 million USD and above) reached over one million in 2014, doubling from only four years earlier.[15] Other sources put the estimated number of dollar millionaires in China at 2.7 million in 2012, implying a rate of increase of more than 30 percent per year for several years in a row.[16] In 2004, there were reported to be only three billionaires in China. In 2015, that number had increased to 213, second only to the United States which, with its 536, is the world's largest economy with a long capitalist history.[17] By 2017, at 318, the number of billionaires in China is the largest in Asia, and is close to that in Europe, 342.[18] In 2004, there were estimated to be just 10,000 people in China who had assets over $10 million. In 2015, in comparison, there were nearly as many (9,555) ultra-rich Chinese whose estimated net worth stood at $50 million and above, an increase of 24 percent from the year before, and at a level of wealth that was five times more than it was just over a decade earlier.[19]

Moreover, wealth accumulation and concentration emerged at a rate that was far faster than rising income and income inequality. Household survey data, which cannot accurately capture the situation of the richest individuals but which can be calculated for the general population, shows that between 1995 and 2002 average urban household wealth increased by four times.[20] A more recent study reported that between 2002 and 2010, the average household wealth level again increased fourfold, while the Gini index of inequality of wealth distribution edged up from 0.538 in 2002 to 0.739 in 2010.[21] Another study, relying on the same household survey data as used in the research on wealth distribution in 2010 above, and bringing in additional information from data sources on the wealthiest, claims a Gini index of wealth distribution of as high as 0.73 in 2012. The same study also found that the richest 1 percent owned one-third of all wealth, with the poorest 25 percent owning only 1 percent.[22] In contrast to a ratio between the top 10 and bottom 10 percent (90/10) in income, estimated at 13.1 to 1 in 2012, the disparity ratio for household wealth was 33 to 1 in the same year.[23] These numbers, as with income inequality, place China not far behind the United States. According to analyses of US household survey data reporting, the Gini index stood at 0.83 in the early 2000s, with the richest 10 percent owning over 70 percent of the wealth. In China, by comparison, the wealthiest segment owned 62 percent of total national wealth in 2012, a proportion not too different.[24]

A systematic analysis, combining data sources from national accounts, surveys, wealth rankings, and taxes, draws a similar conclusion; by 2015, the top 10 percent of households possessed 67 percent of all wealth, having risen from 40 percent in 1995. As of the same year (2015), these preliminary analyses and incomplete data still suggest that wealth concentration in China was approaching that in the United States, at 72 percent, and was substantially higher than that in France, where the corresponding figure was 50 percent.[25]

Rapidly increasing private wealth in China comes from many sources. The Bain & Company study of private wealth reports, for instance, that "55 percent of Chinese millionaires derived their wealth from private businesses, and 20 percent are property speculators who have jumped on the crest of the rapid hike in home prices. About 15 percent are stock gurus, while the remaining 10 percent are high-earning salaried executives."[26] Though these are the sources of wealth among the ultra-rich, for the majority of the people who have accumulated wealth in the last decades, housing assets have been the most important component of their assets. Rapidly escalating real estate prices have been the main contributor to wealth inequality in recent years for the population at large.[27] In 2012, for instance, 73.9 percent of all household wealth nationwide was in housing assets. The share was even higher in urban China, at 78.7 percent in that year.[28] While the high savings rate of Chinese households plays a major role in wealth accumulation, increases in real asset values are almost as important, estimated to account for 40 to 50 percent of the rising wealth-to-income ratio between the years 1978 and 2015.[29]

What makes a person rich and who were among the first beneficiaries of China's broad wealth accumulation due to increases in housing prices? In the greatest wealth boom in modern Chinese history, it was those who occupied advantageous positions in the socialist planned economy years who, building on their preferential statuses, were able to win the race. Specifically, it was the urban population who rode the property market boom, the officials who controlled power, and the businesspeople who had access to political power.

In the postsocialist era of primitive capital accumulation, many urban families obtained their initial private property ownership from the state, and at very low prices. China's 2000 census, which took place shortly after the housing reform implemented in 1998, revealed that nearly three-quarters of all urban households had already managed to take possession of their housing units by then. Thirty percent of all urban households resided in units purchased from their own work organizations (often with heavy subsidies). Of all the properties sold by then, 64 percent were purchased from people's own work organizations.[30] Among those whose occupations were classified as officials, professionals, and staff members of government organizations, who made up 43 percent of all urban employees at the time of the 2000 census, two-thirds to three-quarters bought their housing units from their work organizations.

The average price paid for the whole housing unit was between 50,000 and 70,000 RMB, converting to a per square meter price of around 2,000 RMB.[31] Fifteen years later, by 2015, the average price per square meter nationwide had increased by more than three times, to 6,793 RMB.[32] In China's largest cities, where the property price boom has been much more drastic, average prices rose much faster. The individuals and families in these occupations were clearly among the first beneficiaries of the China wealth boom associated with the property price increase that took place later on. Wealth accumulation in the short time period has created a propertied class in China. While still relatively small for the population as a whole, the share of property income in total income increased from 2.7 percent in 2001 to 4.5 in 2007,[33] with the majority of owned property concentrated in the hands of the relatively few.

Those urban residents in the lower social ranks, and especially the majority of the rural population, including those who moved to cities as migrants, did not get this first leg up in China's new era of wealth accumulation. China's 2000 census shows that only about 40 percent of production workers and 36 percent of those who worked as commerce and service personnel bought housing units from their work organizations.[34]

China's wealth accumulation also contains another distinctive Chinese characteristic, which is the role of political power in generating wealth.[35] In the initial years of the wealth boom, between 1995 and 2002, households headed by Communist Party and government officials accumulated 30 to 50 percent more wealth than other households.[36] What has happened since then, when China's economic boom further took off and when corruption became more systemic, is that obtaining wealth via political power has taken a direction and with a magnitude that is nothing short of astonishing. The roles played by government officials are best described as having progressed from rent-seeking to rent-setting, as they set up policies and institutions from which they alone have the best chance of benefiting. From land acquisition, capital market development, and finance to massive government spending, it has been those who control or have access to political power who have benefited most, based on their monopolizing power.[37]

One needs to look no further than the information provided by the Chinese government, from its anti-corruption campaign between 2013 and 2016, to get a sense of the collusion between power and wealth. In this unprecedented campaign of the Chinese Communist Party, a large number of high-level officials have been investigated and sentenced for corruption, along with other crimes and misbehaviors. In a compilation of publically announced corruption cases between 2013 and August 2016, a total of over 1,100 officials ranked above top county official or division chief had been charged, with a large proportion already sentenced. From this compilation of cases publicized by the Chinese official media, 129 are high level officials, here defined as those above the level of a vice provincial governor or vice central government minister. Of the eighty-four whose sentencing had been announced as of the end of 2016, a large majority, 64 (76 percent), were charged with taking bribes and other illegal payoffs (a smaller percentage, 44 out of 84 individuals, were also charged with having mistresses). The amount these officials took ranged from 0.31 million to 584 million RMB, with a mean of 66.35 million (about 10 million USD) and a standard deviation of 96.89 million. While these numbers offer perhaps only the tip of the iceberg in terms of ill-obtained wealth via political power, they do illustrate the pervasiveness and the magnitude of the marriage between power and money.

CLOSING OPPORTUNITIES

It is safe to say that while excess inequality is always unnecessary and harmful to a society, a certain degree of inequality is unavoidable and may even be desirable. The same cannot be said, however, about opportunities and social mobility. This understanding is clearly the viewpoint and expectation of the general Chinese public.[38] Survey after survey of public perceptions of distributive justice in recent times in China has shown that the public is prepared to accept inequalities in outcome, but not in opportunity.

Largely due to the historical economic transformations that have unfolded in the last three decades, many ordinary Chinese have experienced an impressive chance to enjoy upward social mobility. Such opportunities are considered to be "structural" or relative mobility. What is more telling, however, are the mobility opportunities available after taking the macro structural-level changes into account. True, opportunities for social mobility due to structural changes in the economy have greatly increased, during both industrialization and in the postindustrial era. But when structural changes are examined, the other type of mobility, namely intergenerational mobility, provides a very different picture. As the era of rapid economic expansion and transformation comes to an end, it can be anticipated that the opportunities for overall mobility, and for agency, will also decline. The huge inequalities in wealth mean that the starting lines in life chances are being reset.[39] Not only will individuals' options narrow and agency decline, but a caste-like formation is under construction as people are forced to fall into the social space that their parents occupied.

The first crucial mobility channel is education. Throughout Chinese history, education has always been perceived and honored as a principal channel for social and economic mobility. Economic prosperity and post-reform government policies have ushered in the most drastic expansion in educational opportunities in Chinese history.[40] College admission ratios (admitted versus all examinees) first rose from 4.7 percent in 1977 to 20 percent in 1990, and then again to 34 percent in 1998. With the government's push for mass higher education expansion, annual enrollment increased sixfold in merely a decade's time, from 1 million in 1998 to 6.4 million in 2009. By 2014, that number further increased to over 7 million. With this expansion, the ratio of senior high school students enrolling in tertiary educational institutions also rose sharply, from 43 percent in 1998 to 83 percent by 2005.[41]

Yet analyses of both published government statistics and survey data report either persistent or enlarging gaps in access to education at higher levels. For instance, the rural-urban gap in the share of junior high school students advancing to academic senior high schools, which is the only realistic path to college enrollment, widened from 7 and 50 percent to 9 and 70 percent, respectively, between 1999 and 2005.[42] Moreover, children from families with more educated fathers also benefited disproportionately, as their chances of getting into full-program academic colleges increased following the expansion of educational opportunities.[43] Poor and rural students have been far behind in getting into colleges, especially elite colleges, and are seven and eleven times less likely to gain entry, respectively.[44]

As for enrollment in elite colleges, a competition that has become ever more intense, one study reports that children of parents with a cadre status are more likely to gain admission than are others. This advantage remains after other family and student characteristics, such as parents' education, students' academic performance, and elite high school attendance, are taken into account,[45] reinforcing in a different way the solidity of the barriers being raised against bettering one's station purely on the basis of one's own choice and effort. A study using survey data collected in 2008, which examined trends in school enrollment tracking, reported that while parents' occupation does not make a difference for admission to elite colleges, it does matter at critical stages earlier in the educational trajectory of young people. Thus, for enrollment in key middle and high schools, schools that offer much better chances for students to get into college, parents' residential type, education, and occupation make a significant difference.[46] Combined, these results paint a picture showing that a person's household registration status, parents' education, and political status are all critical elements determining educational mobility, and in some cases, the effects of these factors have only increased with time.

The same can be said about intergenerational mobility across different social strata. Recent studies portray a picture of declining intergenerational mobility and rising prominence in family background in affecting one's job opportunities and standing. As far back as a decade ago, in the mid-2000s, the vast increase in overall mobility was not found to be matched by rising intergenerational mobility.[47] A recent analysis, using data from three waves of national surveys, confirmed a rise in overall mobility across five social strata (defined based on one's relationship to ownership of the means of production: official/managerial, professional, white collar, blue collar, farming labor) over the last several decades, with the most notable rise taking place in the decades between 1978 and 2008. Yet, even during the period when overall social mobility reached its highest level ever during the time of the People's Republic, intergenerational transfer in social status has remained the most dominant feature.[48]

An earlier analysis, using data up to 2008, also found that the increase in job mobility was due not only to economic privatization—namely the expansion of the non-state sector of the economy—but also to working in the informal sector. The job mobility structure, in other words, has become highly segmented. Moreover, as of 2008, there were already signs of a slowdown in overall job mobility.[49] A comprehensive analysis of survey data of personal connections (*guanxi*) in job searches reveals its increasing, not declining, importance.[50] Another study based on an eight-city survey conducted in 2009 of over 7,000 respondents similarly showed diverging opportunities for gaining employment. Among the three types of jobs new job seekers obtained, the best ones went to those located in the formal sector and to job seekers with personal connections (*guanxi*). Meanwhile, the worst went to those who relied only on personal connections or introductions but who had no formal sector affiliation. Occupants in this lowest job category receive lower returns on their educational credential and work experiences and are more prone to switch jobs.[51]

Rising inequality, especially wealth inequality, could further constrain the opportunities provided by these two channels of social mobility, educational and occupational. Families with wealth can now send their children to elite primary and secondary schools to prepare for entrance into elite colleges, or they may even send their children abroad, an option most Chinese families do not have. Wealthy Chinese parents can not only help their children to land in good jobs, some can even create jobs for their children, either in their own firms or by supporting their children in starting new businesses.

THE NOT-SO-BENEVOLENT STATE

In all modern societies, the government is expected to play a role in reducing inequalities that arise from a market economy. In China's post-reform era, especially during the first decade of the twenty-first century, the Chinese government launched a series of major social welfare programs aimed at creating a social safety net. Major examples included public funding for nine-year compulsory education, beginning in 2001; the New Cooperative Medical System (NCMS) for the rural population in 2003; the Urban Resident Basic Medical Insurance (URBMI) for urban residents in the informal sector or for those who are unemployed, introduced in 2007; and the New Rural Pension Scheme (NRPS) and Urban Resident Pension Scheme (URPS), also for informal-sector workers in cities and the urban unemployed, which were piloted in 2009 and 2011, respectively.

By 2010, NCMS had already covered 96 percent of rural residents and the URBMI had reached a coverage rate of 93 percent after three years of promotion. The New Rural Pension Scheme, first piloted in 320 rural counties (which is about 16 percent of the total number of counties) in 2009, was expanded to 838 counties in 2010; through further growth, it covered nearly all rural counties by 2012.

Enabled by a high rate of growth in government revenue, the Chinese government has increased social spending at a rate that surpassed the growth rate of the economy as a whole. Government education expenditure as a percentage of GDP rose from 2.7 percent in 2007 to 3.6 percent in 2014. Health expenditure more than doubled to reach 1.6 percent of GDP in 2014, and social security benefits increased from less than 3 percent to nearly 5 percent by 2013. Public education, health care, and social security expenditures as shares of total fiscal expenditures also increased between 2007 and 2014. This was especially the case for social security, which went from 15.8 to 20.5 percent (in 2013), and in health care, which rose from 4 to 6.7 percent.

Yet, despite these major steps in creating a social safety net and in addressing rising inequality, the role of the Chinese government in reducing inequality continues to be rather limited.[52] First, while the government has increased its efforts in redistribution, its role in initial distribution of income continues to be tilted toward the government and the more privileged. Second, the outcome even of its redistributive programs is that state policy also continues to favor the more privileged members of society. Once again we see that those on top are being anchored there, and the chances for others to penetrate their realm have been closed off.

Over the two decades following 1995, China's hyper-economic growth was combined with government extraction. As shown in figure 1.2, during the first decade of the twenty-first century, the economy, measured by GDP per capita, grew at an average rate of around 10 percent. The rate of government revenue growth averaged about twice as high, at nearly 20 percent. The share that government revenue represented of total national income increased from 13.1 to 14.6 percent between 2000 and 2009, while the share of household income dropped from 67.2 to 58.7 percent.[53] The growth rate of household income, in other words, fell below the rate of overall economic growth, while that of government revenue exceeded the overall economic growth rate. Indeed, in the decade from 1998 to 2008, not counting for inflation, gross domestic product in China grew 3.34 times. In contrast, urban household income rose only 2.91 times and rural household income grew just 2.2 times. During the same time period, government revenue increased 6.21 times.[54]

The third component of national income distribution, in addition to government and household income, is business income. Here, the growth rate also exceeded that of household income, with its share in total national income rising from 19.7 percent in the year 2000 to 24.7 percent in 2009. With a rising prominence of state-owned enterprises during this decade, largely through subsidies from state-controlled banks with low-interest loans, again it has been those associated with the state or state-

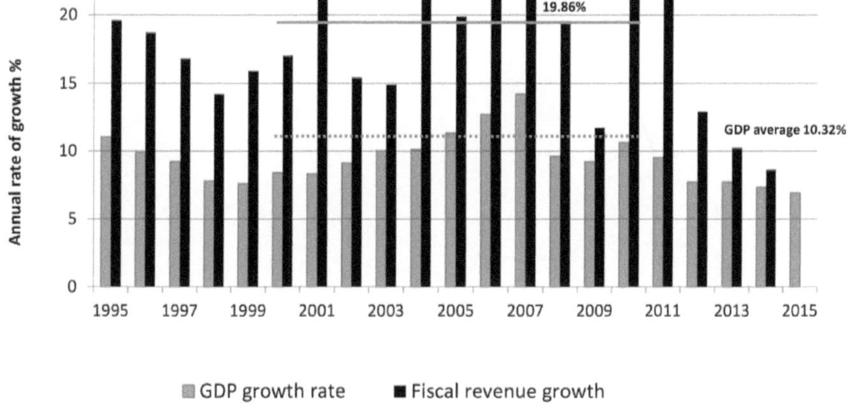

Figure 1.2. Growth with Extraction: Economic and Government Revenue Growth Rates, 1995–2015
***Sources: China Statistical Yearbooks*, various years**

owned enterprises who have enjoyed better economic returns and received higher incomes and benefits, once more contributing to entrenching wealth at the top.

Even with the most direct government intervention in reducing inequality by means of the recently launched and expanded social welfare programs, it has been the more privileged members of society who continue to benefit the most. An in-depth analysis of public transfers over the life course in education, health care, and pension reveals that those who belong to the households of the top quartile of the income groups have benefited more from government redistribution than have other households.[55] As shown in figure 1.3, on a per capita basis, almost at every age throughout a person's life course, those belonging to the top income group receive more public transfers than do those belonging to the other groups, especially those in the bottom half of the population (the lowest two groups).

At the ages of senior high school and college students (from fifteen to twenty-two), the difference in receiving public transfers in education is 3.3 to 1 between the top and the bottom income quartile. The gap between the rich and the poor in receiving public transfers gets larger over the life span, as those in the upper income groups benefit more from public expenditures in health care and in social security. At the peak age

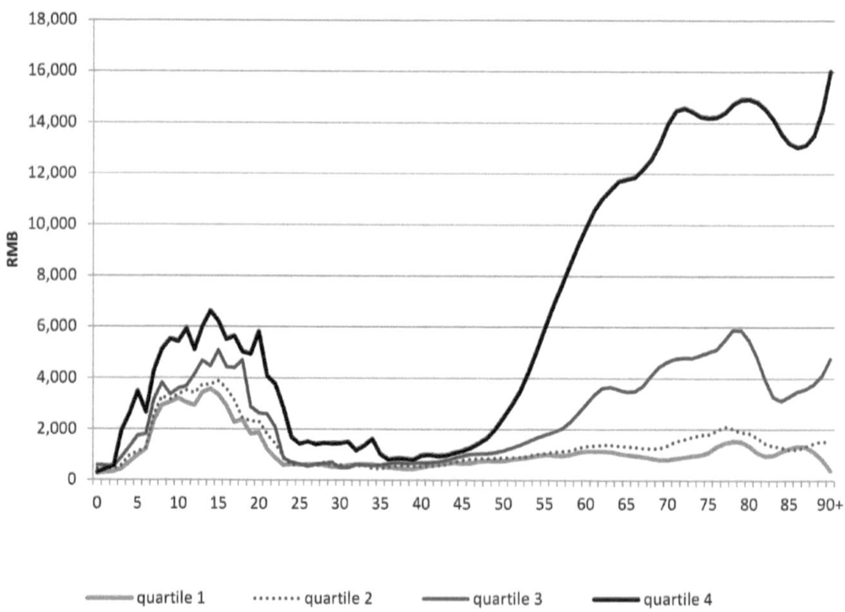

Figure 1.3. Per Capita Public Transfer Received by Income Quartile, 2010
***Source:* Shen et al., 2018**

of eighty and on a per capita basis, the people in the top income quartile received three times the public transfers in health care that those in the bottom income quartile did, one more form of polarization. Of all the public transfers spent on pensions, the top income quartile group received almost 80 percent, versus the 1.3 percent received by those in the bottom income quartile group.[56] Thus, the state is heavily implicated in the extremes of income division in Chinese society.

These regressive redistributions have far-reaching implications for life chances and for future social mobility. In education, the top income group receives substantially more state resources in preschool education and in higher education, two stages of education that set the start and end points. While the much higher pension payout to the top income group is largely a result of past employment histories—namely, those in the higher income groups were employed in the formal sector and are entitled to pensions, the meager pensions received by those at the bottom reveals how inadequate the social safety net is for a large number of the Chinese elderly.

BATTLE UPHILL

Less than four decades since its postsocialist planned-economy turn, China has evolved into a market-based economy best described as state capitalist. Nearly four decades of capitalist development under a socialist state have led to the creation of a society that is highly unequal, embodying features of both its socialist past and its capitalist present.[57] Economic and social inequalities have become systemic, structural, and durable. In contrast to the days of the socialist planned economy, when scarcity and poverty were the features of the day, a vibrant market economy has turned out to be a much better deal for the old communist elite, whose members can continue their reign over both the economy and the state, while profiting handsomely from it.

The structured nature of inequality, and its transferal from income to wealth and from the first to the second generation, makes containing or reducing inequality an uphill battle for China in the years to come. The state, even with its latest campaign to crack down on official corruption, in many ways is still very much a source of, not a cure for, rising inequality. From its control and expansion of the state-sector of the economy to its distribution of the national economic output, the state has played a direct role in generating inequalities between those who are close to the system and those who are not. Its vastly increased social spending, as shown above, has consistently favored the more privileged while inadequately assisting the poor. Good educational and job opportunities increasingly depend on one's family background and family wealth, even as social and political connections grow ever more important. Across most East Asian societies and elsewhere, the level of income inequality has become less severe after government redistribution. In China, however, this has not quite been the case.[58] Socially, wealth has exploded even as it has become concentrated in the hands of a few. Moreover, neither a property tax nor an inheritance tax has been imposed on those who have amassed a vast amount of wealth.

As noted above, at the start of China's postsocialist turn, the slogan used to legitimize inequality was "to let some get rich first." The hope or the promise was that a rising tide would lift all boats, and that income inequality would decline after a period of increase, following the trajectory of the Kuznets inverted U-curve. While some in China may have begun to celebrate a recent leveling off and even a slight drop in the overall level of measured income inequality, after more than three decades of rising inequality, that inverted U has yet to emerge.[59]

Studies based on international and historical data over the last half-century have shown that such an inverted U is best viewed as a mirage. One comprehensive study examining seventy-three countries that account for 80 percent of the world population and 92 percent of the world GDP, for instance, shows that between 1950 and 1995, in all but nine countries, inequality either increased or stayed constant.[60] Even in regions where "growth with equity" was advertised as a new model for the world, recent trends have shown that the period in which this was a reality has become history.[61] Rising inequality has been a global trend and it has only gotten worse in recent years.[62]

China's battle against rising inequality may well become much more daunting in the coming decades with changes in the two fundamental parameters of its so-called new normal: slowing down economic growth and accelerating population aging. China's historical economic boom has created unprecedented opportunities for most, with hundreds of millions of young people leaving farming and getting into manufacturing and services, and moving from the countryside to the cities. But as the hypergrowth era comes to an end, competition for jobs will increase and continued income augmentation will become more elusive, as has occurred in other societies, most relevantly those in East Asia, from Japan and South Korea to Taiwan. As opportunities become scarcer, it is primarily the already privileged who are positioned to seize them, and to stay at the top. As this process unfolds, we see closed doors for those at the bottom.

A slowing economy, coupled with rapid population aging, will also further tie the hands of the government in its attempts to upgrade its new, yet fragmented, social welfare regime. Hyper-increase in government revenue, once made possible by the model of growth with extraction, is affected more by slower growth than by the economic growth rate itself. As shown in figure 1.2 earlier in this chapter, in the last few years a drop in the rate of government revenue growth has far outpaced the drop in the overall growth rate of the economy: the rate of revenue increase between the years of 2013 and 2015 fell from an average annual rate of nearly 20 percent in the previous decade to less than 10 percent, having more than halved. The overall economic growth rate, in contrast, declined by only about 30 percent, from the average annual rate of 10 to 7 percent. With the prospect of further economic slowdown, the era of high revenue growth is also over.[63] Yet the number of elderly aged sixty and over will more than double in the two decades to come, from slightly over 200 million as of 2016 to over 440 million twenty years later. Rapidly escalating costs in health care and pensions will take up a larger and larger share of government revenue and expenditure, and will therefore further constrain the government's ability to address rising inequality.

Failure to address and to contain rising inequality could carry a significant political risk for the Chinese government, which has relied on its paternalistic role as a basis for political legitimacy. Rising inequality has been a great social and political concern, both for the Chinese public and for the government.[64] Yet persistent public concerns have not so far turned into the basis for social discontent and unrest, in part because the rapid economic growth and new economic opportunities have made most Chinese happy about their current state. As opportunities for upward mobility increasingly diminish following the economic slowdown, and as wealth and opportunities continue to transfer from one generation to the next—with poverty also inherited, the Chinese public may no longer view the system as fair and equitable as it has in the past, and it may not tolerate the degree of inequality it once did. Combatting inequality is a battle that China cannot afford to wait to wage, let alone to lose.

NOTES

I wish to thank Tao Ran, Li Yu, and Shi Qian for their kind help in locating and suggesting relevant data sources and literature, and to Dorothy Solinger, Martin Whyte, Deborah Davis, and Su Yang for their careful reading of the draft of the paper and helpful comments and suggestions. I am also indebted to Shen Ke and Cai Yong for their work in producing the results on public transfers, which are used in this chapter.

1. Glenn Firebaugh, "Empirics of World Income Inequality," *American Journal of Sociology* 104, no. 6 (1999): 1597–1630.

2. Carl Riskin, Zhao Renwei, and Li Shi, eds., *China's Retreat from Equality* (Armonk, NY: M.E. Sharpe, 2001); Wang Feng, *Boundaries and Categories: Rising Inequality in Post-Socialist Urban China* (Stanford: Stanford University Press, 2008); Li Shi, Hiroshi Sato, and Terry Sicular, eds., *Rising Inequality in China: Challenges to a Harmonious Society* (Cambridge: Cambridge University Press, 2013); Martin King Whyte, "Soaring Income Gaps: China in Comparative Perspective," *Daedalus* 142, no. 2 (2014): 39–52; Yu Xie and Xiang Zhou, "Income Inequality in Today's China," *Proceedings of the National Academy of Sciences* 111, no. 19 (2014): 6928–33.

3. Deborah Davis and Wang Feng, "Poverty and Wealth in Postsocialist China: An Overview," in *Creating Wealth and Poverty in Postsocialist China*, ed. Deborah Davis and Wang Feng (Palo Alto: Stanford University Press, 2009), 3–19.

4. Martin King Whyte, "China's Dormant and Active Social Volcanoes," *The China Journal* 75 (2016): 9–37.

5. Victor Nee, "A Theory of Market Transition: from Redistribution to Markets in State Socialism," *American Sociological Review* 54 (1989): 663–81; Andrew G. Walder, "Markets and Inequality in Transitional Economies: Toward Testable Theories," *American Journal of Sociology* 101, no. 4 (1996): 1060–73; Zhou Xueguang, "Economic Transformation and Income Inequality in Urban China: Evidence from Panel Data," *American Journal of Sociology* 105, no. 4 (2000): 1135–74.

6. Wang, *Boundaries and Categories*, chapter 6.

7. Wang, chapter 6.

8. Martin King Whyte, "Social Trends in China: the Triumph of Inequality?," in *Modernizing China*, ed. A. Barnett and R. Clough (Boulder: Westview, 1986), 165–84; Andrew G. Walder, "Social Change in Post-Revolution China," *Annual Review of Sociology* 15 (1989): 405–24; Martin K. Whyte, *One Country, Two Societies: Rural-Urban Inequality in Contemporary China* (Cambridge: Harvard University Press, 2010).

9. Xie and Zhou, "Income Inequality."

10. *China Statistical Yearbook* 1982 (Beijing: China Statistics Press, 1982), 440.

11. Thomas Piketty, Li Yang, and Gabriel Zucman, "Capital Accumulation, Private Property, and Rising Inequality in China, 1978–2015," NBER Working Paper. No. 23368 (2017).

12. Piketty et al., "Capital Accumulation."

13. Piketty et al.

14. https://www.forbes.com/sites/pamelaambler/2017/10/30/where-young-chinese-billionaires-are-making-their-wealth-and-spending-it/#6c181a17fb6c, accessed December 17, 2017.

15. http://www.bain.com/about/press/press-releases/2015-china-private-wealth-report-press-release.aspx

16. http://factsanddetails.com/china/cat11/sub70/item157.html

17. http://www.asianranking.com/top-20-richest-people-in-china/; https://en.wikipedia.org/wiki/List_of_countries_by_the_number_of_US_dollar_billionaires020.

18. https://www.forbes.com/sites/pamelaambler/2017/10/30/where-young-chinese-billionaires-are-making-their-wealth-and-spending-it/#6c181a17fb6c, accessed December 17, 2017.

19. http://www.scmp.com/news/china/money-wealth/article/1867321/china-be-top-ten-nation-us-dollar-millionaires-2020. Also a later report gives the number of "ultra-rich" individuals—with net assets of over 100 million RMB or $16 million—at 89,000, a growth rate of 14.1 percent over the past year. http://www.china.org.cn/china/2016-08/17/content_39103826.htm.

20. Xin Meng, "Wealth Accumulation and Distribution in Urban China," *Economic Development and Cultural Change* 55, no. 4 (2007): 761–91.

21. Li Shi and Haiyuan Wan, "Evolution of Wealth Inequality in China," *China Economic Journal* 8, no. 3 (2015): 264–87.

22. Yu Xie and Yongai Jin, "Household Wealth in China," *Chinese Sociological Review* 47, no. 3 (2015): 203–29.

23. Xie and Jin, "Household Wealth."

24. Xie and Jin.

25. Piketty et al., "Capital Accumulation."

26. http://www.bain.com/about/press/press-releases/2015-china-private-wealth-report-press-release.aspx

27. Li and Wan, "Evolution of Wealth Inequality"; Xie and Jin, "Household Wealth."

28. Xie and Jin, "Household Wealth."

29. Piketty et al., "Capital Accumulation."

30. Wang Feng, "Housing Improvement and Distribution in Urban China: Initial Evidence from China's 2000 Census," *China Review* 3, no. 2 (2003): 121–43.

31. This average price (per square meter) is very close to the number published by China's National Bureau of Statistics, which gives the price for year 2000 at 2058 RMB.
32. http://blog.sina.com.cn/s/blog_3f70d8d00102vhnj.html.
33. Shi Faqi, "Analysis of the Macro Structure of Income Distribution in China," in *China Faces Inequality: Studies in Income Distribution*, ed. Song Xiaowu, Wang Tianfu, Li Shi, and Wang Feng (Beijing: Social Sciences Academic Press of China, 2013), 9–34.
34. Wang, "Housing Improvement."
35. Minxin Pei, *China 's Crony Capitalism: The Dynamics of Regime Decay* (Cambridge: Harvard University Press, 2016).
36. Meng, "Wealth Accumulation."
37. Pei, *China 's Crony Capitalism.*
38. Whyte, "China's Dormant and Active Volcanoes."
39. Wang Feng, "Beyond Inequality: Mobility and China's Future," *Chinese Sociological Review* 45, no. 3 (2013): 3–5.
40. Donald Treiman, "Trends in Educational Attainment in China," *Chinese Sociological Review* 45, no. 3 (2013): 3–25; Wei-jun Jean Yeung, "Higher Education Expansion and Social Stratification in China." *Chinese Sociological Review* 45, no. 4 (2013): 54–80.
41. Yeung, "Higher Education Expansion."
42. Yeung.
43. Xiaogang Wu, "Economic Transition, School Expansion and Educational Inequality in China, 1990–2000," *Research in Social Stratification and Mobility* 28, no. 1 (2010): 91–108; Emily Hannum, Xuehui An, Hua Yu, and Sebastian Cherng, "Examinations and Educational Opportunity in China: Mobility and Bottlenecks for the Rural Poor," *Oxford Review of Education* 37, no. 2 (2011): 267–305; Anning Hu and Jacob Hibel, "Changes in College Attainment and the Economic Returns to a College Degree in Urban China, 2003–2010: Implications for Social Equality," *Social Science Research* 44 (2014): 173–86; and Tony Tam and Jin Jiang, "Divergent Urban-Rural Trends in College Attendance: State Policy Bias and Structural Exclusion in China," *Sociology of Education* 88, no. 2 (2015): 160–80.
44. Hongbin Li et al., "Unequal Access to College in China: How Far Have Poor, Rural Students Been Left Behind?," *China Quarterly* 221 (2015): 185–207.
45. Wenhui Yang and Chen Ling, "Political Capital and Intergenerational Mobility: Evidence from Elite College Admissions in China," *Chinese Journal of Sociology* 2, no. 2 (2016): 194–213.
46. Wu Yuxiao, "Educational Tracking System and the Educational Stratification in China," *Sociological Studies* 4 (2013): 179–202 (in Chinese).
47. Meng Chen, "Intergenerational Mobility in Contemporary China," *Chinese Sociological Review* 45, no. 4 (2013): 29–53.
48. Li Lulu and Zhu Bin, "Changes in the Pattern of Intergenerational Mobility in Contemporary China," *Chinese Journal of Social Sciences* 5 (2015): 40–58 (in Chinese).
49. Jun Li, "Job Mobility in Post-reform Urban China," *Chinese Sociological Review* 45, no. 4 (2013): 81–109.
50. Yanjie Bian, "The Prevalence and Increasing Significance of Guanxi," *China Quarterly*, forthcoming.
51. Wu Yuxiao, "Social Connections, First Job Seeking, and Occupational Mobility," *Sociological Research* 5 (2011): 128–52 (in Chinese).
52. Barry Naughton, "Is China Socialist?," *Journal of Economic Perspectives* 31, no. 1 (2017): 3–24.
53. Shi, "Analysis of the Macro Structure."
54. Wang Feng, "The End of 'Growth with Equity'? Economic Growth and Income Inequality in East Asia," in *Asia Pacific Issues*, no. 101 (Honolulu: East-West Center, 2011).
55. Shen Ke, Wang Feng, and Cai Yong, "A Benevolent State Against Unjust Society? Inequalities in Public Transfers in China," *Chinese Sociological Review*, forthcoming.
56. Shen et al., "Benevolent State."

57. Naughton, "Is China Socialist?"
58. Wang, "End of 'Growth with Equity.'"
59. Wang, *Boundaries and Categories*; Whyte, "Soaring Income Gaps."
60. Giovanni Andrea Cornia, ed., *Inequality, Growth, and Poverty in an Era of Liberalization and Globalization* (Oxford: Oxford University Press, 2004).
61. Wang, "End of 'Growth with Equity.'"
62. Joseph E. Stiglitz, *The Price of Inequality: How Today's Divided Society Endangers Our Future* (New York: W. W. Norton, 2013); Thomas Piketty, *Capital in the Twenty-First Century* (Cambridge, MA: Harvard University Press, 2014).
63. This trend of falling fiscal revenue is accelerating: in the last two years, the growth rate of government revenue for the first time since the 1994 fiscal reforms underperformed economic growth, with 5.8 percent of fiscal revenue growth versus 7.0 percent GDP growth in 2015, and 4.5 versus 6.9 in 2016.
64. Whyte, "China's Dormant and Active Volcanoes."

TWO

Convergence and Divergence Among the Rich and the Poor

Li Zhang

It has been widely acknowledged that China is becoming one of the most unequal countries in the world. While per capita disposable income has been rising, the gap in income distribution is soaring. According to an IMF working paper, "the top quintile of earners now pull in nearly half of total income while the poorest quintile of earners account for under 5%."[1] Another measure is the Gini coefficient, which hit 0.469 in 2014 according to China's National Bureau of Statistics. This number is considered alarming (0 being perfect equality, 1 being maximum inequality).[2] Some online surveys of Chinese netizens show that narrowing the gap between the rich and the poor (*pinfu chaju*) is one of the top public concerns. Policymakers in recent years have become aware that this factor, along with corruption and official mistreatment of some citizens, is a main source of social discontent and could be a destabilizing force for Chinese society. Given the glaring chasm between the rich and the poor, the haves and the have-nots, one can hardly recognize contemporary China as a socialist country, as it is claimed to be by the party-state. Many Chinese intellectuals have begun to reflect on the serious social costs of the reforms and the very model of development that is giving rise to what some call *quangui zibenzhuyi* (crony capitalism).[3]

Although the title of this chapter invokes two contrasting notions—"the rich" and "the poor," my aim is not to simply juxtapose them but seek to go beyond traditional class categories by exploring the lived experiences of differently located people. As Solinger argues, while a caste-like formation marked by monumentally disparate lifestyles and access to resources and opportunities is taking place, this is a complex configuration that maintains a varying degree of agency (in this volume). In fact, "the rich" has long been an ambiguous and unstable category that refers to a wide spectrum of social actors in Chinese society, from wealthy business and political elites to mid-level state enterprise managers and private entrepreneurs to urban professionals and intellectuals. "The rich" is constituted in everyday practices and is a shifting, relational, and contested category, which cannot be easily demarcated by income or occupation.[4] Yet this ambiguity can be productive because it allows us to examine why and how people deploy the term for different purposes depending on the specific context. The rich and the poor are meaningful categories only when we examine them in relation to each other.[5]

In this chapter, I explore how the so-called rich and poor in Chinese cities tackle several salient problems given their unequal access to resources, and I discuss the implications of the very different outcomes. The first issue is fighting for the rights to space and land in the city; the second concerns different responses to the worsening air pollution in urban areas and its health effects in recent years; the third example deals with managing psychological distress and emotional problems. In particular, I show that regardless of their position, the rich and the poor all exercise a different degree of agency conditioned by their different socioeconomic circumstances. There exists a hierarchy of agency, ability to choose, and opportunity to escape.

CONTESTING URBAN SPACE

There have been widespread urban land disputes between some real estate developers and urban residents over the past two decades. One prominent form is "Battles Over Green Space" (*Ludi Baoweizhan*). This specific style of spatial struggle is an integral part of the broader rights protection movement in reform China, known as *weiquan yundong*, which includes protecting consumer rights, land rights, environmental concerns, gay rights, and so on. This movement is becoming a powerful force in reshaping popular politics. Rather than invoking the notion of citizen rights (*gongmin quan*), this urban activism draws specifically from two distinct and contested notions—"property rights" and "public common good." These concepts are based on two popular subject positions—"property owners" (*yezhu*) and "the masses" or "ordinary people" (*qunzhong*). *Yezhu* is a newer category that has emerged as a result of the housing reform and the enacting of the 2003 Property Rights Law. By contrast, *qunzhong* is a longstanding political category that gained its salience under socialism and continues to remain relevant and significant today. As Shao Qin and Mun Yung Cho demonstrate, some displaced urban residents and laid-off workers frequently seek to position themselves in terms of *qunzhong* in their struggle to call for state accountability and government assistance.[6]

The case of "Riverside Battle Over Green Space" took place in Kunming where I conducted long-term ethnographic fieldwork between 2000 and 2006 on the privatization of housing and its social and cultural consequences. That struggle represented a kind of fierce battle over the appropriation of communal space within private gated communities (*xiaoqu*). In order to maximize profits, some developers attempt to construct additional commodity housing buildings on the common land within a *xiaoqu*. The existing homeowners believe that this act is a breach of the contract they signed with the developer and thus a violation of their property rights. They feel strongly that they are entitled to the communal space they commonly hold. Therefore, they come together to challenge predatory developers by engaging in protests, legal action, and other oppositional behaviors to block what they see as an illicit appropriation of their land. The residents involved speak often as rightful *yezhu* (private property owners).

I first heard about the Riverside battle from a casual conversation with a friend in Kunming in 2004. I then located reports on it from five major local newspapers. A development firm had just filed a lawsuit against several resident activists. I was able to talk to the two lawyers who agreed to meet with me and to introduce me to some of the residents involved. Riverside Garden was developed by the Dragon Development Company in the Guandu District of Kunming. The focal point of conflict was the use of communal space already designated as the green space within the community. In 1997, before the housing construction was finished, the apartments were already on the market for sale at a price of about twenty-one hundred yuan per square meter. At that time, this property was considered upper-middle-level housing. Most buyers here were small or midsized business owners and urban professionals such as doctors and lawyers who had assembled some wealth from their lucrative practices.

One of the factors that attracted many buyers was the developer's promise that nearly half of the development was to be committed to green communal space—an amount much higher than most of the existing residential communities in the city. The developer promised to create an attractive environment with lots of lawns, trees, flowers, and open space. According to newspaper reports and my interviews, the sales agents verbally promised all the buyers that there would be a large, open green space in their community. Liu Jin, a small business owner in her thirties who planned to buy two apartments there, called the municipal planning office and was assured that no construction of high-rises within the community was planned or would be approved. She was satisfied and finished her purchase. The residential units there were sold quickly within a year.

For the first five years, the residents enjoyed the communal green space, which had become a popular place for kids to play, the elderly to gather, and others to stroll and exercise. But the situation suddenly began to change in late May 2005. One day a group of construction workers arrived at Riverside Garden and started to cut down trees and remove light posts and benches. The residents soon discovered that this green field would no longer belong to them because two new high-rises would be built there. They became furious and had a violent encounter with gangsters sent by the real estate firm. Ms. Liu Jin recalled:

> On the evening of June 1st, the road to our xiaoqu was blocked by dozens of homeowners because they heard that heavy construction machinery was about to move in. On June 2nd, when I came back from work at noon, I saw some five hundred men hired by the developer forming a circle hand by hand around the green space to prohibit anyone from entering. There were still a few elderly people taking a walk within who refused to leave. They were simply carried out forcefully by the hired men. At that moment, a bulldozer was moving in. I jumped out and tried to stop them, but the driver would not listen to me. As some of the residents pushed into the green space, their men began to beat us.

That afternoon, three to four hundred infuriated residents marched to the street and blocked traffic on the busy second ring road. They held large banners with such slogans as "Return Our Garden, Return Our Green Space." They believed that such public action would draw officials' attention and public sympathy. Local government officials and the police came out to persuade the protestors to return home in order to halt this unrest. After a couple of hours, they finally left the street and decided to hang the banners from their home windows. To gain wider public attention and support, a group of activists posted flyers about their struggle throughout the streets in the nearby area and displayed the slogans on their car windows.

The violent confrontation and public protest halted the construction. The developer sought other means to terrorize the residents. A female homeowner who was an activist drove to a nearby supermarket. When she stopped at a red light, two strangers suddenly came up and broke her car window and tried to stab her. She quickly jumped to the other seat and the knife cut her leg. The men vanished into the crowd. This incident terrified Riverside's residents who saw it as a threat to their entire community.

The developer then filed a lawsuit against six activists at the local district court and demanded that the defendants make a public apology and pay a large settlement for damaging the firm's reputation. The two hundred thousand yuan lawsuit against them each was not a small amount. The activists were frightened and mobilized their *guanxi* (personal connection) networks to hire two lawyers to defend them. Even though they had ample photos, videos, and eyewitness accounts that could be used in court to prove the violence against them, they had little confidence in the legal system and were deeply worried about their fate. Individuals fighting against a powerful developer in China rarely have a positive outcome.

City governments tend to take a hands-off approach by staying out of a dispute such as this one unless the situation gets out of control. The official rhetoric today is to let citizens seek justice from the legal system. The judicial system is supposed to be relatively independent from politics, but in reality it is heavily permeated by political and corporate power. Meanwhile, the activists were concerned about the safety of their families as they were sometimes followed and watched by thugs sent by the developer. One of them said: "We sometimes feel like members of an underground party since we have to change our meeting places all the time. We cannot meet at home within the compound as it is under surveillance. We cannot call each other from home as we believe that our phones are tapped."

Despite these obstacles and threats, Riverside residents eventually won the green land battle on two fronts. The developer finally withdrew the litigation due to lack of evidence after two rounds of court hearings. Then some three hundred Riverside homeowners collectively filed a lawsuit at the municipal middle court against the city planning bureau for wrongly issuing Dragon Real Estate a license to develop commodity housing on the green space. Two weeks later, the planning bureau announced that it would withdraw its approval for housing development on the disputed site and put this land under the category of "public green project." It was speculated that the city government was under strong pressure from higher authorities to prevent this highly publicized conflict from escalating into larger civil unrest. This then can be counted as a victory for these better-endowed citizens.

By contrast, the fate of urban spatial contestation involving relatively poor city residents is gloomy. China's urban redevelopment and march to modernity has largely been built on massive destruction of old neighborhoods and large-scale displacement of the ordinary families who had lived in those places for several decades. This is known as *chaiqian* (demolishing and relocating) in order to make space for new commercial centers, fancy hotels, and luxury apartment high-rises. I have documented this ruthless process and conflicts in my second book, *In Search of Paradise*. The cases I analyzed were several old neighborhoods located at the heart of Kunming, which were slated for new development in the 1990s and 2000s.

Tens of thousands of residents who had lived there for decades were forced to leave their homes and relocate to inconvenient suburbs where few hospitals, schools, and markets had been established at that time.

Many families simply refused to move; some demanded a better compensation package than what was given to them by the developers (often significantly lower than the market value). I called this movement "homegrown urban activism," which included "nail households" (*dingzi hu*, a term for persistent troublemakers) standoffs, suicide threats, and spontaneous protests by affected residents. In most cases, these efforts eventually failed and the families were forced out of their homes and displaced in far suburbs. At best, only after a long period of bargaining and deadlock were a few families able to negotiate for somewhat better compensation than the original offers. Their loss was both an economic one and a social and emotional one as they were uprooted from the social fabric in which they were embedded. This type of case can only be classified as a defeat.

Why do we see very different results in spatial struggles? I believe that one of the key factors is the lack of social and economic resources among the relatively poor residents. In comparison with the well-to-do homeowners in gated communities, the evicted residents did not have the money or the social resources to hire strong lawyers to argue on their behalf. They, along with their dilapidated homes, were viewed by the developers and government officials as dispensable and standing in the way of modernizing the city. Their struggle thus received little public attention and sympathy. By contrast, the middle-class homeowners had a strong sense of entitlement and were able to mobilize their social networks to obtain decent lawyers at high legal fees. Further, those evicted were far less organized than the homeowners, who had better communication technologies and media access. The notion of property rights was seldom invoked because rights consciousness had not yet become well developed among most residents in the 1990s. Their spatial struggle was framed simply in terms of the right to a place and the demand for better compensation.

AIR DEMOCRACY?

Our flight was descending for a while and the plane was about to land at Beijing Capital International Airport. But I could not see any cityscape, which made me very worried. As we moved through the dense smog, the runway appeared and the plane landed quickly. It was a late June afternoon in 2015, and Beijing was enveloped in a gray smog that made one easily mistake it for evening. The air quality index in my iPhone showed 218—a number indicating a "very unhealthy condition." For the next five days, I lived under this smog dome and from time to time used the PM2.5 proof mask I had brought from the United States. But that was not the worst. Later in November, the index reached 611, an off-the-chart number, triggering a red alert for severe air pollution. Chinese authorities advised Beijing residents to stay indoors as much as possible. Schools were closed down, construction projects were halted, and traffic was interrupted.

Perhaps in recent decades nothing has posed such a widespread and tangible threat to everyone as the record air pollution in Beijing, Shanghai, and a number of other cities. Some recent studies find that air pollution is one of the major causes of heart and lung diseases, birth defects, and strokes, killing four thousand people every day in China.[7] The situation is getting worse despite government efforts to improve the environment. The reactions of ordinary citizens have ranged from fear, anxiety, anger, vulnerability, and frustration to helplessness, pessimism, and cynicism. As anthropologist Jerry Zee puts it, "To breathe, then, is both a necessity for life and an erosion of it."[8] And air knows no boundary; it moves and permeates every possible corner of space.

For a while, there was a shared public sentiment in affected areas as articulated by a female white-collar professional I met: "The only comfort is that this time we are all suffering—the rich, the poor, the middle class. It does not matter who you are, you cannot stop breathing. If you want to go outside, the air treats everyone equally. Unlike other previous crises during which the rich always found ways to escape the problems, this time at least it is fair to everyone. Maybe it is a kind of air democracy." Many ordinary citizens I spoke to expressed this view with a deep sense of cynicism.

At first glance, it is true that everyone, regardless of his or her position, must breathe in the same air (at least outdoor air). Some have speculated that this shared fate might create a new form of solidarity that will bring the poor, the middle-class, and the rich together to demand change. Chinese media have occasionally featured top Chinese leaders walking outside without wearing any masks to demonstrate that they are not fearful and share a common fate with ordinary people. But this is seen by most people as merely a show since these officials can retreat to their spacious and well-filtered indoor spaces.

Very quickly, different social groups have developed different strategies which, in turn, have created unequal air spaces. In Beijing, it is common for well-to-do families to install expensive air filters at home to ensure indoor breathable air. As anthropologist Matthew Kohrman shows, marketers and manufacturers of air purifiers quickly cash in "at the intersection of pollution and inequality" by offering different levels of products for those with varying consumer power, exploiting both their fears and their dreams of the good life.[9] It is also common for those who have choices to plan for family activities according to the air quality index (AQI), and decide whether they should go out or not.

A small number of people have even begun to carry an expensive personal air supply. In late 2015, a Canadian company, Vitality Air, started to sell bottled Rocky Mountain air to Chinese people as a joke, but to its surprise the first shipment (500 bottles) was sold out in four days. A 7.7-liter can sells for 100 yuan, and there is a huge market for it. Fresh air and portable air filters are now marketed as luxury consumer items (along with other items such as iPhones, flat screen TVs, and high-end cosmetics).

Further, some wealthy organizations and work units have recently begun to create enclosed outdoor areas for their own members to enjoy. For example, the International School of Beijing put up a large, pressurized dome over its playground so that the privileged children enrolled there can still play outside on polluted days. Thus, enclosure and filtration have become important technologies to alter Beijing's cityscape and urban life. Rather than fostering democracy or a "coming together" as some had wished, a new form of environmental injustice that reinforces class inequality is emerging. It creates different "chambers" in the city that can only be accessed by certain advantaged people. This form of exclusivity regarding the very basic necessity of living is unprecedented and troubling.[10]

To escape bad air altogether, one must ultimately move to another place far away. Again, one's financial capacity makes a big difference here. For the rich, there are at least two popular choices. The first is to purchase a second home or to find a job in another Chinese city with good AQI numbers. My hometown, Kunming, known as "the city of eternal spring," is one of the most favored places. When Beijing's air is too bad to breathe, these families fly to their second home and stay for a period of time. But this option is clearly costly. Some middle-class professionals even choose a new job in order to relocate the whole family to another city that has blue skies. For example, out of serious concerns over her young son's health (he had recurring upper-respiratory-related illness in Beijing), Lan Yanfei decided to take a job in a remote tourist town, Lijiang, in Yunnan Province, so as to escape the smog trap altogether. "Of course, there is a sacrifice to make, including giving up social and other resources I have accumulated, but one has to decide what is the most important thing in life," said Lan.[11] Clearly, for her it is the blue sky, health, and the freedom to breath in fresh air.

The second choice is to go as far as North America or Europe for vacations during the worst winter season of air pollution. Some even purchase a home overseas or send their children out of the country for high school or college. Several parents told me that concerns about the detrimental health effects of polluted air and other environmental factors have influenced their decision to choose overseas education for their children. Zhou, for instance, is a successful playwright in his early fifties. His wife, Liu, is a real estate agent who made a fortune a few years ago. I have known them for over twenty years. One day they called me and asked where a good place to buy a small house in the Bay Area would be, because they want to come out several months a year to write and avoid the choking smog. They had first tried to get a place in the suburbs outside of Beijing but soon discovered that the smog spread quite far out. Since they have to get out of the northern plain to avoid bad air and their daughter attends a college in California, they decided to buy a second home in the United States. Obviously not many people can choose this option because it is both financially and socially complicated.

For the majority of ordinary families, an indoor air filter or a personal air bottle is far beyond their financial capacity, let alone relocating away from their original neighborhoods. They often have to go outside and travel—just to their workplaces—by bus or bicycle. Many among the poor who are doing street sweeping, construction labor, sanitation-related work, public gardening, or garbage collecting have few choices but to labor all day outdoors in the pollution.

In Beijing, I spoke to some who can afford to think quite differently. To illustrate, a middle-aged university professor mused: "If I had to choose, I would rather live a life that is a few years shorter and not be confined inside like a prisoner." A young mother wrote: "After two months of checking the AQI every day, I find myself growing more and more anxious . . . The *pollution* index has begun to determine my mood daily. Seeing the words *wuran* (polluted) on the computer screen and looking at the gray sky as if covered by a comforter is enough to ruin my day."[12] Indeed, I was surprised to find that in recent years the correlation between mood and climate change is becoming a frequent topic among Beijing dwellers. A new category, "smog-induced anxiety," is emerging.

In the midst of this toxic air crisis and self-protection mania, some citizens have also chosen to respond by engaging in collective action and voluntary work: creating websites, bulletin boards, and chat groups to voice their concerns and raise public awareness; monitoring air for better self-protection; or calling for government policy changes to curb pollution. Some women believe that anxious mothers can engender positive changes for society and their children. Still others use dark humor to express their desperation and frustration.[13] In sum, the notion of "air democracy" turns out to be a fantasy after all. Facing common environmental threats, the rich are able to afford different strategies to protect themselves and lessen the adverse impact on their health. The poor are once again exposed to multiple hazards but have fewer recourses, or none at all, to help them cope.

MANAGING DISTRESS

The third domain I want to examine is how the rich and the poor deal with the mental and psychological distresses heightened by increasing market competition and rapid social changes. It has been reported that in recent years more and more Chinese people are experiencing varying degrees of anxiety, depression, stress, and other emotional problems.[14] The pressure to become "successful" (*chenggong*) is a leading stressor across a broad range of social strata today. Other stresses, especially for the less fortunate, include but are not limited to unemployment, housing costs rising beyond affordability, uncertain prices for everyday foodstuffs, soaring healthcare costs, and so on. Although it is hard to identify a direct causal relationship between recent societal transformations and the increasing rate of mental distress, research indicates that the need for psychological care is rising rapidly, especially among urban professionals. It is in this broader context that a mass psychological counseling and learning movement is unfolding in Chinese cities over the past two decades.

As the rich and middle-class Chinese are accumulating material wealth and building up their private "paradises" in gated communities, they are beginning to realize that their gains do not necessarily give them a deeper sense of fulfillment and well-being. Many are feeling confused, frustrated, and lost. Among the urban professionals and relatively well-to-do population, a new therapeutic language of personal emotions, self-fulfillment, and self-care is emerging and reshaping the way the individual psyche and the social are conceived and managed. This phenomenon raises important questions of how Chinese people in different socioeconomic situations manage their mental well-being.

Over the past several years, I have been working on a project that explores how the new "psy fever" is transforming selfhood, sociality, and techniques of governing in urban China.[15] What I have termed the "inner revolution" (*neixin de geming*) is a bottom-up attempt to address mental distress, psychological health, and subjective feelings by moving such concerns to the forefront of discussions on personal and national well-being. In this emerging realm, psychology is often branded as "psychological science" (*xinli kexue*) to give this discipline validity and credibility.[16] During the summers from 2010 to 2016, I went back to the city of Kunming to conduct ethnographic research based on extensive interviews and participant observation.

What is really interesting about this trend in China is a combination of two simultaneous processes: The first is the psychologization of social and economic issues, through which many societal or structural problems have come to be interpreted in personal and psychological terms. This development is quite new to China since, under socialism, psychology was regarded as a bourgeois practice and was largely banned, and psychiatry was limited to treating severe cases of psychosis.

The second trend is the demedicalization of emotional distress.[17] Rather than focusing on treating mental illness, what is at the center of this "inner revolution" is the promise of achieving well-being, resilience, optimism, and feeling happier with the aid of professionals and imported Western therapeutic methods. Thus, a significant part of the "psy fever" is taking place far beyond hospitals and clinics and has spread into other arenas such as professional training centers, families, corporations, police forces, schools, and so on.

What is most relevant to my concern here is the class and gender dimension of this "inner revolution." The primary consumers of the new profitable psy industry are the members of the younger urban middle classes and especially women. What motivates these people to embrace psychology and counseling is the desire to enhance their familial and social relationships, to engage in better self-care, and to improve the quality of their lives beyond material comfort. I met numerous young mothers who brought their single child to counseling in order to find a quick fix for their kid's school or behavior problems through expert help. Common difficulties children confront include troubles in socializing, internet addiction, poor school performance, depression, and parent-child conflicts. Among the women I interviewed, many were eager to improve their family relations so as to live a harmonious family life, improve their interpersonal skills (especially in communicating with their children), or become more successful in their careers.

But professional intervention for emotional well-being is expensive. Already in 2005 the average cost for a one-hour counseling session in Kunming was 300–500 yuan; in Beijing and Shanghai it was even higher—around 500–800 yuan. A two- to three-day workshop on psychological training and counseling techniques can cost 2,000–3,000 yuan, depending on the content and the status of the lead trainer/therapist. In the summer of 2016, I attended a workshop in Kunming on cultivating "Non-Violent Communication Skills" through psychological training, which was largely based on the Satir family counseling model.[18] Twenty-six people (mostly school teachers, doctors, state enterprise employees, and private business owners) aged between twenty-two and thirty-five participated in it with great interest. The price tag was 1,500 yuan for two days—half of a school teacher's monthly salary. But most of the participants felt that it was worth it if they could learn how to improve their family dynamics and emotional outlook through professional help. The leader of the workshop was a well-known psy expert specializing in family therapy.

The working-class, the poor, and others on the margins of society are left out of this highly commercialized realm, as they do not have the time or the money to engage in these therapeutic experiments of self-care and self-actualization. Therefore, "psy fever" is a very class-specific phenomenon in China.

But in some areas, government-led therapeutic interventions among the poor have taken place and been integrated into social work. Jie Yang's recent book, *Unknotting the Heart,* documents the psychologization of governance among the urban poor in reform China.[19] In contrast to my research focus, her project traces the top-down efforts by some local governments to utilize psychology and counseling techniques in order to transform disgruntled laid-off workers into happier, stable, and self-reliant citizens.

Yang details how the newly trained community psychosocial workers are playing an increasingly important role in reemployment programs. Their goal is to harness the positive potential of the unemployed and deliver emotional care to distressed workers while promoting the image of a nurturing reform-state. Rather than directly tackling the structural problems of unemployment itself, laid-off workers are encouraged to accept their harsh reality while, supposedly, pursuing happiness through positive thinking and self-reflexive practices. For example, they are taught by social workers how to manage anger and create a positive relationship with the self in challenging times. Much of the teaching is done in the spirit of Martin Seligman's positive psychology.[20] By giving the distraught workers the opportunity to learn how to transform themselves and gain optimism, Yang argues, the state is exercising a form of "kindly power" that might help to alleviate the negative impact of mass unemployment through psychotherapeutic care. This form of "therapeutic governing" is innovative yet has its own limits.

REFLECTIONS

From urban space, to air quality, to affect politics, China's urban better-off and poor citizens have very different relationships to each of these spheres. Despite people facing common dilemmas, so far, my ethnographic evidence suggests that the divergence in situation between those with means and those without is far greater than any convergence. The ultimate driving force behind this disparity is the vastly unequal access these groups have, respectively, to social and economic resources. As my research shows, relocation or seeking psychological help are usually voluntary actions for the wealthy. In stark contrast, the residential moves of the poor and the psychological treatment they receive are largely involuntary, as these changes are pushed upon them by real estate developers or government agencies. At the same time, the ramifications of the existing inequality in the reconfigurations of urban space, the altered lived experiences, and the disparate inner landscapes of the rich and the poor are not merely transformations within the economic domain. Instead, they extend to the social domain. Although some Chinese people have the necessary agency to manage to improve their life trajectories, the obstacles for the impoverished to move up are unsurmountable. That is why Solinger opts to refer to "a caste-like" formation constituting Chinese society. Poverty remains a tough and pressing issue to be tackled by the Chinese government.[21]

With growing unequal distribution of resources and alarming social polarization, it is no surprise to see that the Chinese party-state is deeply concerned about the potential instability and social discord that may be occasioned by the profound redistribution of wealth that has appeared in the cities—especially now that the threat of instability and discontent comes from not only the poor but also from the relatively rich and the middle classes. Thus, the Chinese state is eager to find quick fixes to quell the anger and unease by adopting unconventional tools such as psychological intervention.

In the context of mounting inequality and public concerns over air quality, food safety, and income distribution, recent official attempts to build a "harmonious society" (proposed by former president Hu Jintao) and to advocate for a new "China Dream" (by the current president Xi Jinping) can be regarded as efforts to reduce social conflict and reunite a diverging and polarized society in distress. But whether such efforts will turn out to be effective and reach their intended goals remains to be seen.

NOTES

I am grateful to the volume editor, Dorothy Solinger, and to Karl Gerth, Mei Zhan, Ann Anagnost, Jeffrey Wasserstrom, Feng Wang, Anne-Christine Tremon, Jieun Kim, and Roberta Zavoretti for their helpful engagement with my work. A small portion of the ethnographic material used in this chapter was previously published in my book *In Search of Paradise: Middle-Class Living in a Chinese Metropolis* (Ithaca and London: Cornell University Press, 2010).

1. Ian Talley, "China Is One of the Most Unequal Countries in the World," *Wall Street Journal*, March 26, 2015.

2. See also the alarming analysis of China's glaring inequality and its implications by Li Qiang in his article "How Big Is China's Inequality?," http://mp.weixin.qq.com.

3. Hengfeng Capital Research Institute, "How Is China Falling Into the Trap of Crony Capitalism?" http://mp.weixin.qq.com.

4. David Goodman, "The New Middle Class," in *The Paradox of China's Post-Mao Reforms*, ed. Merle Goldman and Roderick MacFarquhar (Cambridge: Harvard University Press, 1999), 241–261; John Osburg, *Anxious Wealth: Money and Morality Among China's New Rich* (Stanford: Stanford University Press, 2013); Li Zhang, *In Search of Paradise: Middle-Class Living in a Chinese Metropolis* (Ithaca and London: Cornell University Press, 2010).

5. Jie Chen, *A New Middle Class without Democracy: Economic Growth and the Prospects for Democratization in China* (Oxford University Press, 2013); Deborah Davis, ed. *The Consumer Revolution in Urban China* (Berkeley: University of California Press, 2000).

6. Shao Qin, *Shanghai Gone: Domicide and Defiance in a Chinese Megacity* (Rowman & Littlefield Publishers, 2013); Mun Young Cho, *The Specter of "The People": Urban Poverty in Northeast China* (Ithaca: Cornell University Press, 2013).

7. See "Air Pollution in China Is Killing 4,000 People Every Day, A New Study Finds," *Guardian*, August 13, 2015.

8. Jerry Zee, "Breathing in the City: Beijing and the Architecture of Air," *Scapegoat* 8 (2015): 54.

9. See Matthew Kohrman, "Filtered Life: Air Purification, Gender, and Cigarettes in the People's Republic of China," paper presented at the conference on "A Better Life

through Science and Biomedicine?," Cambridge, Massachusetts, Harvard University, April 15–16, 2016.

10. The concept of "environmental justice" emerged in the United States in the 1980s. Its aim is to ensure that people of different backgrounds have equal protection from health hazards and access to decision-making for a healthy environment to live in.

11. See "Three Mothers' Choices under the Smog," published online at https://www.thepaper.cn/. December 30, 2016.

12. Luo Jia, "I am Middle-Class, But I am Powerless," *Sanlian Weekly* 16 (2015): 74.

13. See "Air Pollution in China: The Causes, Impacts, and Responses to an Environmental Crisis," http://sites.dartmouth.edu/anth491/.

14. S. Lee, "Depression: Coming of Age in China," in *Deep China: The Moral Life of the Person*, ed. Arthur Kleinman et al. (Berkeley: University of California Press, 2011), 177–212.

15. See Li Zhang, "The Rise of Therapeutic Governing in Postsocialist China," *Medical Anthropology* 36, no. 1 (2016): 6–18; see also Li Zhang, "Bentuhua: Culturing Psychotherapy in Postsocialist China," *Culture, Medicine, and Psychiatry* 38, no. 2 (2014): 283–305.

16. Li Zhang, "Embracing Psychological Science for the Good Life?," paper presented at the conference on "A Better Life through Science and Biomedicine?," Cambridge, Massachusetts, Harvard University, April 15–16, 2016.

17. A similar argument is made by Junko Kitanaka in her research on Japan. See *Depression in Japan: Psychiatric Cures for a Society in Distress* (Princeton: Princeton University Press, 2012).

18. The Satir family therapy model was developed by an American psychotherapist Virginia Satir (1916–1988). It has a distinct approach to interpersonal communication and family dynamics. Imported into China about fifteen years ago, this is one of the most popular counseling models adopted by Chinese therapists.

19. Jie Yang, *Unknotting the Heart: Unemployment and Therapeutic Governance in China* (Ithaca: Cornell University Press, 2015).

20. Martin E. P. Seligman, *Authentic Happiness: Using the New Positive Psychology to Realize Your Potential for Lasting Fulfillment* (New York: Atria, 2002); see also, Martin E. Seligman, *Learned Optimism: How to Change Your Mind and Your Life* (New York: Knopf, 1991).

21. See Cho, *The Specter*.

Part II

Portraits of the Urban Poor

THREE

Banish the Impoverished Past

The Predicament of the Abandoned Urban Poor

Dorothy J. Solinger

Tales of the miraculous "Rise of China" abound. And commentators marvel ceaselessly over the country's pulling millions up from poverty, yet another oft-mouthed piece of rhetoric rehearsed when that nation is the subject. But these stories of success generally have one of two foci: if the story is of "rise," then the (domestic) locus of attention is the urban middle and rich classes; if the point is to look at poverty, it is just the peasants, the rural people, whether in the countryside or as migrants in the cities, whose situation is examined. Besides, most investigation of Chinese privation has focused on the phenomenon of poverty itself, or else on the efficacy of particular efforts at reducing or eliminating indigence.[1] Thus, all we get, in the main, is about positive, upward trajectories.

Perhaps the regime has willed it so. For this has been a government—much like its predecessors going back some two hundred years—that aims for progress, prosperity, and productivity, not just to display to its own populace but also to present to the world-at-large. Indeed, much of the legitimacy of the current political order has been tethered to achievements in amassing wealth, stimulating national pride, and fabricating a new, so-called high-quality citizenry, all aimed at permitting China to be conceived, finally, as fully "modern." What does not—most likely cannot—be forced into that mold is best cast aside, pitched out of the range of watching gazes and robbed of agency. China is proud but it is also self-conscious; its dreams must be glorious, its path seen as ever pushing onward, toward modernity.

In such a context, poverty in the cities is simply out of place. It is not to be available for viewing. And yet, the poverty-stricken, urban-registered in the cities—much of their condition of penury manufactured by the state itself in and after the late 1990s—cannot be merely left to expire in situ immediately. So the Party has devised a mode of maintaining these indigents. But in doing so it employs a method that more or less clamps the cities' poor into a space of exclusion from which they cannot escape. It forges them into a caste.

Fashioned, then, as the "other" side of the "modern," I submit, these unfortunates thus must be shucked away.[2] I ground my argument in some comparative statistics, setting the urban poor of today (and of the past decade) alongside three social segments that are—or have been—officially treated differently from how the current, caste-like impecunious are served: China's city-based, urban-registered unemployed of the late 1990s and early 2000s; the destitute in the Chinese countryside in recent years; and the impoverished in other countries, whether "developing" or "developed."

I pose the question: Why are the ill-off in the urban places of China now managed so much more meagerly, in relative terms, than are or were these other groups with which they can be contrasted? I make the case that China's municipally situated and registered needy have been shunted away because of the state's obsession with forging stability and with sustaining the appearances that its political elite deems necessary for attaining its own vision of modernity. This form of modernity is a site of aspiration regarded by the powerful as suitable for realizing its own illusions and imaginaries of rejuvenation, regeneration, and renovation.

The crux of my claim lies in a sorry appraisal of the state's "Minimum Livelihood Guarantee" (*zuidi shenghuo baozhang*, or for short, *dibao*). This is a program that was initiated formally in 1999, at a time of crisis for the urban working class—many of whose members were turned into the recipients or "targets" (*duixiang*) of this welfare, and in Chinese are often termed the *dibaohu* (*dibao* households). This guarantee is a social assistance scheme whose urban component especially has been steadily downgraded in the past several years.

I begin by tracing the early days and the rules of the program, and consider how it has changed of late. I then draw some comparisons with the way these other three sets of subjects have been officially dealt with. I finish with a cultural explanation about the motivating drivers that have left the *dibao* takers for most purposes out of the metropolitan picture. Again, my basic question is this: Why is social assistance in Chinese cities so stingy, especially at present, compared with comparable projects?

BACKGROUND OF THE *DIBAO* PROGRAM

Urban social assistance in PRC cities goes back to the 1950s, when a program entitled the "three withouts" (*san wu*)—which referred to those with no source of livelihood, no legal supporter, and no work ability—was instituted. That scheme sufficed for an era in which most other urban dwellers were employed and serviced by their firms (*danwei*). This set of destitute-in-three-ways, to whom an embarrassingly tiny pittance was doled out, has not been forgotten, despite an entirely new platform devised in the 1990s, the Minimum Livelihood Guarantee. That new plan was meant to shore up all of China's urban indigents' (not only the old "three-withouts" but also the newly impoverished) sustenance, thus extending allowances to substantially larger classes of recipients than in the earlier era.

As—in the 1980s and 1990s—the country's political economy shifted from state planning, the plants that made up the industrial portion of that economy were forced to cope with an unaccustomed market. Soon the planned model of business arrangement began to falter and crumble under the onset of rivalry between state-owned (on the one hand) and private, collective, and foreign (on the other) factories, especially because the latter grouping had no welfare responsibilities. The result was that the state-funded-enterprise social security system cracked apart, completely unable to cope.[3] The political elite then decided that tens of millions of workers had to be abruptly cast aside, and that a new welfare model would also be a necessity. According to Athar Hussain, as many as 68.9 million jobs were "sacrificed" to the economic marketization project between 1994 and 2003, if one adds up all those dismissed from state- and collectively-owned sectors in enterprises, public institutions, and the government.[4]

Besides introducing competition among firms, market economics increased both the price level and the scale of fees that beset the public.[5] There was an initial effort to handle the extremities of the people who had been pushed from their work posts, named the Reemployment Project of 1998–2001. But its promised supply of a "basic living allowance" to all laid-off state workers failed, with many firms unable to assemble the required resources to meet the need. At the same time, the numbers of the urban poor far outpaced the capabilities of the old "three-withouts" program.[6] And to add to the disaster, by 2001 in twenty-one of China's thirty-one provinces, the official *People's Daily* announced that the "reemployment rate" (percentage of the laid-off who found new jobs) had plunged to under 19 percent.[7] This statistic in itself must be an exaggeration, for untold numbers of those who achieved placement quickly discovered that the jobs they landed turned out to be short-term and quite irregular.[8]

As of the early 1990s, Shanghai's leaders had already become aware of the protest upheaval against job losses going on in the northeast, the core of the outdated heavy industrial base of the country, where, by far, the greatest numbers of dismissals were occurring.[9] Hoping to forestall such disorder in their own metropolis, Shanghai's politicians developed the *dibao* to tend to their city's discarded labor.[10] By the mid-1990s, many cities nationwide were following suit, and in 1997 the State Council issued a draft document setting up a national urban residents' Minimum Livelihood Guarantee System.[11] Two years later, that draft became the formal set of regulations specifying the program's rules and procedures.[12]

THE PROGRAM[13]

This program's stated aims were to "maintain the basic living standard for urban residents," defined as meeting the "necessary costs of food, clothes, and housing, giv[ing] reasonable consideration to water and power and fuel bills, and [providing for] the educational costs for children."[14] Soon after then-premier Zhu Rongji had signed the empowering order, a Ministry of Civil Affairs official referred to the 1997 Fifteenth Party Congress as having authorized the project to "perfect the traditional social relief system [a reference to the "three-withouts" program], establish a wholesome modern social welfare system, and guarantee that the economic system reform, especially the state enterprises' reform, could progress without incident (*shunli jinbu*)."[15]

These hopes revealed that—in addition to (or, better put, on the foundation of) sustaining the needy, the paired objectives of securing "stability" in the cities and facilitating the firms' restructuring lay at the core of the program. One Chinese writer went so far as to refer to the *dibao* as a "tranquilizer" which, it was hoped, would permit the "reorganization" of the state enterprises in Shenyang's Tiexi District (a site of massive layoffs) to go forward without obstruction. For without it, this essayist unabashedly wrote, "these people must become a burden that the enterprises would find it hard to throw off . . . even to possibly arousing even larger social contradictions."[16] Thus, the *dibao* had not just a goal of preserving livelihood; it was also meant to "ensure no threats to social order" even while its "benefit levels were set low so as not to be a disincentive to work."[17]

But the program failed to fulfill its goals within its first two years in operation.[18] Besides, at that point China was soon to join the World Trade Organization, which it did in December 2001. Many Chinese policy analysts expected that this accession would lead to millions more workers being thrown from their plants, as new and intensified international competition overcame their employers' ability to stay afloat.[19]

At its early stage, the undertaking called for municipalities to design and then finance their own programs after creating a local means norm (*dibao biaozhun*) which was to define eligibility just for that one city. Households whose members' average per capita income fell below that line were to be accorded monthly allowances to lift their per-person income up to the norm in their city (or sometimes city district). Dependence on localities let each city work out a "scientific determination" of the norm, based on its economic conditions. The factors to be taken into account comprised the following: that city's residents' basic livelihood needs; its price level; its degree of development; and its financial ability to contribute to the program.

This reliance on cities' calculations and decisions, however, opened a loophole for municipal officials to contrive "local conditions" or "local policies" limiting eligibility and excluding some needy individuals.[20] Thus, significant disparities grew up among cities in the way the program was managed; for instance, poorer urban jurisdictions set their norm low to minimize the numbers they had to serve, whereas in cities with more revenue and where, often, the numbers of the poverty-stricken were fewer, the line was pegged at a higher level.[21] In an endeavor to iron out such disparities to some degree, in 1999 the central government stepped in to subsidize the more indigent cities. The upshot was that the portion borne by the different localities varied significantly.

Yet, alarmed by ongoing demonstrations by the laid-off even after that boost, in 2001 Premier Zhu called for an enormous on-the-ground survey of the plight of the furloughed throughout the country, involving some 800,000 officials, in which he himself participated.[22] The insufficiencies uncovered (both in the size of the allowances and in the miniscule number of recipients) led him to order a massive increase in the funding for and the numbers served by the *dibao* program. Investment leapt from 1.5 billion yuan in 1999 up to 10.5 billion by 2002, as beneficiaries ballooned from 2.8 million in 1999 to 19.3 million in the latter year. (See tables 3.1 and 3.2.) Despite these boosts, the program as implemented far from succored the needy (neither did it manage to reach all those who were eligible, nor could it meet even the basic needs of those it did "cover"). So, in the early 2000s, large-scale central governmental transfers began to reverse an initial reliance on often inadequate local budgets.[23]

But one team of scholars found that as early as the mid-2000s, as many as 7.7 percent of the total urban-registered population had a net income below the relevant *dibao* line in their cities of registration. And yet the program was serving just about 22.5 million people at the time, which amounted to under 4 percent of the country's then-current city population. Thus, the researchers discovered, only about half of those eligible to receive the *dibao* were actually getting it. Besides that malfunction, "leakage" had resulted in an absurd situation in which "about 40 percent of the [program's actual] recipients [were people who were in fact] ineli-

Table 3.1. *Dibao* Expenditures as Percentage of GDP, 1999–2015 (billion *yuan*)

Year	*GDP*	*DB Expdtr.*	*DB Expdtr. as % of GDP*
1999	9,018.70	1.50	0.02
2000	9,977.60	2.70	0.03
2001	11,027.00	5.40	0.04
2002	12,100.00	10.90	0.09
2003	13,656.00	15.10	0.11
2004	16,071.00	17.30	0.11
2005	18,590.00	21.73	0.12
2006	21,766.00	26.70	0.12
2007	26,802.00	37.90	0.14
2008	31,675.20	61.50	0.19
2009	34,563.00	82.70	0.24
2010	40,890.30	97.00	0.24
2011	48,412.40	132.77	0.27
2012	53,412.00	139.20	0.26
2013	58,802.00	162.39	0.28
2014	63,646.30	159.20	0.25
2015	67,670.08	141.47	0.20

Sources: For government expenditures and GDP: Zhonghua renmin gongheguo guojia tongjiju bian [People's Republic of China State Statistical Bureau, ed.], *Zhongguo tongji nianjian* [*China Statistical Yearbook*] (Beijing: Zhongguo tongji chubanshe [China Statistics Press], various years); All China Data Center, China Data Online, selected years, retrieved from http://chinadataonline.org.
For *dibao* expenditures: Ministry of Civil Affairs Yearbook, All China Data Center, China Data Online, selected years. Retrieved from http://chinadataonline.org.
For 2015, calculated from http://www.360doc.com/content/16/0119/16/502486_529117704.shtml (for GDP) and http://www.askci.com/news/finance/2015/12/30/163331xfkf.shtml (for total national expenditure on the *dibao*).

gible" for it. The team also noted that "29 percent of all poor urban people [without specifying how a figure for the total poor was derived] were actually obtaining the *dibao*."[24] It is important to clarify here that there is no official urban poverty line.

Martin Ravallion did discover some improvement by 2007, when 39 percent of the *dibao*-eligible poor were recipients, and when just 1.2 percent of the non-poor were.[25] Thereafter, the number of urban recipients climbed up to 23.5 million at the program's peak in 2009; within six years, however, at year-end 2015, the number had fallen to just 17.216 million in

Table 3.2. Number of *Dibao* Participants, Urban and Rural, 1999–2015 (millions)

Year	*Urban*	*Rural*	*Total*
1999	2.80	N/A	2.80
2000	3.24	N/A	3.24
2001	11.70	N/A	11.70
July 2002	19.30	N/A	19.30
December 2002	20.60	4.08	24.68
2003	22.50	3.70	26.20
2004	22.10	4.90	27.00
2005	22.30	8.25	30.55
2006	22.40	15.93	38.33
2007	22.70	35.66	58.36
2008	23.30	42.84	66.14
2009	23.50	47.60	70.60
2010	22.90	52.28	75.18
2011	22.80	53.06	75.86
2012	21.40	53.45	74.85
2013	20.60	53.82	73.88
2014	18.77	52.07	70.84
2015	17.22	49.33	66.50

Sources: Zhongguo minzheng tongji nianjian [*China Civil Affairs Statistical Yearbook*] (Beijing: Zhongguo tongji chubanshe, various years).
For 2011, 2012: Minzhengbu wangzhan, retrieved from http://cws.mca.gov.cn/article/tjbg/2011210/20121000362598.shtml, accessed January 2013.
For 2015, retrieved from http://www.askci.com/news/finance/2015/12/30/163331xfkf.shtml.

the cities.[26] Adding up the beneficiaries in urban and rural areas together, the total amounted to a national sum of 66.55 million that year,[27] a significant decline from 2011's peak of 75.86 million.[28] (See table 3.2.)

CURRENT TREATMENT OF *DIBAOHU*: THREE COMPARISONS

Not only are the numbers of beneficiaries down. In general, today's urban-registered poor are faring worse in a relative sense than are three other similar groups. I go on to support this claim by contrasting the treatment recipients in cities are accorded now with three comparable groups: the current *dibaohu* as against those assisted in the early years of the program; urban "targets" as opposed to rural ones; and Chinese urban poor as opposed to similarly situated people in other countries.

Comparing Today's Recipients with Those of the Dibao's *Early Days*

True, local administrations have been finding make-work positions for the unemployed in recent years, tasks that often keep them out of sight, such as sweeping the lanes of community courtyards, standing "guard" at the gates of these quarters, and peeling shreds of old notices from the common walls. And yet, even if some of the originally poverty-stricken have seen their incomes go up, there is evidence that the drop in beneficiaries in recent years did not necessarily signify that indigence has been disappearing. Some evidence for this statement comes from poverty expert Peter Townsend, who estimated in 2009, at the height of the program's generosity, that, "If the poverty line were drawn 50 percent higher than the very stringent threshold in fact adopted, the figure of 4.7 percent [then the percent of the urban population being served by the program] in poverty becomes 20 percent of the city population, or nearly 90 million in urban areas."[29]

In another analysis, two social scientists estimated that as of early 2013, over 30 million urbanites should have been counted in the category of the poor as a conservative estimate.[30] And this was a time when just 21.23 million city people were receiving the welfare, only about 70 percent of those who should have been on the rolls.[31] (See table 3.2.) Besides, over the years the average urban *dibao* norm has come to represent a steadily declining percentage of the average disposable income of ordinary registered (but non-*dibaohu*) city folk nationwide. Similarly, that average norm has also amounted to a falling percentage of the average state factory wage: In 2002 the mean *dibao* norm, averaged across urban China, represented 28 percent of the average monthly per capita disposable income in large cities. (See table 3.3.) By November 2011, however, that proportion stood at a mere 15.8 percent. (See table 3.4.) And in 1998, the average *dibao* norm nationally equaled 20.5 percent of the mean wage in the largest cities. But by 2007 that proportion had already sunk by a full 50 percent, down to 10.3 percent. In 2011, the norm amounted to a tiny 7.8 percent of the mean wage in state firms.[32]

Another kind of calculation reveals a second way the *dibao* appears to have diminished in significance for budget writers: In 2007, urban *dibao* expenditures accounted for .113 percent of GDP, a proportion that rose in 2008, but up to just .128 percent (during the Great Recession). In 2012, however, the percentage dropped to just .108 percent. By 2015, it was back up, but only to 2007's .113 percent. (See table 3.5.) One could argue that GDP was rising, along with average incomes which, perhaps, could account for the diminishing proportion represented by the funds for the *dibao*. But my exercise here is meant to draw attention not to absolute

Table 3.3. *Dibao* Norm as Percentage of Average Disposable Income, Various Cities, July 2002 (unit = *yuan* per month)

City Name	*Dibao Norm*	*Avg. Disp. Inc.*	*Dibao as % of Avg. Disp. Inc.*
Beijing	290	1,038.67	28
Tianjin	241	778.17	31
Shenyang	205	587.50	35
Dalian	221	683.33	32
Changchun	169	575.00	29
Harbin	200	583.67	34
Taiyuan	156	614.67	25
Jinan	208	748.42	28
Qingdao	205	726.75	28
Shanghai	280	1,104.17	25
Hangzhou	285	981.50	29
Nanjing	220	763.08	29
Wuhan	210	651.67	32
Changsha	190	751.75	25
Chongqing	185	603.17	31
Chengdu	178	747.67	24
Xi'an	156	598.67	26
Lanzhou	172	N/A	N/A
Shenzhen	317	2,078.42	15
Xiamen	290	980.67	30
Guangzhou	300	1,115.00	27
AVERAGE			**28**

Sources: For the dibao norm, *Quanguo 36ge chengshi zuidi baozhang biaozhun yilan* [General survey of 36 cities' Minimum Livelihood Guarantee norm], retrieved from http://china.com.cn/city/txt/2006-11/25/content_7406758_2.htm, accessed August 17, 2007.
For disposable income, Chengdu Statistical Yearbook 2003, China Data Online, accessed May 29, 2008.

amounts but rather to how budgeting choices and *relative* allocations can be figured.

Thus, it does seem that the scheme (as well as its initially announced objective—to keep the urban laid-off quiet in order to avoid wrecking enterprise restructuring) constitutes a lesser concern for central-level decision-makers in recent years than it did a decade-plus in the past, when

Table 3.4. Average Urban *Dibao* (DB) Norm as Percentage of Average Disposable Income, 2003–2015

Year	*Nat'l. Avg. Urban Disp. Inc.*	*Nat'l. Avg. Urban Dibao Norm*	*Avg. Urban Dibao Norm as % of Avg. Disp. Inc.*
2003	8,472	1,788	21.0
2004	9,422	1,824	19.0
2005	10,493	1,872	18.0
2006	11,760	2,035	17.0
2007	13,786	2,189	16.0
2008	15,781	2,464	15.6
2009	17,175	2,734	16.0
2010	19,190	3,014	15.8
2011	21,810	3,451	15.8
2012	24,565	3,961	16.0
2013	26,955	4,476	16.6
2014	28,844	4,932	17.0
2015	31,195	5,268	16.9

Sources: For average disposable income, *Zhongguo tongji nianjian*, various years, online from All China Data Center, China Data Online, selected years, retrieved from http://chinadataonline.org.
For *dibao* expenditures, see table 3.1.
For 2015, for average *dibao* per person per month, see http://news.xinhuanet.com/politics/2016-01/25/c_128666296.htm; for average disposable income in 2015, see http://www.stats.gov.cn/tjsj/zxfb/201602/t20160229_1323991.html.

raucous discharged workers thronged the roads. This is in line with Lynette Ong's work that shows that, whereas protests related to state-owned enterprise labor disputes accounted for over 37 percent of eighteen different grievance types in 2003, in the years 2010 to 2012 these disturbances amounted to between a mere 6.3 and 8.4 percent of the total.[33] Eli Friedman has also charted a drop-off in labor disputes from 2008–2011.[34] While these figures pertain to actions by workers at work, the drive of the "furloughed" or "laid-off" seems to have lost steam as well.

Perhaps along these same lines, a slew of new restrictions and regulations, already brewing for several years, have become formal policy. An official sign was a State Council "Opinion" published in late September 2012 containing several mandates that were either novel to the program at that time or that had been present in practice but much less accentuated officially earlier. The first of these was that the emphasis in social assistance was changed to demanding that local *dibao* workers arrange

Table 3.5. Urban *Dibao* as Percentage of GDP, 1999–2014

Year	*% of GDP*
1999	0.016
2000	0.027
2001	0.049
2002	0.090
2003	0.111
2004	0.108
2005	0.103
2006	0.103
2007	0.103
2008	0.142
2009	0.139
2010	0.128
2011	0.163
2012	0.126
2013	0.129
2014	0.113

Source: Calculated from tables 3.1 and 3.6.

employment, not offer allowances, for the able-bodied impecunious. Secondly, this announcement urged localities to take the seriously and chronically diseased and disabled, the totally destitute and the deserted—in short, those who amounted to the recipients of the former "three-withouts" policy—as the "keypoint" of assistance.

Also, this September 2012 Opinion for the first time formally ordered that household assets, including bank savings, securities and other financial assets, vehicles and housing, be taken into account in assessing a family's eligibility to receive the *dibao*. The outcome was that now one's local urban residence registration, one's family income, and, in addition, the full amounts of one's household property and resources have become the new three basic conditions for obtaining the allowance.[35]

Fieldwork supports this altered slant. In Wuhan interviews in summer 2012, community officials mentioned a new stringency greeting applications. As one leader explained,

> A person who is under 50 years of age and has work ability can't get the *dibao* now; the policy has become very strict. If s/he can't find work, that's not a condition for getting the *dibao*. We encourage them to go work.[36]

In a different Wuhan community the same summer, the *dibao* manager asserted that,

> Now, it's almost impossible for a healthy laid-off person to obtain the *dibao*. Only the seriously ill and disabled can get it. Receiving the allowance depends on age and ability to work; it's only for the old, weak, those with ill health and the disabled. If one has working ability, he's unlikely to get it. In the past, the policy was more relaxed and there were lots of laid-off people [receiving it].[37]

And in Shanghai in 2013, a seventy-two-year-old woman with two grown daughters explained that, "If you have work ability you have to work, unless you're a veteran, a child, or disabled."[38]

By late 2014, the views of informants in Beijing, Wuhan, Lanzhou, and from a small Heilongjiang city all concurred with this information. In Beijing, Tang Jun, the foremost *dibao* scholar in China, noted that, "Around 2010 the policy got tighter with regard to the able-bodied." Scholars in Wuhan related that, "Recently we especially care about work ability." More confirmation comes from a street committee cadre in Lanzhou, who held that, "Policy has gotten stricter . . . if you have work ability you should work." And the interviewee from Heilongjiang observed that, "At first the qualifications for the *dibao* were easier [to meet], but it's gotten harder now."[39] Nailing this trend down even more securely, State Council Document No. 649, issued in early 2014, decreed that even for households in which every adult member was without employment, if all had labor ability, the responsible locality was to guarantee that at least one person becomes employed, and not that the family be given an allowance.[40]

To illustrate the change that has taken place since the end of the last decade, we can compare the percentages of two kinds of recipients over the years—the needy and the unemployed able-bodied. Near the start of the program, in 2002, "three-withouts" (*san wu*) people constituted just 4.5 percent of the total beneficiaries of the *dibao*.[41] There was no separate category for the "disabled" listed then; perhaps such people were sorted with the *san wu*. By 2009, though, the disabled, now counted, and the *san wu*, added together, had jumped up to 11.7 percent of the national total recipients (2.6 times as large a percentage as seven years before).[42] That percentage dropped just a bit, to 11 percent, in the first half of 2015.[43] Perhaps illuminating this trend is a remark of a scholar of social work, who explained in Shanghai in June 2013, "The government fears that the *san wus*' psychology (*xin*) is unbalanced, so it uses the *dibao* to keep them quiet."[44]

Meanwhile, the total percentage occupied by the registered and unregistered unemployed constituted just 38 percent in 2009. These data appear to bolster a claim that the totally pauperized and bereft, plus those physically incompetent to work, began to get a boost, perhaps at the expense of the able-bodied nonworking who, for the most part, have more and more been shunted off to depend on their own devices in what interview subjects have described as an unfriendly labor market.

For instance, as conveyed in the words of a nearly fifty-year-old Guangzhou recipient, half-paralyzed and suffering from high blood pressure and diabetes but still yearning to somehow be gainfully at work: "Because I'm too old and sick, if you were a boss you wouldn't look for a forty-plus-year-old sick person, it's this simple." As a one-time state-owned oil-depot employee, later laid off, he summed up the general situation of the laid-off (*xiagang*) thusly:

> Everything requires a high educational background, I have only primary school education, naturally they won't hire me, talented people are numerous, so they won't take me. You say go sell things, that needs start-up money (capital), private businesspeople wouldn't invite us, private bosses have no reason to ask a both sick and old person to work, right? I've already tried to find work, but it's no use, no one hired me, I'm too old, and I'm sick. The main reason is sickness, when the boss hears you're sick he wouldn't want you; being young is much better, this is the way it is.[45]

So these people, even as they are urged to work, are as if banned, as if they belonged to a caste, when they attempt to do so. And, for whatever reason, the cities' impoverished appear to have become less relevant to the budget designers than they were at the time of the enormous layoffs and accompanying street demonstrations that took place around the turn of the century.

THE RURAL POOR: A SHIFT TO THE COUNTRYSIDE

A second relative comparison is with the rural poor. A recent switch to a relative prioritization of poor residents in the agricultural regions could be a move to shore up the government's (and the Party's) legitimacy in these localities, as clashes between farmers and authorities have been rife for years. Indeed, an attempt to placate the restive rural areas has been official policy for some time, one associated mainly with the tenure of leaders Hu Jintao and Wen Jiabao in the first decade of the century. These leaders presided over moves to terminate rural taxes and fees, to institute new, cheap, and free health and schooling services, and to create pension schemes for the countryside.[46] So, quite possibly in line with this effort, in 2006–2007 what had been just an urban minimal livelihood scheme for many years was extended to the villages after a brief trial period.

An unequivocal rural bent with respect to the *dibao* began in the period I am chronicling here.[47] Back in 2008, when the rural *dibao* was just being extended nationally, the urban pot of outlays far, far surpassed that for the countryside: 23.34 million urbanites got 38.5 billion yuan, an average of 1,650 yuan per person per year. Meanwhile in the countryside, 42.84 million people shared 22.23 billion yuan, at an average rate of just 520 yuan per person per year, a mere 31.5 percent of what an urban recipient was given. This was an imbalance that was maintained through 2010. In 2011, however, the sums for the rural and urban areas were nearly equal, with 66.77 billion yuan going to the rural areas and 66 billion yuan to the urban poor, which was a big improvement for the farmers despite the fact that the numbers of recipients in the two regions were vastly different, with 22.8 million in the cities and 53.06 million in the countryside. Thus, the individual's share remained far greater in urban places.

In 2012, however, 67.43 total billion yuan for cities was split up among 21.43 million urban dwellers, an average of 3,146 yuan per person per year, while the 53.44 million destitute rural residents got 71.8 billion yuan, or 1,340 yuan per person per year.[48] This means that the ratio changed substantially, since a rural beneficiary thereby received 43 percent of what an urban one did. And in both 2013 and 2014 the rural areas got larger amounts of funding than did the urban (86.69 billion yuan in 2013 and 87 billion in 2014 went to the rural poor). Meanwhile in the cities, 75.7 billion yuan was allocated in 2013 for 20.6 million people, a figure that dropped to 72.2 billion yuan in the next year (2014) for 18.77 million beneficiaries.

This means that in 2014 average urban recipients—presuming they remained on the allowance for the entire year, which may not have been the case—got 3,846 yuan per year while an average rural *dibaohu* got 1,670 yuan per year which, interestingly, again—as in 2012—amounted to about 43 percent of the urban indigent's take (could that have been a mandated proportion?). That is by no means an equalizing allocation, but it is a significant *relative* improvement for rural recipients. (See tables 3.2 and 3.6.)

One last type of indicator compares the rate of annual increase in allocations to urban and rural poor residents, respectively. In 2013, for instance, the total funds issued to the urban-registered *dibaohu* amounted to an increase of 12.2 percent over the year before while in the countryside, the total sum increased by 20.7 percent over the amount issued in 2012.[49] For another recent example, in 2015, the average urban per-person monthly norm rose by 9.5 percent, while the rural one went up by 14.7 percent, and the monthly subsidy level for urbanites rose by 12 percent. In the countryside, by contrast, the payout increased by 15.8 percent.[50]

At the March 2015 National People's Congress meeting, then-premier Li Keqiang's speech indicated the rise in importance of the rural *dibao* program, in his pledge to "continue to raise subsistence allowances for rural and urban residents," notably naming those in the countryside first. Li also announced projected increases in subsistence allowances (which refers to the *dibao*) per person by 9.97 percent for the urban impoverished

Table 3.6. Government Expenditure on the *Dibao*, Urban and Rural, 1999–2014 (billion *yuan*)

Year	*Urban*	*Rural*	*Total*
1999	1.5	N/A	1.50
2000	2.7	N/A	2.70
2001	5.4	N/A	5.40
2002	10.9	N/A	10.90
2003	15.1	N/A	15.10
2004	17.3	N/A	17.30
2005	19.2	2.53	21.73
2006	22.4	4.30	26.70
2007	27.5	10.41	37.90
2008	39.3	22.23	61.50
2009	48.2	34.50	82.70
2010	52.5	44.50	97.00
2011	66.0	66.77	132.77
2012	67.4	71.80	139.20
2013	75.7	86.69	162.39
2014	72.2	87.03	159.23

Source: Ministry of Civil Affairs website, http://www.mca.gov.cn.

but by as much as 14.1 percent for the rural needy.[51] This emphasis was echoed by the Beijing city government, which publicized in June that year that, "We will put emphasis on the rural areas, pay attention to strengthening the readjustment of the rural *dibao* norm, to reduce the gap between the cities and the countryside."[52] Even if this shift is aimed purely at moving to narrow the benefit chasm across types of areas, it clearly signals a tilt to the rural areas.

In July 2015, another striking sign emerged that (at least some of) the rural areas were to be served in a new way: the Chinese News Network broadcast that many places had equalized the *dibao* norm in their urban and rural areas, that is, they had raised both their city and country poverty lines to the same level. Though only a handful of major cities, including Beijing, Shanghai, Nanjing, Hangzhou, Changsha, Chengdu, and Hefei, had fulfilled the plan as of midyear, other cities were said to be considering the move as they carried out their own trials or set up experimental districts. Others, such as Guangzhou, were still collecting opinions from the public as of early July that year. In one case, Beijing raised its urban level from 2011's 480 yuan per person per month to 710 yuan, an increase of about 50 percent, while its rural standard over the same years went from 300 up to 710 yuan, a rise of over 233 percent.

It is likely that the "rural areas" that received this hefty increment were suburban places on the outskirts of the large cities. But the reform remains substantial, even if for a rather limited clientele. This new measure was specifically touted as a means of cutting back the much-criticized income divide between urban and rural areas. Perhaps the subtext of the move was that it amounted to a way of addressing the larger issue of gross inequality in the country that has attracted such censure at home and abroad. Or, maybe, it was aimed at trying to tackle the anger over the large-scale land dispossessions assailing farmers for well over a decade.

Regardless of this priority to improving rural allocations, in the past couple of years even the countryside component of the program is declining: After the initial rise, the numbers of recipients dropped off in the countryside with time as well: Just before the program's official extension into the agricultural regions in 2007, figures of beneficiaries there stood at just 15.9 million. (According to Ministry of Civil Affairs yearbooks, some ruralites got a *dibao* allowance before 2007, presumably in trial programs, but the formal roll-out of the program in the countryside was not until 2007).[53]

But rural *dibaohu* increased speedily once the scheme was in place, going from 35.66 million in 2007 up to 53.8 million in 2013. Figures fell to 52 million in the following year (2014), and down to 49.3 in 2015, however.[54] (See table 3.2.) Remarkably, after years of data, no figures have been released either for numbers of recipients or for funding amounts thereafter, whether for the cities or for the countryside. But it does appear that the regime has chosen of late to distribute its funding for penury more to the peasants than to the urban poor.

Comparisons with Social Assistance Elsewhere

A third line of comparison is with programs of social assistance outside China. That the *dibao* program is ungenerous in comparative terms becomes evident when considering the percentage of GDP devoted to the scheme. This is a significant statistic precisely because it symbolizes the level of largesse a government is willing to shower on its poor. In China that percentage for the urban *dibao* has wavered around 0.12 percent of GDP[55] (reaching a high of .14 percent in 2009, during the financial crisis) after rising from under 0.1 percent, where it stood before 2003. Even with the funds for the rural *dibao* added in, the two allowances together amounted to just .25 percent of GDP in 2014.[56] In 2015, the percentage dropped to .20 percent of GDP.[57] (See table 3.4.) Again, we have no statistics thereafter.

By contrast, the percent for targeted poverty programs elsewhere spanned from 0.5 to 1.0 percent of GDP in Latin America in the early

2000s[58] to an average 2.5 percent of GDP spent on cash transfer programs. According to Armando Barrientos, as of 2013 expenditures on anti-poverty programs typically were ranging between 1 and 2 percent of GDP there.[59] Mexico fell below this proportion, but still was investing 0.3 percent of GDP in its poverty reduction programs as of 2008, and Indonesia's similar program cost 0.5 percent of its GDP in 2005.[60]

Besides this, in China in 2015, the average *dibao* handout nationwide was a mere 439 yuan per person per month in the cities, or 5,268 yuan per year. Urban average disposable income that year was 31,195 yuan per person, so that *dibao* represented just 16.88 percent of China's average urban disposable income that year, a drop from the previous year's 17.1 percent. This is not to mention a long-term drop from the 28 percent of average urban disposable income in 2002 among the country's major cities.[61] (See tables 3.3 and 3.4.)[62] And, whereas Barrientos' study reports a rising trend in social assistance budgets as a proportion of GDP in most countries over the past decade-and-a-half,[63] in China the percentage has steadily fallen since 2011. In that year, the figure amounted to .274 percent of GDP, but four years later, in 2015, the amount was .20 percent. The only exception to the trend was the year 2013, when it rose, but just to .277 percent. (See table 3.4.)

Another critical way in which at least the urban portion of China's program suffers by comparison with social assistance around the world is in its failure to essay to raise its recipients out of poverty. As a general rule, Barrientos reports, "anti-poverty transfer programs [which] provide direct transfers in cash and/or in kind" carry the "aim of facilitating [their targets'] permanent exit from poverty."[64] By upgrading household consumption and, correspondingly, productive capacity, such programs (usually in the form of so-called "conditional cash transfers") "lead to poverty reduction and, over time, facilitate exit from poverty."[65]

Crucial components of these transfer efforts elsewhere include a bargain according to which parents must see to the primary health care, nutrition, and education of their young; a work requirement for the parents is often a part of obtaining the benefit. In all, the schemes entail investments in human development, even as they also lessen the social exclusion that all too often accompanies poverty.[66]

But in China, neither is there an effort to encourage indigent parents to improve the endowments—whether physical or cultural—of their offspring nor is there a work requirement for adult welfare recipients (more likely those able to work are written off the rolls, as noted above). These are telling contrasts, suggesting that perhaps the Chinese leadership has no real intention of bettering the long-run lot of its urban poor. Perhaps it is seen as best to confine them and their offspring to a separate social segment, as a sort of caste.

Why, after all, is this the case? Can we create a larger commentary to explain these three comparative cases of relative stinginess for the Chinese urban-registered destitute? Why are they not doing as well as they did a decade ago? Why are they sidelined, at least relatively, as compared to funding for their rural counterparts? And why are they getting less attention from their government than do impoverished people elsewhere in the world? A turn to a cultural account could provide some insight.

A CULTURAL EXPLANATION FOR CHINA'S DIFFERENT APPROACH TO ITS INDIGENT

A bevy of Chinese intellectuals, from political figures and thinkers going back to the early nineteenth century[67] through the 1919 May Fourth Movement, harbored a "faith in a march from backwardness to modernity," penned Gail Hershatter.[68] This aspiration was not confined to scholars but echoed strongly at the pinnacle of the state, over and over. The powerful wish for showy sophistication animated national leaders of the twentieth century, with both Mao Zedong and Deng Xiaoping sustaining an ardent, unquenchable vision, what Ruth Rogaski has labeled an "intense longing for modernity," which she claims informed a "struggle to achieve what seems to be an ever-elusive state of modernity."[69] Certainly leaders' desires had a major role in determining how those who did not fit in were handled.

Even before the Western colonial powers and Japan came onto their soil from the 1840s,[70] Chinese people have striven for a formula that would transform the nation from its relative "backwardness" (relative to the "advanced" West) into a "modern" place that could become one of the colonial countries' peers. The colonials' coming, of course, intensified that striving immeasurably, as those foreigners perceived the country as behind, delayed, and thereby deficient and arrested in development, resulting in a severe rattling of the country's ancient sense of superiority.

A century later, the Guomindang government—despite its highest hopes—managed to induce just the more southern portions of the coast into the then-contemporary world, with that regime's thrust for progress to be propelled by productivism.[71] In his time, Mao—both in his unacknowledged awe of the West and also in his heated determination to catch up with and surpass it—imagined that ever-higher productive output, to be attained by corralling peasants and workers into a gigantic state-driven industrial project, could "propel [the nation] into the modern world."[72] The obsession with being au courant in the world likewise galvanized Mao's successor, Deng Xiaoping, who also battled to position the nation for strength and affluence, and was probably the influence behind amending the state constitution in 1993 to this effect.[73]

Global recognition, what Ann Anagnost has termed "the evaluative gaze of global capital," along with the push lent by what she characterized as "the rigorous norms of discipline and skill of the global market," and the unquenchable urge to match up to the guidelines of global competition, with its "sophisticated products," have been among the most potent drivers of this demanding drumbeat at the level of the state to remake the place.[74] This has been especially the situation once China entered the global economy in force in the 1990s and thereafter. But how best to accomplish this phantasmagoric future?

There has been broad agreement in China that human improvement and industrialization—perhaps, for those musing on this issue in the twentieth century, rooted in the writings of Karl Marx's faith in material changes propelling human transformation—lie at the root of the quest for modernization. Thus, according to a 1988 piece in the Chinese (as of that era, intellectual) daily, *Guangming ribao*, modernization had to include human modernization.[75] In recent decades, this notion has been translated into a preoccupation with "quality" (*suzhi*), which amounts to roughly the same thing.[76] Most critically, this often has to do with elevating the quality of the workforce.[77] So state power, economic growth, and nation-building were to grow on the backs of an imagined "bettered" people.

There have been, over the past century or so, at least three models for engendering a major, upward alteration of human quality at the level of the populace as a whole. The first of these has been by eradicating signs of human social decay, that is, by removing, marginalizing, and confining, putting out of sight, in short, excluding those whose being evokes backwardness—and who, thereby, are viewed as holding back the nation's onward momentum.[78] The second approach has involved mandating labor, even from the less qualified, in the interest of converting unproductive persons into, at a minimum, drudges for the benefit of the nation.[79] And the third strategy has been to remodel, educate, and uplift the less endowed in order to upgrade the nation collectively by way of elevating the entire populace.

Sometimes an amalgam of these techniques has been attempted: for example, there has at times been an effort to remake "useless" people into ones "useful," especially for production purposes,[80] as in the fantasy that characterized Guomindang state policy in the main. But the state at that juncture varied its tactics, trying to empty major cities of those considered derelicts or the otherwise unsightly, thereby at best marginalizing the poor, and yet also, at times, endeavoring to raise up those deemed capable of improvement.[81]

I propose that this long-term Chinese bent toward contriving contemporaneity through elevating (or excluding) the nation's lowest-class slice of humanity has been responsible for neglecting the urban poor in the present, and not essaying to absorb them into the mainstream populace. Such a method today appears to obviate endeavoring to include or advance such persons. Indeed, there is a clear disinclination to seriously bestow adequate financial and administrative resources on bringing them and their offspring within the general fold. It would appear, in this perspective, that their presence could threaten to derail the track to modernity along which the nation is racing, especially now, when the goal would seem so near.

CONCLUSION

I have presented three contrasts with regard to how social assistance, that is, the *dibao* allowance, is handled these days in urban China as compared with three other "spaces" where such assistance is (or was) given: to the laid-off workers in China as of a decade-and-a-half or so ago (1999–2004), to China's rural poor, and to the impoverished in other countries. I am now in a position to use these comparisons to provide my account for the circumstances surrounding urban poor policy today. By underlining the connection or, better put, the lack of a link between the destitute and China's dreams, I can build my conclusion.

The crux of the issue is that the indigent in China today cannot have a place, cannot conceptually be present in the grand "Dream" that President Xi has proposed for the country. For whatever else that dream might embody, it—as did the fancies of thinkers and political figures of the past—must surely embrace modernity and omit the searing destitution of the days long gone, whether under Chairman Mao or before him. If anything, these people, the impoverished of the present, stand as a kind of metaphor for Maoist society which, along with themselves, is viewed now as best obliterated, both mentally (and rhetorically) as well as physically. The imaginaries in these visions were surely of wealth and power, always, and now, more specifically, of the marketplace (in which, presumably—true or not—anyone of fit body can find a posting), of a thriving middle class, whose members alone stroll along trim and tidy, clean avenues, presumably enabling stability and order for society at large.

Though, in fact, modernity with its markets, as the world has witnessed, can also mean inequality, layoffs, bankruptcies, and impecuniousness, exclusion, and marginalization for many. But surely such features are decidedly *not* the stuff of forward-oriented aspiration. Those phenomena are the underside of the current drama, the portion that dredges up memories of past nightmares that must be purged. Indeed, they are the makings of bad, black dreams; China's reverie is instead to shine with the light of bright images, the glorious ones.

Indeed, the poor are the very antithesis of all the Chinese dream consists of domestically—the inversion, one might say, of the market (for they were fostered under the state plan, and it is plans that cast them away), the opposite of the modern, of economic growth and prosperity, of productivity, of progress. As such, neither poverty nor the poor can be "modern."

Thus, today's *dibaohu* are, or were, yesteryears' *xiagang*, or laid-off staff and workers. According to one account, as of the early 2000s, these laid-off workers amounted to some 70 to 90 percent of the total urban poor (probably this large percentage included not only those who themselves were laid off but also the members of their families).[82] The training they received and the old daily practices they lived, along with the machinery and technology they managed to master, mark them as obsolete in today's terms.[83] As such, they represent a past best put to rest and banished.

Unsurprisingly, when they were severed from their positions, multitudes raged in the roads, severely jarring the political elite of the turn of the century. But once the *dibao* was devised and its allowances distributed, trifling as its sums amounted to, it seemed to calm these former workers down. A policy designed for stability has appeared to wane as its beneficiaries wandered back to their homes, more or less placated or, surely, pacified. My supposition is that a project meant for forging peacefulness lost its prominence once it had achieved its purpose. This, to me, is why the funds allocated to the program are in steady decline. As for the seeming state preference for the rural needy over the urban *dibaohu*: these country paupers are the persons whose land confiscations have become the most prominent prods of protests in the nation nowadays. Could it be that the farmers are meant to be mollified by the meager monies of this social assistance as once the urban poor were in their turn?

Finally, it is notable that most welfare allotments around the world (outside of China) are aimed at improving household consumption and productive capacity, at reducing poverty and at facilitating people's exit from it. Thus, unlike in China, such programs are geared to enhancing the human development of households and individuals and hence their productive capacity and not just (as in China) to keeping these people, turned silent, from perishing outright.[84] In Latin America, for instance, there is an affirmed objective of breaking the intergenerational cycle of poverty,[85] an aim never mentioned in the "People's Republic."

Might it be, then, that the Chinese government, even as it advocates throwing the labor-able from the welfare rolls, is not seriously concerned with lifting up the employability of the indigent, or with seeing them depart from destitution? If the state truly is concerned about these matters, there needs to be a fundamental revamping of the allowance scheme, as well as an upgrading in its funding.

No source can be nailed down for these ruminations. One could not find them in official documents, nor were such words voiced in interviews with bureaucrats or even in conversations with most scholars in China. So these thoughts are meant to be only my suppositional hypotheses. Nonetheless, I venture, they do fit and also illuminate the bare facts we have at hand. The impoverished poor of Chinese cities have been abandoned, and when their generation finally passes, the Chinese nation, its leaders believe, will finally more fully have "stood up."

NOTES

1. Albert Park, Sangui Wang, and Guobao Wu, "Regional Poverty Targeting in China," *Journal of Public Economics* 86, no. 1 (2002): 123–53; Cheng Fang, Xiaobo Zhang, Shenggen Fan, "Emergence of Urban Poverty and Inequality in China; Evidence from a Household Survey," *China Economic Review* 13 (2002): 430–43; Azizur Rahman Khan and Carl Riskin, *Inequality and Poverty in China in the Age of Globalization* (New York: Oxford University Press, 2001); and Xin Meng, Robert Gregory, and Youjuan Wang, "Inequality and Growth in Urban China, 1986–2000," IZA Discussion paper series, no. 1452, 2005. Qin Gao has written extensively on the topic; a few of her relevant pieces are: Qin Gao, S. Yang, and S. Li, "Welfare, Targeting, and Anti-Poverty Effectiveness: The Case of Urban China," *Quarterly Review of Economics and Finance* 56 (2015): 30–42; Qin Gao, "Public Assistance and Poverty Reduction: The Case of Shanghai," *Global Social Policy* 13, no. 2 (2013): 193–215; and Qin Gao, "Redistributive Nature of the Chinese Social Benefit System: Progressive or Regressive?," *China Quarterly* 201 (March 2010): 1–19. See also Qin Gao, *Welfare, Work and Poverty: Social Assistance in China* (New York: Oxford University Press, 2017).

2. See Lisa Rofel, *Other Modernities: Gendered Yearnings in China after Socialism* (Berkeley: University of California Press, 1999), xiii, 3; and Ann Anagnost, *National Past-Times: Narrative, Representation, and Power in Modern China* (Durham: Duke University Press, 1997), 77.

3. X. Shang and X. Wu, "Changing Approaches of Social Protection: Social Assistance Reform in Urban China," *Social Policy and Society* 3, no. 3 (2014): 260, 265.

4. Athar Hussain, "Urban Poverty in China: Measurement, Patterns and Policies," manuscript (Geneva: International Labour Office, 2003), 107.

5. Bjorn A. Gustafsson and Deng Quheng, "Di Bao Receipt and Its Importance for Combating Poverty in Urban China," *Poverty & Public Policy* 3, no. 1 (2011): 2.

6. Daniel Hammond, "Explaining Policy Making in the People's Republic of China" (PhD diss., University of Glasgow, 2010), 33–48, 71, 76; C. K. Chan, "Re-thinking the Incrementalist Thesis in China," *Journal of Social Policy* 39, no. 4 (2010): 633.

7. Fulong Wu and Ningying Huang, "New Urban Poverty in China: Economic Restructuring and Transformation of Welfare Provision," *Asia Pacific Viewpoint* 48, no. 2 (2007): 173.

8. I base this on dozens of street-side and in-home interviews with laid-off workers, mostly in Wuhan, in the years 1999 through 2004.

9. Hammond, "Explaining," 71; William Hurst, *The Chinese Worker After Socialism* (New York: Cambridge University Press, 2009); Ching Kwan Lee, *Against the Law: Labor Protests in China's Rustbelt and Sunbelt* (Berkeley: University of California Press, 2007).

10. Linda Wong, *Marginalization and Social Welfare in China* (London: Routledge, 1998), 200; Hammond, "Explaining."

11. Guowuyuan [State Council], "*Guowuyuan guanyu zai quanguo jianli chengshi jumin zuidi shenghuo baozhang zhidu de tongzhi*" [Circular of the State Council on the national establishment of the urban residents' Minimum Livelihood Guarantee System], Guofa [1997] 29 hao [State Council Document No. 29], accessed August 13, 2013, dbs.mca.gov.cn/article/csdb/cvfg/200711/20071100003522.shtml.

12. "Chengshi jumin zuidi shenghuo boazhang tiaoli" [Urban residents Minimum Livelihood Guarantee regulations], accessed August 13, 2013, dbs.mca.gov.cn/article/csdb/cvfg/200711/20071100003522.shtml.

13. What follows draws upon Dorothy J. Solinger, "Dibaohu in Distress," in *China's Changing Welfare Mix*, ed. Beatriz Carrillo and Jane Duckett (London: Routledge, 2011),

36–63; Dorothy J. Solinger, "The Urban Dibao," in *Marginalization in Urban China*, ed. Fulong Wu and Chris Webster (Houndmills, Basingstoke: Palgrave/Macmillan, 2010), 253–77; Dorothy J. Solinger, "The Miserly Minimum Livelihood Guarantee: Social Assistance (Just to) Stave Off Starvation," in *Handbook of Welfare in China*, ed. Beatriz Carrillo Garcia, Johanna Hood, and Paul Kadetz (Cheltenham, UK: Edward Elgar, 2017), 144–62; and Dorothy J. Solinger and Ting Jiang, "When Central Orders and Promotion Criteria Conflict: Implementation Decisions on the Destitute in Poor vs. Prosperous Cities," *Modern China* 42, no. 6 (2016): 571–606.

14. Shang and Wu, "Changing Approaches," 261.

15. Z. Wang, "Chengshi jumin zuidi shenghuo baozhang" (Urban residents' Minimum Livelihood Guarantee), *Zhongguo minzheng* (Chinese Civil Affairs) (hereafter *ZGMZ*) 11 (1999): 18.

16. L. Ding, "Cong danwei fuli dao shehui baozhang—ji zhongguo chengshi jumin zuidishenghuo baozhang zhidu de dansheng" [From unit welfare to social security—recording the emergence of Chinese urban residents' Minimum Livelihood Guarantee System], *ZGMZ* 11, (1999): 7.

17. R. Lindqvist, J. Tang, and J. Li, "Social Assistance in China and Sweden," *China Journal of Social Work* 6, no. 3 (2013): 313, 316.

18. Shang and Wu, "Changing Approaches," 261; Hammond, "Explaining," 120–23.

19. Dorothy J. Solinger, "Urban Jobs and The World Trade Organization," *China Journal* 49 (January 2003): 61–87.

20. Shang and Wu, "Changing Approaches," 265; D. Hong, "Recent Developments in the Minimum Living Standard Assistance Policy for Urban Residents," in *Poverty and the Minimium Living Standard Assistance Policy in Urban China*, chapter 3 (Beijing: Social Policy Research Center, Chinese Academy of Social Sciences, 2005), accessed (in Chinese) http://www.chinasocialpolicy.org/Paper_Show.asp?Paper_ID=38, 12.

21. Y. Du and A. Park, "The Effects of Social Assistance on Poverty Reduction," second draft, September 7, 2006, 4; S. Zhang and J. Tang, "*Chengxiang zuidi shenghuo baozhang zhidu jiben xingcheng*" (Urban and rural Minimum Livelihood Guarantee System has basically taken form), in *2008 nian: Zhongguo shehui xingshi fenxi yu yuce* (2008: Analysis and forecast of China's social situation), ed. S. Ru, X. Lu, P. Li (Beijing: Social Sciences Academic Press, 2008), 62. This appears to be consistent with global norms: according to Armando Barrientos, "High-income countries with low poverty incidence show relatively high levels of social assistance expenditure compared with low-income countries with high poverty incidence," in his book, *Social Assistance in Developing Countries* (New York: Cambridge University Press, 2013), 169.

22. D. Ge and T. Yang, "Minimum Income Schemes for the Unemployed," *International Social Science Journal* 5, no. 179 (2004): 47–56; Hammond, "Explaining," 86ff.

23. Joe Leung and Yuebin Xu, *China's Social Welfare: The Third Turning Point* (Cambridge: Polity Press, 2015). I have not seen any data specifying the amount of central transfers in the various localities.

24. S. Chen, M. Ravallion, and Y. Wang, "Does the Di Bao Program Guarantee a Minimum Income in China's Cities?," in *Public Finance in China*, ed. Jiwei Lou and Shuilin Wang (Washington, DC: World Bank, 2006), 18.

25. Martin Ravallion, "A Guaranteed Minimum Income: China's Di Bao Program," PowerPoint presentation, n.d. Draws on research with Shaohua Chen and collaborators in China's National Bureau of Statistics (obtained from the author).

26. Accessed April 28, 2016, http://www.askci.com/news/finance/2015/12/30/16333 1xfkf.shml.

27. Accessed August 5, 2015, http://finance.people.com.cn/n/2015/0611/c.

28. Same as previous note, accessed August 10, 2015, http://cws.mca.gov.cn/article/tjkb/201102/20110200133593.shtml.

29. Peter Townsend, "Social Security in Developing Countries: A Brief Overview," in *Building Decent Societies: Rethinking the Role of Social Security in Development*, ed. Peter Townsend (Houndmills: Palgrave Macmillan 2009), 250.

30. Zhang Ruli and Peng Qing, "Zhongguo chengshi gaigezhong pinkun qunti zhengce de zhuanxing ji qi tedian" (In China's urban reform, the transformation of policy for the poor masses and its characteristics), *Shehui kexue jikan* (Social science journal) 4 (2014): 44–50.

31. Accessed August 7, 2015, http://files2.mca.gov.cn/cws/201304/20130424180247244.htm.

32. Calculations are from various editions of the *Zhongguo tongji nianjian* (*China Statistical Yearbook*).

33. Lynette H. Ong, "Reports of Social Unrest: Basic Characteristics, Trends and Patterns, 2003–2012," in *Handbook of the Politics of* China, ed. David S. G. Goodman (Cheltenham: Edward Elgar, 2016), 352.

34. Eli Friedman, *Insurgency Trap: Labor Politics in Postsocialist China* (Ithaca: Cornell University Press, 2014), 4.

35. Guowuyuan (State Council) (2012), "*Guowuyuan guanyu jinyibu jiaqiang he gaijin zuidi shenghuo baozhang gongcuo de yijian*" (State Council's Opinions on Progressively Strengthening and Improving the Minimum Livelihood Guarantee Work), *Guofa* 45 (2012) [State Council Document, no. 45], accessed September 15, 2012, http://www.gov.cn/zwgk/2012-09/26/content_2233209.htm. See also a commentary on that decision issued by the Ministry of Finance: Caizheng bu, minzhengbu tongzhi (Ministry of Finance, Ministry of Civil Affairs Circular), "Guanyu yinfa 'Chengxiang zuidi shenghuo baozhang zijin guanli banfa' de tongzhi" [On issuance of the circular on the management of urban and rural minimum livelihood funds], *Caishe* 171 hao (2012) [Finance and society, no. 171], http://baike.baidu.com/view/9452029.htm.

36. Interview, Huazhong shifan daxue community, June 26, 2012.

37. Interview, Wuhan, Hongshan District, June 30, 2012.

38. Interview, Shanghai, June 25, 2013.

39. Interviews, Beijing, October 10, 2014; Wuhan, November 3, 2014; Lanzhou, November 21, 2014; and with a resident from Heilongjiang, in Hong Kong, November 14, 2014.

40. Accessed August 2015, www.sourcejuice.com/.../People-Republic-China-State-Council-Order-64.

41. Through 2006, "disabled" was not a separate accounting category.

42. Zhonghua renmin gongheguo, 2010.

43. Zhonghua renmin gongheguo minzhengbu, bian [Ministry of Civil Affairs of the People's Republic of China, ed.], *Zhongguo minzheng tongji nianjian* [*China Civil Affairs' Statistical Yearbook*] (Beijing: China Statistics Press, 2012), 478–79.

44. Interview, Shanghai, June 24, 2013.

45. Interview, Guangzhou, June 30, 2010.

46. Jeremy Wallace, *Cities and Stability: Urbanization, Redistribution, and Regime Survival in China* (New York: Oxford University Press, 2014), chapter 5.

47. Over the past two decades there has been a significant fall in the size of the rural population, so the rapid increase in the numbers of rural recipients is especially important in this context.

48. *Minzhengbu fabu 2012 nian shehui fuwu fazhan tongji gongbao* [Ministry of Civil Affairs announces 2012's social services development statistical bulletin], June 19, 2013, Renminwang. For the year 2011, the sums for the two sorts of regions were closer, with the rural pot slightly greater for the first time.

49. Zhonghua renmin gongheguo minzheng bu [Ministry of Civil Affairs of the People's Republic of China], *Minzhengbu fabu 2013 nian shehui fuwu fazhan tongji gongbao* [Ministry of Civil Affairs announces social services development communique].

50. See http://www.askci.com/news/finance/2015/12/30/163331xfkf.shtml.

51. "China NPC 2015: The Reports," China Real Time Report, WSJ (blog), regarding speech delivered by Li Keqiang at the Third Session of the Twelfth National People's Congress on March 5, 2015, 29 and 2–6, accessed March 6, 2015, http://blogs.wsj.com/chinarealtime/2015/03/05/china-npc-2015-the-reports.

52. Beijing chengxiang dibao biaozhun tongyi zhi meiyue 710 yuan [Beijing's urban and rural dibao norm unified to 710 yuan per month], *Xin jing bao* [New capital paper], June 27, 2015.

53. Huawei Han, Qin Gao, and Yuebin Xu, "Welfare Participation and Family Consumption Choices in Rural China," *Global Social Welfare* 3, no. 4 (2016): 223–41, notes that local experiments with rural *dibao* began in the early 1990s.

54. The cost of living in rural areas is far lower than in the cities. Thus, a certain level of inequity in *dibao* norms between city and countryside is reasonable.

55. Alfred M. Wu and M. Ramesh, "Poverty Reduction in Urban China: The Impact of Cash Transfers," *Social Policy and Society* 13, no. 2 (2014): 291, state that the average spending on the urban allowance from 2000 to 2009 amounted to .12 percent of GDP, "considerably below other countries in East Asia."

56. Calculated from *Renmin ribao*, June 11, 2015, accessed August 10, 2015, http://finance.people.com,cb.b.2015;0611/c.

57. Calculated from http://www.360doc.com/content/16/0119/16/502486_529117704.shtml (for GDP) and http://www.askci.com/news/finance/2015/12/30/163331xfkf.shtml (for total national expenditure on the *dibao*).

58. Stephan Haggard and R. R. Kaufman, *Development, Democracy, and Welfare States: Latin America, East Asia, and Eastern Europe* (Princeton: Princeton University Press, 2008), 217.

59. Armando Barrientos, *Social Assistance in Developing Countries* (New York: Cambridge University Press, 2013), 5, 168, 221.

60. J. A. Hanlon, A. Barrientos, and D. Hulme, *Just Give Money to the Poor* (Sterling, VA: Kumarian Press, 2010), 22, 40, 42.

61. A list of China's thirty major cities in 2015 shows that their *dibao* distributions averaged .165 of the national average disposal income in cities. The table displaying these *dibao* norms is at http://www.566job.com/shebao/zhengce-1877.hmtl, accessed in April 2016.

62. For average *dibao* per person per month, see http://news.xinhuanet.com/politics/2016-01/25/c_128666296.htm; for average disposable income in 2015, see http://www.stats.gov.cn/tjsj/zxfb/201602/t20160229_1323991.html, accessed in April 2016.

63. Barrientos, *Social Assistance*, 221.

64. Barrientos, 1.

65. Barrientos, 14.

66. Barrientos, 85, 104.

67. Orville Schell and John Delury, *Wealth and Power: China's Long March to the Twenty-first Century* (New York: Random House, 2013), 18, on Wei Yuan in 1826; 50, on Feng Guifen in 1860; 97 on Liang Qichao in 1897; and 98 on Yan Fu, also in the late 1890s. These thinkers wanted to ground China's future in wealth and power (Wei); warned that "those who confine themselves to the old will . . . become weak" (Liang); appealed to the social Darwinism notion of "survival of the fittest for understanding China's plight" (Yan); and pointed to shame as a possible catalyst to strengthen the nation (Feng).

68. Gail Hershatter, *Dangerous Pleasures: Prostitution and Modernity in Twentieth-Century Shanghai* (Berkeley: University of California Press, 1997), 255.

69. Ruth Rogaski, *Hygenic Modernity: Meanings of Health and Disease in Treaty-Port China* (Berkeley: University of California Press, 2004), 250, 2.

70. Rogaski, *Hygenic Modernity*, 9, 168.

71. Janet Y. Chen, *Guilty of Indigence: The Urban Poor in China, 1900–1953* (Princeton: Princeton University Press, 2012), 90.

72. Hershatter, *Dangerous Pleasures*, 324; Schell and Delury, *Wealth and Power*, 238; Rofel, *Other Modernities*, 27.

73. Borge Bakke, *The Exemplary Society: Human Improvement, Social Control, and the Dangers of Modernity in China* (Oxford: Oxford University Press, 2000), 60.

74. Joseph W. Esherick, "Modernity and Nation in the Chinese City," in *Remaking the Chinese City: Modernity and National Identity, 1900–1950*, ed. Joseph W. Esherick

(Honolulu: University of Hawai'i Press, 1999), 4; Anagnost, *National Past-Times,* 123; Chen, *Guilty,* 22; David Strand, "New Chinese Cities," in Esherick, *Remaking,* 216; and Markus Eberhardt and John Thoburn, "China, the World Trade Organization and the End of the Agreement on Textiles and Clothing: Impacts on Workers," in *Marginalisation in China: Perspectives on Transition and Globalisation,* ed. Heather Xiaoquan Zhang, Bin Wu, and Richard Sanders (Aldershot, England: Ashgate, 2007), 180–81.

75. Bakke, *The Exemplary,* 3, 60; Lee McIsaac, "The City as Nation, Creating a Wartime Capital in Chongqing," in Esherick, *Remaking,* 185.

76. Bakke, *The Exemplary,* 1.

77. Bakke, 62.

78. Bakke, *The Exemplary,* 3; McIsaac, "The City," 183, 186; Zwia Lipkin, *Useless to the State: "Social Problems" and Social Engineering in Nationalist Nanjing, 1927–1937* (Cambridge, MA: Harvard University Asia Center, 2000), 18.

79. Janet Chen records that this was the strategy used by the Guomindang government, in *Guilty,* 90, 92.

80. Lipkin, *Useless,* 16, 54.

81. Lipkin, 60, 87.

82. According to Ka Lin, "Institutional Responses to the Changing Patterns of Poverty and Marginalisation in China Since 1949," in Zhang, Wu, and Sanders, *Marginalisation in China,* 122.

83. Eberhardt and Thoburn, "China," 178, found that as of the beginning of the 1990s, only 1 percent of China's textile machinery met international standards!

84. Barrientos, *Social Assistance,* 14, 84, 104, 129, 151.

85. Barrientos, 123.

FOUR

The Passionate Poor

Foxconn Workers Invited as Volunteers

Mun Young Cho

Tian Yu is a former employee of Foxconn, the world's largest electronics contractor manufacturer. She is one of the few survivors of the tragic serial suicides that occurred in the factory in 2010. In Tu Qiao's 2015 documentary film, *Fei Sheng* (Fly to Transcend), a seventeen-year-old girl with paralyzed legs, having returned to her rural hometown, looks back on her factory labor, in which she could not find any meaning at all. "As it [my work on the assembly line] was done over and over every day, there was nothing there to learn. My movements were just repeated like that day after day, bring it here, and taking it there . . . work on it and put it back." She contrasts her factory work with shoemaking, in which she now participates, while sitting in her wheelchair. Unlike putting a label on an Apple iPad, crafting shoes allows Tian Yu to know exactly what she is doing and what the significance of her work is.

Factory labor at Foxconn comes not just from a Taylorist legacy and its reach for perfect efficiency. It is, in addition, a product of violent management, which results from the harsh demands coming from global brand owners, arbitrary managerial power, and various types of segregation of employees.[1] Under this management, the suffering of frontline workers like Tian Yu had a structural root: their workday was prolonged to meet the global production schedule; labor disciplines were strict enough to maintain secrets relating to the IT industry; the dormitory system was carefully arranged to meet just-in-time production and cut off regional networks among workers. Local governments often ignored the enforcement of labor laws to boost GDP growth in their jurisdictions; they even fostered the use of low-paid student—so-called intern—labor in alliance with Foxconn.[2]

What intrigues me is that such structural violence within and outside the factory coexists with the explosion of various social activities and programs that many factory workers in China have embraced. Beginning in the summer of 2013, conducting fieldwork in a Foxconn town in Shenzhen, I have witnessed migrant youth spend considerable time and effort as registered volunteers at local community service centers. After long hours working at the Foxconn factory, many of them simply filled their stomachs with street food and then went off to visit these centers, still wearing their Foxconn uniforms. Those who worked on the night shift headed to the centers after sleeping only a few hours in their small rental housing.

Some workers spent their time in the centers just playing ping pong or reading the books furnished there. But there were others who pitched in and helped social workers prepare for daily programs or special events for their charges. These workers were willing to put up a banner, hand out flyers, take photos, display goods for a charity bazaar, or clean up the event hall. Their volunteer labor seemed to be different from the repressive factory labor, which Tian Yu's days at Foxconn had painfully embodied. Indeed, though it was unwaged labor, for her, volunteering was pleasurable. Foxconn workers-cum-volunteers whom I interviewed proudly narrated how their labor contributed to the production of programs or events at the centers. This unwaged labor was rewarded, if only with volunteer records, applause, prizes, gifts, media reports, or photos on their SNS (social network services).

What kind of "the poor" are these migrant youths who do both factory labor and volunteer labor? Michael Hart and Antonio Negri conceptualize the poor as neither destitute nor repressed but embodying "the ontological condition of productive life itself."[3] Their argument that the poor are excluded from wealth and yet included in its circuits of social production[4] is based on these authors' novel attention to the growing dominance of the informational economy across the world. Replacing industrialization and modernization, "informatization" has prompted the hegemony of immaterial labor as "the social form of networks based on communication, collaboration, and affective relationships."[5] Immaterial labor relies on the creativity and inventiveness of the poor, or "the multitude," who constitute the foundation of every possibility of humanity despite their deplorable situation in material production.[6]

Yet China's position as the world's factory leads us to pay attention to the coexistence between material and immaterial labor, and not merely the latter's predominance over the former. Whenever I visited labor nongovernmental organizations (NGOs) in Guangdong Province, activists brought up Chun Tae-il, whose suicide protest in 1970 awakened South

Photo 4.1 Foxconn workers-cum-volunteers are displaying goods for a charity bazaar. (July 13, 2014) Mun Young Cho

Korean workers to a political awareness of their miserable condition. They also referred to a book entitled *Korean Workers*[7] which analyzed the rapid formation of the working class in South Korea. Unlike South Korea in the 1970–1980s, however, today's China faces the simultaneous growth of the secondary and tertiary industries that, together, involve both material and immaterial labor. Between 1980 and 2013, the nation's secondary industry increased from 18 percent to 44 percent of GDP; the service industry grew even more meteorically, from 13 percent to 46 percent of GDP.[8]

Young factory workers are subject to low wages, overtime work, and militaristic labor discipline in their workplaces. Still, they are also exposed to immaterial labor along with the nation's rapid industrial transformations and its involvement in the worldwide digital revolution. The class subjectivity of migrant youth, who daily experience global scapes through SNS and who easily switch to service industries, should be more fluid than that of factory workers under Fordism or under the socialist planned economy of previous decades. However, as I will detail, this fluidity does not promise workers liberation from the structural, institutional barriers that they nonetheless continue to experience in the city as well as in their workplaces. Consequently, fluidity does not mean they have any hope of breaking away from the class—or, as this volume argues the "caste"—in which they are situated.

In this chapter, I contextualize the conditions of poverty that Foxconn workers experience as they intersect waged, robot-like, material labor in factories and non-waged, immaterial, humanized labor in China's booming social sector.[9] My focus on the social sector[10] among various niches for immaterial labor arises from the outburst of discourses, strategies, policies, or programs relating to "society" (*shehui*) in China.

In response to the grave inequalities and contradictions that economic development has brought about, both the number of NGOs and their participation in dealing with social problems have dramatically increased over the last two decades. These organizations include not only labor NGOs, which aim at enhancing workers' rights (*weiquan*), they also include social work organizations, voluntary associations, and other types of social organizations[11] that approach labor issues in terms of "public welfare" (*gongyi*) and that receive financial and institutional support from the government.

Particularly concentrating on government-funded "public welfare" organizations, I call the Foxconn workers whom these organizations invite as volunteers "the passionate poor." As volunteers, these workers are given "ethical citizenship," that is, a mode of cultivating care for others as the new citizen's ethic.[12] As "producers of their ideas at the same time as their material life,"[13] they also seek different forms of life through their active participation in volunteering, regardless of how they are regulated and expected to perform in the field.

However, their vitality becomes enmeshed in the particular politics of recognition, which prompts them to pursue individual strategies for self-development rather than collective efforts to achieve social membership. Furthermore, four years' observation of Foxconn workers who participated in volunteering has uncovered the inexorable reality that most of them are stuck in precarious life conditions. Imbued with neither social nor political rights, the possession of merely an ethical citizenship ends up lubricating the social suffering that these migrant youth endure as their life boundaries turn out to be fixed, despite that possession (see introduction). They remain, therefore, unable to break through the barriers that exclude them from those other forms of rights.

What is at stake is that the production of ethical citizenship sustains social inequality, not by dehumanizing workers but by working through their choices, desires, and aspirations, echoing the productive feature of power.[14] Many scholars have emphasized the ambivalent feature of immaterial labor, arguing that the cultural, affective production that is gained through it is both pleasurable and exploitative.[15] Yet, the exploitative part of immaterial labor is elided by many migrant youth who tend to locate volunteer labor as the opposite other of "gruesome" factory labor. The unwaged labor of "the passionate poor" contributes to the spectacle of social stability while its owners continue their precarious lives.

In what follows, I briefly introduce the expansion of the social sector in China, pointing to the ways in which state actions relating to social governance reconfigure the politics of labor. I then turn to my ethnographic research in Shenzhen's Foxconn town, where social workers invite migrant youth to act not only as service recipients but also as volunteers for community activities. The first part of my ethnography examines the workings of social work practices, in which these volunteers are assumed to be "flawed" youth, no longer imbued with the "worker" identity. The next part is a description of Foxconn workers-cum-volunteers, who engage in various forms of affective, relational labor that go way beyond the government's expectations.

Rather than concluding that their active participation is a manifestation of new possibilities, I will probe the multilayered dimensions of poverty by tracing the life trajectories of three volunteers. Their stories shed light on the persistence of the precarious lives of "the passionate poor" and problematize the politics of recognition, which individualizes workers' responses to the structural and institutional barriers which they cannot penetrate.

LABOR POLITICS RECONFIGURED AMIDST THE EXPLOSION OF THE SOCIAL SECTOR

For the last thirty years, China, as the world largest industrial base of manufacturing, has steered global production and trade. Since the country's fame for this accomplishment has come about largely (though not entirely) thanks to the mobilization of migrant youth from the countryside for low-paid, long-hours' labor, "Made in China" has become a catch phrase simultaneously representing the nation's rapid economic growth and the exploitation of labor.[16] Labor exploitation has been made possible by the combination of the global supply chains based on massive outsourcing of labor and the nation's enduring rural-urban divide. As Ngai Pun and Jenny Chan succinctly argue, the "proletarianization" of Chinese workers is characterized by "a spatial separation between production in urban areas and social reproduction in the countryside," under which the reserve army of internal migrant workers contributes to lowering not only production costs but also social reproduction costs in host cities.[17] The power of this amalgam of forces becomes evident when we consider that, although the Labor Contract Law was newly implemented in 2008 as a state action against workers' social suffering, labor disputes and strikes by disgruntled workers have *increased* rather than decreased, as have unpaid or underpaid social insurance, chronic wage arrears, and the expansion of dispatched labor.[18]

It is in this context that labor NGOs have blossomed in southern China, particularly in Guangdong Province. Unlike northeast China, where the collapse of the manufacturing sector inherited from socialist planning has not yet fully dissipated the importance of state-owned enterprises, southern coastal areas have attracted foreign investment and absorbed a large number of rural migrants into a growing labor-intensive economy. Socialist workers in the northeast, who once benefited from the urban work-unit system, seek protection by invoking the claim of "the people," that is, by using the very language with which the party-state had once identified and venerated them.[19] In contrast, most workers in the south—not "the people" but a population group reduced to what mass media often call "the new generation of migrant workers" (*xinshengdai nongmingong*)—increasingly draw on political discourses of class, citizenship, law, and rights in order to cope with their vulnerable situation.[20]

Grassroots labor NGOs have engaged in this rights-based activism since the 1990s. Often with financial and organizational support from Hong Kong labor NGOs or foreign foundations, they have taken the place of the official trade union—long crippled by its conflicting mission of protecting workers' rights and, at the same time, representing the nation's interest[21] —in encouraging lawsuits, strikes, education, or communal activities for migrant workers.

However, beginning in the late Hu-Wen period, many labor NGOs began to face a new predicament as the Chinese government relaxed its controls over social organizations and promoted their expansion in particular ways. To begin with, the government loosened the registration regulations for social organizations[22] and introduced a scheme by which local governments could purchase social services from them (*zhengfu goumai fuwu*). Yet this state support has been concentrated just on social work organizations, community-based associations, volunteer associations, and charity foundations, which identify their mission in terms of "public welfare." By encouraging local governments to incubate social organizations and provide those organizations with opportunities to apply for state-funded community projects, higher-level governments have attempted to foster civil participation and, at the same time, share government functions without undermining state authority.[23]

Importantly, this action has occurred in parallel with sanctions on NGOs that raise more explicitly political claims. After the accession of Xi Jinping as supreme leader in late 2012, the activities of many of these NGOs have been curtailed and even repressed. A new Foreign NGO Management Law, effective as of January 2017, stipulates that any group wishing to operate in China must register with the public security bureau as well as refrain from engaging in political or religious activities that damage "China's national interests."[24] This so-called supervision attacks labor NGOs that have inevitably relied on financial support from outside. They are on the edge between dangerous confrontation with the state and limiting their activities to safe agendas, for instance, to what Jude Howell calls "welfarist incorporation."[25]

In all, this mode of governing social organizations raises a new dilemma for labor NGOs that try to maintain distance from or fight against the state. However, by offering secure funding it also provides new opportunities to emerging "public welfare" social organizations that want to do something "good" or "meaningful," in the words of my interviewees. Under the broad and opaque title of "public welfare," the organizations have engaged in various activities for a range of target groups, including young migrant workers. How differently do these organizations, compared to labor NGOs, embrace migrant workers in their programs? I will probe the workings of social governance with an ethnographic eye to a Foxconn town in Shenzhen. There, social work practices are most salient among the various forms of "public welfare" activities.

SOCIAL WORK AND THE "FLAWED" VOLUNTEERS IN SHENZHEN'S FOXCONN TOWN

The serial suicides incident at Foxconn in 2010 coincided with the period when social work, which had remained just an academic discipline for about twenty years, emerged as a full-fledged profession across the nation. With its increasing attention to social stability around this same time, the party-state proposed an "urgent need to train talented troops of social workers," who were expected to alleviate inequalities and contradictions.[26] Rapid economic growth and geographical proximity to Hong Kong[27] enabled the city of Shenzhen to actively pioneer the government model of purchasing the services of social workers, who had been recruited on a contractual basis, into social work organizations.[28]

The development of social work in Guanghua,[29] a Foxconn town in Shenzhen, started with a media blitz that highlighted the Foxconn incident; later, this profession was pushed through a nationwide project of "social construction" (*shehui jianshe*). When the serial suicides aroused global attention in 2010–2011, more than four hundred social workers were quickly dispatched to the two Foxconn compounds in Shenzhen to consult with frontline workers.[30] The Shenzhen government, with Foxconn, supplied funding to purchase social work services from external agencies. After about a year, Foxconn chose not to renew this contract, instead hiring its own social workers and psychology counselors.[31]

Thereafter, rather than entering the walled compound of the factory, local governments centered their efforts on the management of Foxconn workers who were living within their jurisdictions. In December 2011, the district government[32] (financial sponsor) and the street office (project manager) made an official agreement with a social work organization (service provider). The government paid 500,000 yuan per annum to each organization so that it could create two community projects under a three-year contract. In the contract, the district government set out service goals, plans, and targets, stipulating that the main purpose of the organization would be "providing a series of advice and programs to young migrant workers who come to Shenzhen, particularly those who go to work in Foxconn, to help them to relieve stress, extend social networks, and build a sense of belonging to the city."[33]

Accordingly, the social work organization set up two Community Service Centers (hereafter, CSC), one in Daxing and the other in Xinyi, and dispatched six social workers to each of them. These social workers went on to cultivate further social organizations in the community and organized various activities, such as community clean-ups, picnics, karaoke events, cooking contests, and a group blind date event. Of those activities, the group blind date (*xiangqin*) was the biggest and most popular function.

In mid-August 2013, for example, the group blind date for 150 migrant workers—mostly Foxconn workers—was held in one of the largest nightclubs in Guanghua. The occasion was co-organized by Foxconn as the primary sponsor, the nightclub as the venue provider, and the CSC in Xinyi as program manager. An official from the Foxconn Trade Union[34] gave a speech:

> This event started a couple of years ago. Its purpose is more than dating. I hope that through this kind of opportunity, you can extend your personal network beyond a factory or a dormitory. On July 7th in the lunar calendar last year, seven couples were born thanks to the same event that we held. One of these couples has even gotten married and I officiated [at] their wedding! (applause)

Her speech was followed by complimentary messages from the district government official in charge of social construction. After that, the main event lasted almost four hours, copying the pattern used in TV dating reality shows. In the report of the Xinyi CSC, the purpose of the group blind date was described as follows:

> With the accelerated pace of life, work pressure, and the contraction of social networks, many young people who come of marriageable age miss their chance to date and end up becoming "leftover men" (*shengnan*) and "leftover women" (*shengnü*). As the numbers of single men and women are rising rapidly in all cities, their marriage has received increasing social attention. In the processes of social construction, the youth play a vital role; society thus has the responsibility and obligation of taking care of their marriage and happiness. The majority of the population in Guanghua consists of young migrant workers, most of whom are of marriageable age. Due to some factors like work, personality, and environment, most workers experience difficulty in loving or being loved. The CSC-led activity for associating single men and women serves as a platform for making true friends and lovers. It helps them to expand their interpersonal relationships and thus create a happy life.

It is important to note how social workers in the above report—who are subject to the government's supervision and evaluation—characterize and problematize Foxconn employees. Their report recognizes these employees in terms of their value as *youth*; a label of "workers" simply indicates an occupation or a movement from rural to urban. And whereas the value of youth (which the report terms "a vital role") may be elusive, the problem of workers is clear: workers spread to cities (and thus may exacerbate urban problems); they do not marry at a proper time (and thus may damage social reproduction); and they are lacking in social intercourse ability (and thus this is a status that may give rise to suicidal impulses). In short, with massive support and supervision from the state, social work programs in Guanghua have highlighted the "youth" identity of Foxconn workers while at the same time assuming a certain "lack" or "problem" among those workers, one which needs to be filled or solved through social activities.

Importantly, social work programs in Guanghua invite migrant youth not only to be service recipients but also to act as volunteers. Recruiting volunteers at the main gate of the Foxconn cluster, or through internet-based public relations programs or promotion campaigns, has become one of the regular routines for social workers. During my fieldwork in the summer of 2013, the number of volunteers who were registered in the two CSCs reached almost six hundred. According to the directors of the two CSCs, about sixty to seventy volunteers in each of them were active enough to show up regularly.

To be a volunteer in each center also meant to be a member of the Shenzhen Volunteer Association, which was established by the Chinese Communist Youth League. Migrant youth signed up for courses required for registered volunteers, helped social workers to prepare for or clean up after various program activities, and displayed each other's activities through an online platform (QQ zone) titled "Guanghua Volunteers." In 2015, "Perfect Life: Realizing Old Dreams," initiated by a director in the Daxing CSC, was even selected as one of the top ten venture philanthropy projects in the district because more than three hundred Foxconn workers-cum-volunteers helped old and disabled residents to carry out their family wishes, thereby "contributing to the building of a harmonious family and harmonious community."[35]

This activity raises a fundamental question: What does it mean for government-supported social organizations to assume migrant workers are "flawed" youth, yet at the same time to grant them ethical citizenship as volunteers who contribute to building a harmonious society? The work of Andrea Muehlebach brings this question to the surface. Muehlebach defines citizenship as "a process, social position, or orientation that can be precarious and that must be repeatedly asserted and attained." In this sense, volunteer activities allow people to perform ethical citizenship, that is, to exhibit the capacity to live as valued members of society, not as "dependent" figures.[36]

However, the human agency, affect, and will of volunteers, which Muehlebach argues are newly manifest in the framework of ethical citizenship, are rarely expected in the case of Foxconn workers-cum-volunteers. Supposing that they lack cultural and educational capital, social workers exclude these "flawed" volunteers from the planning work of the programs and expect them to merely assist social workers.[37] Frequently mobilized in ritualistic performance under the glare of the cameras, Foxconn workers-cum-volunteers are acknowledged, if at all, for the sake of appearances, not for their actual contributions. Thus, they remain outcast for purposes of social inclusion.

Nevertheless, it is significant to note that such performance has, after all, opened up a new space available to them. In the following section, I turn to Foxconn workers, focusing on their own participation in the social sector and their life paths after (or in the midst of) volunteering. How do these workers act on the particular ways in which the migrants are represented in social work programs? In what ways do volunteering experiences affect (or not affect) their life trajectories? How do those trajectories help us to understand poverty and inequality facing young migrant workers today and their ultimate place in the larger social formation?

"THE PASSIONATE POOR"

On August 10, 2013, I participated in an activity at the Daxing CSC entitled "Happy Kitchen: Making Nutritious Fruit Smoothies with Young Workers." This was one of ten activities targeting young migrant workers that month. In short, the two-hour program involved social workers and Foxconn workers divided into two groups, pureeing fruits in a blender and tasting smoothies together. To complete this simple activity, however, social workers were required to fill out fifteen-page documents, including their activity plans, schedules, budgets, participants' opinions, related media reports, and so on.

During the event, as a senior social worker was busy following bureaucratic guidelines, migrant participants were chatting, exchanging contact information, and taking photos together. As registered volunteers, these migrants of course knew the expectations of the social workers and the local government officials and tried to satisfy them to some extent by listening to boring speeches from the government leaders, offering positive feedback, and taking official group photos. However, their actual performances did not necessarily meet the authorities' hopes and expectations. One Foxconn worker, for instance, utilized the gathering as an opportunity to try out a digital camera he had purchased after saving his wages for months. The other worker, who dreamed of opening a restaurant in his hometown, was more interested in cooking for other participants after the event than in making simple smoothies. Many participants tried to create new spaces for social production in which they could exchange SNS information, demonstrate their hidden talents, and introduce their side jobs, such as multilevel marketing and insurance sales.[38]

In particular, the feverish digital sphere has opened an attractive space in which young volunteers rewrite the narratives of their presence by deliberately interweaving their private and public lives. The internet has prompted "a continuous production of value that is completely immanent to the flows of the network society at large."[39] New personal networks made possible by volunteer activities have rapidly expanded as people continuously add friends of friends to their QQ or Weixin accounts. Various photos and video files—the products of volunteer labor—have filled their "public" diaries in SNS, in telling stories in which their position as Foxconn workers is almost invisible.

The never-ending digital work of uploading, writing, reading, managing, and participating in chatlines has often immersed these volunteers in competition related to their passionate activities. A Foxconn worker proudly showed me a set of video clips about traffic volunteering when we met again half a year later. "I volunteered three hundred hours for the last six months! After work, I spend most of my time in renewing my volunteer records. Friends keep uploading prizes, records, and photos about their activities. I feel subtle pressure . . . ha ha."[40] Indeed, in contrast to factory labor at Foxconn, the volunteer labor which crisscrosses digital scapes has allowed him to feel a sense of delight and accomplishment through the process of production as well as in the finished product. Accordingly, many Foxconn workers I met at the two CSCs in Guanghua have tried to seek their passion not inside the factory but in the emerging social sector outside it. Inviting them as volunteers, social work programs seemed to absorb their affective and relational labor by rescuing them from the atomized and isolated forms of life they live in the factories.

However, a critical point here is this: migrant workers are granted ethical citizenship in the city but without any of the normal political rights or economic entitlements attached to it. To explore the possibilities (or impossibilities) that social production through volunteer labor provides to migrant workers, we need to situate it in the life histories of these workers. The following stories of three Foxconn workers-cum-volunteers—Zuo Mei, Yang Hui, and Wang Xin—lead us to give attention to the social suffering which emerges as social production is not accompanied by the elimination of structural, institutional barriers that lock out what are, after all, socially immobile urban outsiders.

Zuo Mei: A Faded Memory of Volunteering in the City

Twenty-four-year-old Zuo Mei was a Foxconn worker in Guanghua when I first met her in January 2013. Born in a remote village in Jiangxi and graduated from a high school near her hometown, she worked in a small textile factory in Wenzhou for three years and then moved to Shenzhen in 2011 "to find a new path to develop myself in the south," as she recalled. When I met her, Zuo had just relocated from a dormitory inside the Foxconn compound to rental housing in Guanghua despite having to pay a higher rent. "In the dormitory, I'm not allowed to wash my clothes. Our company says that it's a waste of water. Its managers collect things for laundry and then send them to a cleaning company. But I don't want to treat my clothes, which I bought at great cost to myself, in that way."[41]

Although the Foxconn trade union sometimes organized various programs like birthday celebrations, counseling, guest lectures, and volunteering activities, Zuo was so exhausted by the strict discipline under which she was forced to exist and the high intensity of the factory labor that she never thought of the factory as an intimate place for cultivating sociality. As she remarked, "I'm terrified by excessive inspection. I have to be careful (to check for) sleep in my eyes or earwax in my ears. Time is too tight. I have to switch work clothes into plain ones, have a meal, then put on (my) working uniform again, and finally get (to) inspection within only an hour. Foxconn raised our wages after the suicide incidents, but it also increased the intensity of labor."

Instead of remaining a faceless worker in the factory, Zuo decided to devote her affective efforts to volunteering at the Daxing CSC. Returning to her room after the night shift at 8:00 a.m., she slept only three hours, and then went to the center to participate in regular programs or to help the social workers with their preparation for events. When I met her again in July 2014, Zuo told me that she had finally quit Foxconn and started to sell insurance. She was introduced to this new job by another volunteer at the CSC. According to her, the sale of insurance provided her with what she could not access in Foxconn: "freedom" (not surveillance), "openness" (not secretiveness), "useful knowledge" (not a repetitive skill), "entrepreneurship" (not working (*dagong*) for others), and "the expansion of personal networks" (not their reduction). When her sales were not good, Zuo returned to a factory (not Foxconn) in order to sell insurance to those whom she met there.

I was unable to meet Zuo Mei when I returned to Shenzhen in January 2015. A social worker in Guanghua told me that she had left for Jiangxi. She also mentioned that Zuo Mei's hope to become a social worker was not fulfilled due to "her lack of professional knowledge and conduct." But I did renew my connection with Zuo Mei through SNS. Tired of unsuccessfully selling insurance and overwhelmed by her parents' pressure to get married, she eventually returned to her hometown and began to work in a gas station. She sent me a recent photo that showed her in a blue uniform, with a genial smile, unfolding a few 100 yuan notes that she had received as her salary. Her QQ zone was no longer filled with numerous activity photos of her and her friends wearing the red-colored vest with the logo of "Guanghua Volunteers." Instead, it occasionally showed conventional phrases attuned to traditional Chinese holidays or the photos of some cosmetics she was selling on the side. Her central concern was that her relationship with a boyfriend had seemed to fall apart after her parents, who had only two daughters, urged him to live with them after marriage.

In November 2016, Zuo Mei eventually broke up with the boyfriend and got engaged to a man to whom her cousin had introduced her. Still working (*dagong*) in Guangdong, the man was nine years older than she was. Zuo Mei proudly sent me several photos of him, an engagement ring he had given her, and a three-storied house he was building in his village, which was close to her hometown. Because of the big house, Zuo Mei's parents eventually allowed her to live with her in-laws; the house also prompted her to decide to marry this older man whom she had met only once. Zuo Mei made no comment when I told her that I would visit Shenzhen. Instead, she sent me beautiful photos of Mount Lu (*Lushan*), asking me to visit her hometown. Her four years in Shenzhen, including her volunteering activities in Guanghua, no longer emerged in our online conversations. Yet, numerous photos of urban lifestyle in her SNS implied that her decision to live a "simple" life in the village might have resulted from a compromise due to harsh realities.

Yang Hui: Volunteering as a Flexible Activity that Costs No Money

In July 2015, I first met twenty-three-year-old Yang Hui in the Xinyi CSC. Born in a poor village in Guangxi, he helped his parents raise pigs after dropping out of high school. "I wasn't thinking seriously at that time. I just thought that I would rather make money early." In 2010, he and his cousin came to work in a light bulb factory in Zhongshan, Guangdong, where they received only five yuan per hour. In October 2011, he moved to Shenzhen to join his parents as an employee in a food processing factory, but moved to Foxconn by himself in July 2013.

As he related, "People said that Foxconn was sizable and systematic enough not to delay payment of wages." His real wage, including overtime pay, increased from 2,450 yuan in 2013 to 3,500 yuan in July 2015. However, no income was left over after he paid his rent and utility bills, ate out a few times, and sent some money for building a new house in his hometown. "I was quite lonely and depressed at first in Foxconn. A thousand people in our workshop were changed so often that I couldn't make any friends. I even sought help from a counselor in the plant," he recalled.

After he got a chance to volunteer in some PR campaigns, Yang Hui spent most of his time outside his working hours in the Xinyi CSC, where he could engage in diverse activities. On the day shift, he participated in evening programs particularly for Foxconn workers—for example, a karaoke contest, cooking, or watching movies. On the night shift, he slept a few hours and then appeared in the center where, before going to work, he played ping pong or volunteered to help social workers prepare for programs for the elderly and children.[42] On weekends Yang Hui said proudly, he never skipped the outdoor activities in Xinyi.

Yang Hui described volunteering as an activity in which "I could discover my own values without spending money." Although the Foxconn town was full of restaurants, street bars, internet cafes, and night clubs, he had little money for frequenting those places. When we met again in January 2016, Yang Hui showed me his paycheck from the previous month. Although the basic salary (*dixin*) increased in response to a rise in the minimum wage in Shenzhen from 1,800 yuan to 2,450 yuan, his real wage after deducting his payments into social security and to the housing fund was only 2,022 yuan. This amount was a radical decrease from what he had earned six months earlier because there was not enough work for him to work overtime. "I had no opportunity to do overtime work for about a couple of months.[43] As you might know, Apple iPhones (6s) were not selling well" at the time.

Indeed, Yang Hui's remarks about Apple bring to light another aspect of labor exploitation in addition to the low basic salary, that is, the great flexibility of the production cycle that workers are forced to endure. In response to a request from Apple, which pays close attention to the market, Foxconn hires fewer workers around the Chinese New Year and more during the summer in preparation for the Apple product launch. This general cycle is further complicated by just-in-time production for Apple in order to protect its technology secrets and to respond to customers quickly in its competition with other suppliers. The duration of work—whether an extension or a reduction in working hours—is not subject to workers' discretion. Such uncertainty reinforces the forced flexibility that migrant workers already face under the rural-urban divide, and highlights their total lack of agency on the job.[44]

In this sense, the flexibility of project-based social work programs, which volunteers can choose selectively, corresponds to the forced malleability of Foxconn workers' routines. Although he complained of harsh labor conditions, Yang Hui was reluctant to change his workplace because "business depression is everywhere, and other small factories don't even offer social security benefits." Instead, he tried to overcome loneliness, recuperate his self-esteem, and, above all, *survive* by devoting himself to volunteering (but also depriving himself by underconsuming). He knew he had little real hope of ascending the social ladder, whether socially or occupationally.

Wang Xin: In Search of Equal Membership in Society

I met twenty-two-year-old Wang Xin in August 2013, when social workers in the Daxing CSC introduced him to me as "one of the best volunteers in Guanghua." Born in a village in Henan, he passed through several factories in Jiangsu, Henan, and Guangdong after dropping out of high school. Right before Chinese New Year in 2012, he came to work at Foxconn on a suggestion from a remote relative in Shenzhen. "Due to the Foxconn regulation that new employees are allowed to take vacation for only four or five days, I couldn't return to my hometown at New Year's. You don't know how lonely I felt in a strange environment," he observed.

Like the other two workers, Wang Xin tried to overcome loneliness and expand his personal network by participating in volunteering in and outside Guanghua. Not satisfied with the "volunteer" position, he managed to establish his own social organization by March 2015, which he called the "Longhua New District Green Outdoor Sports Association." Volunteer experience over several years as well as increasing government support prompted him to develop his personal interest by creating this organization and recruiting more than ten thousand members. To carry out the complicated processes of registration during the day, Wang Xin worked the night shift at Foxconn for about a year.

Wang also obtained a mid-level certificate in mountain climbing as well as a Red Cross relief squad license to prove that he was qualified to supervise outdoor activities. In 2014–2015, his organization arranged large-scale outdoor activities for environmental protection with financial support from the district government and local companies. Through these activities, Wang quickly thrust himself into the media spotlight. Praised as a "rare" individual from the post-90s generation or "a worker who acted for workers,"[45] he deliberately used his "worker" identity as represented by the media to get government funding or collect donations from corporations for the sake of his organization.

Yet the primary reason that he surfed the waves of social organization was his aspiration for equal membership in society. "I meet numerous people in this organization. We come from different regions and work different jobs. But here, we are all volunteers and friends. I'm fascinated by this equality."[46] He never insisted on an equal relationship between the employers and the employees in his workplace which, he admitted, was "unimaginable." Compared to this, an equal partnership at least among the volunteers, all imbued with the notion of ethical citizenship, did seem imaginable and achievable.

Nevertheless, Wang Xin was quite aware that this "equal" membership that he proudly spoke of had an expiration date: It was valid only as long as he operated social organizations and stayed in the city of Shenzhen. Accordingly, Wang began to collect media reports about his organization, hoping that those documents would increase his leverage when he returned to his hometown in Henan: "I plan to show all I did in Shenzhen to the leaders of my home village's township government. I will persuade them to build local social organizations that I can take charge of," he imagined.

His resolution was mixed with anxiety, however, as his words betrayed: "Last year, I visited the township government to introduce my work. To my disappointment, the local officials didn't even set up a division for social organizations. Neither my parents nor other relatives are interested in what I'm doing. On the phone, I've talked to my mom about my volunteering activities. But her only response was to scold me, saying that we poor peasants have barely enough money to live on. Although I told her how volunteering was good for my health and vitality, she simply retorted that I would be healthier if I started farming." Evidently, others of his station, even outside the city, were keenly aware of the unscalability of the societal boundaries that encased them all.

The stories of Zuo Mei, Yang Hui, and Wang Xin all demonstrate a craving to realize their own values through volunteering. Yet these tales also reveal structural obstacles that this activity cannot on its own resolve. Volunteer labor, as my interviewees described it to me, lends its workers high aspirations for equality, self-esteem, respect, recognition, belonging, delight, and achievement. Absent in their descriptions of factory labor, these wishes are, at bottom, dreams for what amounts to social membership, that is, for having their own *place* in society. However, the social membership they yearn for has only a limited chance of being granted through ethical actions; indeed, it can even be dangerous to strive for, since the effort brings with it the social suffering that low-paid workers experience in the factory and as involuntary nomads in the city.

For the past three years, I have traced the life trajectories of twenty Foxconn workers, including Zuo Mei, Yang Hui, and Wang Xin, who actively participated in volunteering activities in Guanghua in 2013. A few of them created unique and divergent paths for themselves in doing so; for example, one became a Buddhist nun and others immersed themselves in Eastern philosophy. However, most workers simply moved from one precarious job to another in the industrial or service sector. In moving, volunteering remained a faded memory (Zuo Mei), a survival strategy (Yang Hui), or a precarious achievement (Wang Xin).

Eventually, the life trajectories of Foxconn workers-cum-volunteers unfolded across fragmented landscapes with a recent dwindling of discussions of rights and entitlements, which many labor NGOs had insisted on, in tension with the party-state. These landscapes show us some of the consequences that can result from "cultural recognition" displacing "socioeconomic redistribution," in the words of Nancy Fraser.[47] Fraser argues that two conditions, in addition to formal legal equality, must be satisfied to realize parity of participation as the heart of justice. These are, first, that the distribution of material resources must be such as to ensure participants' independence and "voice." And second, institutionalized cultural patterns of interpretation and evaluation in society at large must express equal respect for all participants and guarantee equal opportunity for achieving social esteem.[48] In order to secure the "parity of participation" that Foxconn workers long for, social workers in Guanghua have focused only on the second condition and even that is severely bounded—and even impossible outside the NGO.

The particular politics of recognition, which these professionals stimulate under state support, has reframed migrant youth not as rightful workers but as "flawed" ethical subjects. Material inequality and economic exploitation, serious barriers that impede true parity of participation, are not an issue when these youths are immersed in self-development and individualize their life paths, but they lurk threateningly just behind the scene.

STRUCTURAL EXCLUSION AND INDIVIDUAL INCLUSION

In July 2014, I returned to Guanghua after staying in South Korea for several months. During this time, the World Cup fever had reached its peak. At dinner with some social workers and Foxconn workers who had volunteered in the Daxing CSC, regardless of the topic of conversation that was raised, the talk always ended up with a reference to "World Cup." Overinflated housing prices also became the target of "World Cup" jokes. A volunteer brought up something he had recently heard: "Numerous rich people ruined themselves by World Cup betting. Now is the right time to buy a house since many of the owners have put their houses up for auction. Some even killed themselves. The price of their houses must have plunged!" This sort of humor represents not just a parody but, more importantly, a vain attempt to collapse what is in fact the inescapable polarization between wealthy homeowners and the sometimes suicidal members of the Foxconn workforce.

The phrase "killing themselves" reminded another volunteer of the 2010 series of suicides at Foxconn. "Do you know when Guo Taiming [Foxconn's CEO] raised workers' wages? He only acted when a worker jumped to death: 900 yuan at first, and then 1,200 yuan, 1,800 yuan . . . Now the basic salary is 2,100 yuan." A social worker introduced a rumor she had heard in relation to "suicides": "Foxconn tried to compensate for a series of suicides with money. That's why so many workers jumped to their deaths. Their suicides were a kind of life insurance for their families. The rate of suicide has decreased since Foxconn decided not to pay any more money for [suicide] death[s]."

How can we understand the trivialization of suicide, or that another's death hurts no one as a dinnertime topic? In Guanghua, Foxconn suicides are caricatured even in the streets. Several stores sell all their inexpensive clothes and shoes with a catch phrase such as, "I will immediately jump off the building if anyone offers lower prices!" (*Shei biwo dijia mashang tiaolou!*). In fact, deaths at Foxconn have never ended. Between 2011 and 2014, fourteen more suicides, including one at Guanghua, were reported in the media.[49] This official number does not cover deaths from overworking or suspicious causes, which I myself witnessed during my fieldwork.

Regardless of numerous criticisms, Foxconn has continued to grow while assembling about 40 percent of all consumer electronics products sold.[50] Although its revenue growth showed fluctuations as of late 2016 due to the decline of iPhone sales,[51] the corporation was strong enough to be ranked as thirty-first in 2015 and twenty-fifth in 2016 on the Fortune 500 list of the largest companies in the world.[52] To increase its revenues, Foxconn has diversified its business into e-commerce or telecom services at one level and, at another level, has sought to lower labor costs by introducing robots or by moving production plants to inland areas in China: No longer centered on Guangdong, it expanded production bases to western and central China, including to Henan, Sichuan, Chongqing, Hubei, Guangxi, and Shanxi.[53]

Public narratives about the Foxconn suicides lead us to consider the fragmented view of "the passionate poor" who do not have the means to elevate their enormous contributions to social production into common actions against market-driven violence. The martial-like drive of Foxconn, which replaces the human machine with the robot machine, leads

Photo 4.2 The sign on the shop reads: "I will immediately jump off the building if anyone offers lower prices!" (December 4, 2014) Mun Young Cho

us to rethink the role of social organizations that invite Foxconn workers to serve as their volunteers. As I have detailed in this chapter, social organizations that approach labor issues in terms of "public welfare" have attempted to unveil the human faces of workers by granting them an "ethical citizenship." However, these agencies turn out to be completely worthless up against the dehumanizing process of material production, in which those human faces are literally expelled by robots as part of "innovative manufacturing technologies."[54]

Furthermore, and more importantly, social governance actually serves as an anti-friction apparatus with regard to the issues of inequality by converting class-based relationships between capitalists and workers into moral relationships, in which the former appear as generous sponsors of the latter. Drawing public attention to the passion and vitality of the poor, the spectacle of social governance makes it difficult to realize that the workers are increasingly marginalized from government schemes, as Dorothy Solinger vividly describes in this volume. It steers "the passionate poor" to seek individual strategies for survival or self-development rather than forging collective struggles for a social membership that could elevate them out of their "caste-like" position. Their social suffering nevertheless leads us to recognize the simultaneous occurrence of their *structural* exclusion in material production but their *individual* inclusion in social production.

NOTES

This research was funded by the National Research Foundation of Korea (NRF), Grant 2014S1A5A2A03066084. My deepest thanks go to people in Guanghua for the hospitality they have shown me. I am also thankful to Dorothy Solinger for her insightful guidance and editorial help.

1. Thung-Hong Lin, Yi-Ling Lin, and Wei-Lin Tseng, "Manufacturing Suicide: The Politics of a World Factory," *Chinese Sociological Review* 48, no. 1 (2015).

2. Ngai Pun and Jenny Chan, "Suicide as Protest for the New Generation of Chinese Migrant Workers: Foxconn, Global Capital, and the State," *Asia Pacific Journal* 37, no. 3 (2010); Ngai Pun and Jenny Chan, "Global Capital, the State and Chinese Workers: The Foxconn Experience," *Modern China* 38, no. 4 (2012); Ngai Pun and Jenny Chan, "The Spatial Politics of Labor in China: Life, Labor, and a New Generation of Migrant Workers," *South Atlantic Quarterly* 112, no. 1 (2013); Ngai Pun, Jenny Chan, and Mark Selden, *Pingguo beihou de sheng yu si* (*Dying for an iPhone: Apple, Foxconn and Lives of the Chinese Workers*) (Hong Kong: Zhonghua shuju, 2015); Ngai Pun and Anita Koo, "A 'World-Class' (Labor) Camp/us: Foxconn and China's New Generation of Labor Migrants," *positions* 23, no. 3 (2015).

3. Michael Hardt and Antonio Negri, *Multitude: War and Democracy in the Age of Empire* (New York: Penguin Press, 2004), 133.

4. Hardt and Negri, *Multitude*, 152. In their analysis, today's production is conceptualized not merely in economic terms but as social production, that is, not only as the production of material goods but also as the production of relationships, communications, affects, and forms of life.

5. Michael Hardt and Antonio Negri, *Empire* (Cambridge: Harvard University Press, 2001), 289; Hardt and Negri, *Multitude*, 66.

6. Hardt and Negri, *Multitude*, 135.

7. Hagen Koo, *Korean Workers: The Culture and Politics of Class Formation* (Ithaca: Cornell University Press, 2001).

8. Prableen Bajpai, "China's GDP Examined: A Service-Sector Surge," *Investopedia*, October 31, 2014, http://www.investopedia.com/articles/investing/103114/chinas-gdp-examined-servicesector-surge.asp#ixzz41VqT8UHx.

9. Given the fact that not all Foxconn workers engage in volunteer activities, I note here that this chapter is not about Foxconn workers in general but Foxconn workers invited as or motivated to become volunteers. Though relatively small in numbers compared to the entire population of workers, Foxconn workers-cum-volunteers are worthy of scholarly attention because the party-state's actions in dealing with poverty and inequality by mobilizing "the social" have been greater than ever in recent times, and the trajectories of those volunteers lead us to better understand the complex dimension of social suffering that they experience over time.

10. In this chapter, I use the term "the social sector" as a generic term for all the independent NGOs, most of which are not registered with the government, as well as other types of registered social organizations that work closely with mass organizations as well, or with party and government organs.

11. In the late 2000s, the term "social organizations" (*shehui zuzhi*) began to be used broadly in the process, wherein the party-state regulated various groups in the social sector, like NGOs, NPOs (nonprofit organizations), grassroots organizations (*minjian zuzhi*), and so on. Refer to Yanling He, "'Huigui shehui'—zhongguo shehui jianshe yu guojia zhili jiegou diaoshi" (Back to Society: Social Construction and National Governance in China), *Kaifang shidai* (*Open Times*) 3 (2013): 31.

12. I draw on the concept of "ethical citizenship" from the work of Andrea Muehlebach. In her ethnography of voluntarism in Italy, Muehlebach argues that ethical citizenship signals "the emergence of a new mode of social and moral subjectivity" at the heart of neoliberal reform and it enables citizens to imagine themselves "as bound together by moral and affective rather than social and political ties." See Andrea Muehlebach, *The Moral Neoliberal: Welfare and Citizenship in Italy* (Chicago: University of Chicago Press, 2012), 17, 43. Of significance is that the Chinese state, unlike the state in Italy, secures transcendental authority in the working of ethical citizenship. I will detail the working of ethical citizenship in China later.

13. Jacques Rancière, *The Philosopher and His Poor* (Durham: Duke University Press, 2005), 74.

14. Michel Foucault, *The History of Sexuality: An Introduction* (New York: Vintage Books, 1978).

15. Maurizio Lazzarato, "Immaterial Labor," in *Radical Thought in Italy*, ed. Paolo Virno and Michael Hardt (Minneapolis: University of Minnesota Press, 1996), 133–47; Tiziana Terranova, "Free Labor: Producing Culture for the Digital Economy," *Social Text* 18, no. 2 (2000), 33–58; Paolo Virno, *A Grammar of the Multitude: For an Analysis of Contemporary Forms of Life* (London: MIT Press, 2004); Muehlebach, *The Moral Neoliberal*.

16. Ngai Pun, *Made in China: Women Factory Workers in a Global Workplace* (Durham: Duke University Press, 2005).

17. Pun and Chan, "The Spatial Politics of Labor in China," 181.

18. Chris King-Chi Chan, *The Challenge of Labour in China: Strikes and the Changing Labour Regime in Global Factories* (New York: Routledge, 2010); Seung-Wook Baek, "Increase of Labor Dispatching in China as a Combined Effect of the Global Financial Crisis and the 'Labor Contract Act,'" *Industrial Labor Studies* 19, no. 1 (2013); Parry P. Leung, *Labor Activists and the New Working Class in China* (New York: Palgrave Macmillan, 2015).

19. Mun Young Cho, *The Specter of "The People": Urban Poverty in Northeast China* (Ithaca: Cornell University Press, 2013).

20. Ching Kwan Lee, *Against the Law: Labor Protests in China's Rustbelt and Sunbelt* (Berkeley: University of California Press, 2007).

21. Joseph Y. S. Cheng, Ngok Kinglun, and Zhuang Wenjia, "The Survival and Development Space for China's Labor NGOs: Informal Politics and Its Uncertainty," *Asian Survey* 50, no. 6 (2010); Ivan Franceschini, "Labour NGOs in China: A Real Force for Political Change?," *China Quarterly* 218 (June 2014): 474–92; Jude Howell, "Shall We Dance? Welfarist Incorporation and the Politics of State-Labour NGO Relations in China," *China Quarterly* 223 (September 2015): 702–23.

22. Experimentation with relaxing the registration requirements for selected social organizations first began in Shenzhen in 2008. It was extended and promoted across China in 2012. Refer to Howell, "Shall We Dance?," 707–8.

23. Jessica C. Teets, "Reforming Service Delivery in China: The Emergence of a Social Innovation Model," *Journal of Chinese Political Science* 17 (2012); Patricia M. Thornton, "The Advance of the Party: Transformation or Takeover of Urban Grassroots Society?," *China Quarterly* 213 (March 2013): 1–18; Mun Young Cho, "Unveiling Neoliberal Dynamics: Government Purchase of Social Work Services (goumai) in Shenzhen's Urban Periphery," *China Quarterly* 230 (June 2017): 269–88.

24. Christy Yao, "China Passes Law Imposing Security Controls on Foreign NGOs," *Guardian*, April 28, 2016, https://www.theguardian.com/world/2016/apr/28/china-passes-law-imposing-security-controls-on-foreign-ngos.

25. Jude Howell defines "welfarist incorporation" as "a political and economic arrangement between the state and organized society, whereby selected civic organizations are invited by the state to assist in the implementation of policy." See Howell, "Shall We Dance?," 704–5.

26. Tom Chan Kam Tong, Keung David Ip Fu, and Mei Ava Lau Siu, "Social Work Professionalization in Shenzhen," *China Journal of Social Work* 2, no. 2 (2009), 85.

27. Shenzhen was also a novel city where private or foreign-funded enterprises overwhelmed state-owned enterprises, and the traditional work-unit system was less influential than in other cities. Drawing a new design for the city's legibility may have been easier than in other cities that were forced to struggle with the old mode of urban governance under the planned economy.

28. The social work organization is categorized as a "private non-enterprise unit" (*minban feiqiye*) among social organizations. In Shenzhen, its numbers increased from 13 in 2009 to about 200 in 2015 while the numbers of social workers skyrocketed from 96 in 2007 to 5,260 in 2014. Refer to "Shenzhen shegong weishenme liushi?" (Why do social workers in Shenzhen leave?), *Sznews*, September 3, 2015, http://www.sznews.com/news/content/2015-03/09/content_11271330_2.htm.

29. In this paper, with the exception of large areas like Shenzhen and well-known names like Foxconn, all names of places, persons, and institutions are pseudonyms. Foxconn has constructed two plants in Shenzhen. The Guanghua (pseudonym) plant is one of the two.

30. Xiaofeng Li, "Qiye yuangong shehui gongzuo fudao jieru moshi chutan" (Exploring the mode of counseling employees in social work), *Shehui gongzuo* 9 (2010).

31. Interview with a director of a social work service agency in Shenzhen (August 5, 2013).

32. I will not disclose the name of the district in order to protect my informants.

33. Internal material from the Daxing CSC (December 1, 2011).

34. The Foxconn trade union is one branch of the All-China Federation of Trade Unions (ACFTU). At Shenzhen, it was first set up in 1996 under the pressure of media and the mobilization of the Shenzhen Federation of Trade Unions. Refer to Pun and Chan, "Global Capital, the State and Chinese Workers," 404.

35. A pamphlet on the "Top Ten Brands of Venture Philanthropy Projects" (August 2015, Social Construction Bureau of Longhua New District, Shenzhen).

36. Muehlebach, *The Moral Neoliberal*, 18.

37. In addition, despite the near impossibility of realizing expertise due to excessive requests from the government, social workers are often preoccupied with it in order to secure their legitimacy from volunteers who often question the difference between volunteer work and social work. Refer to Cho, "Unveiling Neoliberal Dynamics."

38. Despite working long hours at Foxconn, some volunteers with whom I met engaged in side jobs, particularly on the weekend. These youth were familiar with the e-commerce platform, which insurance sales or multilevel marketing were mostly based on.

39. Terranova, "Free Labor," 34.

40. Interview (January 10, 2016).

41. Interview (January 26, 2013).

42. In general, Foxconn workers on the day shift go to work at 7:30 a.m. and leave at 4:30 p.m. (6:30 p.m. in the case of working overtime), while those on the night shift begin at 7:30 p.m. and leave at 4:30 a.m. (6:30 a.m. if working overtime). Yet, attendance time varies slightly in each unit within the plant.

43. As of January 2016, overtime pay was 21 yuan per hour. Eight yuan per day was added in the case of the night shift. In February 2015, the secretary of the ACFTU blamed Foxconn for hampering the psychological health of its workers by forcing them to do overtime work. Foxconn refuted his charge, arguing that workers could not do overtime work (even though they wanted to) because there was little work to do. See Xiliang Zhang and Qiang Li, "Cong fushikang gongsi de shengming shuokaiqu" (From Foxconn's Statement), *Zhongguo gongren* (*Chinese Workers*) (March 2015). The vice president of the Shenzhen Federation of Trade Unions criticized Foxconn about this controversy, insisting that Foxconn should increase the basic salary so that workers could survive without working overtime. Interview (January 15, 2016).

44. Mun Young Cho, "Forced Flexibility: A Migrant Woman's Struggle for Settlement," *China Journal* 61 (2009): 51–76.

45. Tao Qian, "Guanlan liushui xianshang de 90 hou xiaohuo zhili daidong jinqian gongyou tubuxing" (A post-90s boy travels on foot, leading about a thousand workers), *Longhua News*, August 13, 2015, http://ilonghua.sznews.com/content/2015-08/13/content_12079669.htm.

46. Interview (January 12, 2016).

47. Nancy Fraser, "Social Justice in the Age of Identity Politics: Retribution, Recognition, and Participation," The Tanner Lectures on Human Values delivered at Stanford University (1996).

48. Nancy Fraser, "Social Justice in the Age of Identity Politics," 30–31.

49. Lin, Lin, and Tseng, "Manufacturing Suicide," 17–20.

50. Pun, Chan, and Selden, *Pingguo beihou de sheng yu si*, 28.

51. Eva Dou, "Foxconn Profit Slumps Along with iPhone Sales," *Wall Street Journal*, August 11, 2016, https://www.wsj.com/articles/foxconn-profit-slumps-along-with-iphone-sales-1470930889.

52. "Hong Hai Precision Industry," *Fortune*, January 7, 2017, http://beta.fortune.com/global500/hon-hai-precision-industry-25.

53. Thung-hong Lin, "Governing Foreign Capitalists in the Name of Workers: Foxconn as a Case Study of the Implication of Labor Issues for China's Industrial Policy" (conference paper) (2015), 10.

54. Jane Wakefield, "Foxconn Replaces '60,000 Factory Workers with Robots,'" *BBC News*, May 25, 2016, http://www.bbc.com/news/technology-36376966.

FIVE

On the Rough Edge of Prosperity

Informal Migrant Recyclers in Beijing

Joshua Goldstein

Few images better crystalize the dehumanizing inequities that haunt our modern global economy than that of a scavenging waste picker rooting through an overflowing trash can for bottles to recycle in the middle of a high-rent urban district. This routine scene with its vivid portrayal of polarity, repeated millions of times daily throughout cities on our planet, makes plain the obvious link between two contemporary problems: the gap that yawns between wealthy consumers and the desperately poor in our contemporary consumer culture and the squandering of environmental resources upon which that culture is based. In China, with a Gini coefficient among the highest in the world and health-threatening pollution pervading air, water, and land, these problems are perhaps a bit starker than in some other places.

This chapter offers a brief sketch of the contemporary history of China's informal recyclers, focusing on urban Beijing. China has an estimated 3.3 to 5.6 million people working in the informal waste collecting and recycling sector, with 130,000 to 300,000 in Beijing, gathering and processing several million tons of recyclables annually in Beijing alone.[1] Of course, a comprehensive picture of this sector is beyond the scope of a short chapter, so the focus here is on some of the economic and policy conditions against which Beijing's migrant recyclers have been contending, conditions that have had a particularly powerful impact on their sector: urban government efforts to uproot their businesses; rising urban real estate prices; and the current multibillion dollar wave of investment in incineration. While these conditions are interwoven and overlap chronologically, the narrative here will be roughly chronological, beginning with a sketch of the emergence of Beijing' migrant recycling sector in the 1990s and ending with the new challenge posed by incineration today. Up to now the migrant sector has proven remarkably durable, bringing much-needed cash to millions of rural households—both through remittances sent back by urban migrants to their still-rurally-based families, as well as in cash spent by these urban workers while living in the cities—and providing a path towards economic success for a substantial minority. While informal recycling surely is a manifestation of China's gaping inequities, the fact that it remains a huge and profitable sector which the state has thus far been unable to displace or replace also sheds light on the extent and limits of municipal government control and of migrant community agency.

TOP OF THE HEAP: GUSHI COUNTY MIGRANTS IN BEIJING'S WASTE TRADE

There are few barriers to entry in the scrap trade. At the low end all you need is a willingness to pick through trash, a bag to carry it in, and somewhere to sell the recyclables you collect. But before the 1990s few people in Beijing took up the trade: consumerism was in its infancy, recyclables were scarce, and the collection and buying of scrap was mostly handled by a dense network of government-run recycling depots under the management of the Gongxiaoshe (the official Federation of Supply and Marketing Cooperatives).

This situation began to change rapidly in the 1990s as private shops opened, consumer products surged, urban demolition and construction boomed, and rural migrants poured into the city to work in construction and hunt for gray market employment. Construction sites were both rich mines for valuable recyclables (rebar, copper wiring, radiators, brick) and useful temporary sites for floating waste markets. Many of the first rural migrants to enter the scrap trade in Beijing started out as workers on construction crews who realized they could make more money, have more freedom, and even find profitable business opportunities scavenging scrap from work sites.[2] Others, taking advantage of the huge and palpable discrepancy between their own existence and that of the wealthy, found that the city's new high-end hotels and tourist facilities disgorged enough valuable wastes to support clusters of pickers.

Beijing's burgeoning consumer culture created a waste stream municipal authorities were hardly prepared to manage. The city relied on a World Bank loan to build its first landfill, completed in 1994, and this too soon hosted a migrant waste-picking community. Throughout the 1990s large, unmanaged dumpsites became common on the outskirts of China's larger cities, often with migrant pickers or local farmers living in their midst, perhaps raising pigs that grazed on the food wastes. Overall, postconsumer waste in urban China is estimated to have grown at 8 to 10 percent annually since the late 1980s,[3] and current estimates for Beijing are between .85 and 1.09 kg (1.8 and 2.4 lbs.) per capita.[4]

While at first all this postconsumer scrap was great news for the Gongxiaoshe's recycling business, by the mid 1990s it was becoming apparent that migrant recyclers were not just collecting recyclables, they were also creating their own alternative marketing network that competed with that of the Gongxiaoshe. Where most Gongxiaoshe employees sat in their depots waiting for residents to bring their scrap to trade for small amounts of cash, migrant recyclers went directly to offices, construction sites, and shops, as well as door-to-door to residents, and were paid for recyclables on the spot at prices comparable to or even higher than those offered by the Gongxiaoshe.

Waves of urban construction and real estate investment sent land prices rising and many depots managed by the Gongxiaoshe were cashed out for a tidy profit and demolished in the turnover. These same waves of construction circled the city with debris fields that became convenient spaces for temporary informal waste trade markets. By the late 1990s the Gongxiaoshe's recycling infrastructure had nearly disappeared; its network of several hundred government-managed recycling shops in central Beijing had dwindled to six by 1998.[5] The state-run recycling system had been replaced by a highly resilient network of an estimated 80,000 rural migrant collectors and their scrap markets.[6]

While theoretically open to anyone, Beijing' informal recycling sector soon came to be dominated by specific migrant communities. Waste collecting at landfills, dumps, and garbage transfer stations—the grueling work of picking through tons of putrefying garbage—came to be dominated by migrants from Sichuan's Bazhong County. Community recyclers, on the other hand, overwhelmingly came from Henan's Gushi County, the most populous rural county in all of China. Unlike landfill pickers, informal community recyclers (by far the largest and most enduring segment of the informal waste trade sector and our focus here) were more like petty traders than scavengers, buying all kinds of recyclables (newsprint, cardboard, bottles, cans) from residents and businesses, then carting them to rubbish markets where they resold them at stalls that specialize in particular commodities (PET plastic, Styrofoam, iron, copper, etc.). Stall bosses were also mostly from Gushi, typically being collectors who had become successful enough to rent market spaces and bankroll larger-scale trade (in the realm of several tons per week). Like all over the world, China's street-level scrap trade was, and remains, an all-cash business.

Few scholars paid attention to this phenomenon in the 1990s, but there were some exceptions. In *Contesting Citizenship in Urban China*, Dorothy Solinger provided a thoughtful sketch of migrant pickers, describing their poverty, vulnerability to police abuse, and propensity to band into native-place gangs for protection.[7] And a group of researchers in Beijing spent a year doing fieldwork and wrote an excellent two-part study in *China Perspectives* trying to understand how it was that the rural migrants living in what had come to be called Henan village in the city's Bajia neighborhood rose to dominate the city's informal recycling. It was not for lack of competition, as Hebei migrants were also active and seemed to have a head start and the advantage of geographic proximity to Beijing.

The researchers hypothesized that Henan migrants, having few options in Beijing—being further from home and also having on average far smaller land allotments than the Hebei migrants against whom they competed—were more willing to take economic risks and throw themselves tirelessly into their work. These traits were most acutely true of the business leaders of the Gushi community who, in the authors' words, demonstrated a "powerful desire to improve their lot [and] the determination to pay any price to achieve it."[8] These entrepreneurial "trash barons" (*polan wang*) made large and risky investments and gray market deals with Beijing local governments and industrial buyers, and they reinvested their winnings to grow their businesses. In their success they then patronized fellow provincials, further impelling chain migration. Here, unlike for the Foxconn workers-cum-volunteers whom Cho documents or the laid-off workers in the Solinger chapter, we begin to see a form of agency that could progress to a degree of social mobility.

While the exact reasons why Gushi migrants gained command of the sector in the 1990s are debatable, the general conditions under which their rise occurred are clear. Informal recycling markets in the 1990s as a rule were temporary and set up in demolition sites, yards in peri-urban villages, or just by the side of a road or open dump at the city's outskirts. Migrant collectors rented housing near these markets where, at day's end (typically closer to midnight than sunset), they brought their daily haul of scrap. Housing was typically jerry-built brick shacks with shared taps and toilets in the alley. Some scrap markets rather unobtrusively merged into their peri-urban village surroundings. Other markets, particularly those that took root in temporarily idle demolition sites, tended to transform the surroundings into little better than a sprawling dump.

Informal recycling did offer dynamic opportunities for economic mobility in the 1990s, but the sector was also highly stratified and starkly unequal. At the lowest rung were thousands of roaming trash pickers who lived in dire conditions. Though they might pick in the same neighborhood daily, these scavengers had no "turf," no contractual or customary arrangement giving them regular access to a community's or a shop's waste stream, and so resorted to scrounging through street-side trash cans, dust heaps, and construction sites. Their work regimen left them vulnerable to injury and health problems, particularly skin and digestive ailments. Lacking access to the necessary cash or connections to buy or borrow a bike cart, these scavengers could be identified by the large sacks they shouldered as they roamed. The one positive side of scavenging was that there were no business expenses; any recyclables found were sold for pure profit. Such individuals likely remained stuck at the bottom of the social heap.

The next level up were recyclers who managed to secure fairly reliable access to a community's waste stream and, therefore, a regular daily income. In the 1990s these community collectors became, and today still are, the bulwark of the informal recycling sector and the conduit through which huge tonnage gets sorted, packed, and shipped daily. They rarely scavenged and, unlike scavengers, did not get their recyclables for free but rather bought them from residents and businesses and then sold them for a slightly higher price at recycling markets. Their income derived from the difference between the buying and selling prices of different kinds of scrap. Their favored vehicle was the three-wheel bike cart which, if properly loaded, could carry up to 150 kilos (330 pounds) of mixed scrap, including used furniture and appliances. To make the leap from scavenging to community collecting, a migrant needed seed money to buy recyclables and get a cart, requisites not generally so easily acquired.

Living in single room brick shacks near recycling markets, collectors' household objects were usually composed of discards from Beijing's middle class residents—old furniture and used appliances they picked up at work. Their dawn commutes to their collection sites could range from five to as many as twenty kilometers (three to twelve miles), and the return trek during evening rush hour, their carts piled with scrap, could be a public spectacle of endurance. What money these collectors managed to save they typically remitted home or banked for educational expenses for their children. Some recyclers in Beijing today have worked in the same community for over twenty years, but despite their being among the most familiar faces in the communities they serve, they remain socially marginalized and, of course, still lack Beijing *hukou* (household registration). They live in Beijing, but are not of Beijing—finding housing in de facto segregated communities, their children attending segregated migrant schools or being raised back in the village. So while they did not occupy the very lowest social rung among their coworkers, their status in society-at-large and their difficulty in saving up the wherewithal for advancement would seem to place them within the same humble social segment as the group just below them.

Near the top of the migrant sector hierarchy was a small group (maybe 5 percent) of recyclers who, by the late 1990s, had taken the plunge into scrap entrepreneurship, the possibility of which does suggest an upgrading of agency. These recyclers moved from collecting and hauling recyclables to running stalls in trash markets. The economic risks (including theft, dislocation, confiscation of goods, fire, and extreme market volatility) were daunting, but the potential returns could be life changing.

In the 1990s, scrap markets were chaotic with little if any physical infrastructure. Paved yards were a rarity and roofing unheard of. The larger markets were divvied up into a few separate stalls, indicated (if at all) by waist-high unmortared brick walls, each stall specializing in one commodity. A trader who ran a market stall was known as a "little boss" and was said to have a "sitting" job, implying a relatively leisurely lifestyle compared to the exhausting commute confronting collectors.[9] Stall bosses typically lived in a small shack in the market stall they rented; this way they were always there when collectors came by and, just as important, they could guard their stalls. Stall bosses and their handful of workers (often just a family member or two), sorted and minimally processed the scrap they aggregated from collectors, and from there it was trucked to factories, primarily in rural Hebei (where environmental regulations were lax) where it was reprocessed for industrial use or into new products.

Finally, at the apex of the urban recycling sector were a handful of migrant bosses, known as "big bosses," who had accumulated enough economic and social capital in Beijing to negotiate for use rights over real estate for junk markets. While these markets were usually fairly small, accommodating between a few to perhaps a dozen stalls in the early 1990s, by the early 2000s some were large enough to host several dozen stalls. The "big bosses," also mainly from Gushi, were well-known names in the recycling community and shouldered a certain paternalistic responsibility for handling the inevitable relocation of markets and recycler communities that transpired each time a market was demolished (an inevitable occurrence described in greater detail below). Thus, a form of mobility that could even promote a picker up and out of the poorer echelon was obtainable by those skilled enough to make the climb.

The rather acute stratification and differentiation of roles within the migrant recycling sector that emerged by the 1990s has, in large part, remained in place up through today, with some noticeable general trends. For instance, as Beijing has expanded, many community collectors have replaced their bike carts with trucks. And, as municipal authorities changed their policies regarding recycling markets, the infrastructure in them improved somewhat with paving, walls, truck scales, and even roofing becoming increasingly common. These changes, if anything, have made the divide between the poorest and most successful recyclers wider, as purchasing trucks, accessing neighborhoods, and renting market stalls all require greater up-front capital today than they did back in the 1990s. The alluring dynamism of economic mobility of the 1990s has all but disappeared from the sector—it is no longer an attractive sector to migrants hoping that hard work might raise them to a better socioeconomic status. Despite these important changes, the informal recycling system is essentially organized along the same lines today as it was in the 1990s. That this system has endured through over two decades of urban expansion, demographic shifts, and antagonistic municipal regulations speaks to the resilience of this basic model and of the migrants who have created it.

POLICY SHIFTS: FROM ATTEMPTS AT ELIMINATION TO LIMITED TOLERATION

Though the 1990s was in one sense a heyday for informal migrant recyclers—being the years during which they wrested control over urban China's multi-billion-dollar recycling sector from the state—it was also, up until around 2003, a period during which they faced the government's most concerted efforts to ban their activities. These moves by the state took two primary forms: police harassment and district campaigns to eliminate scrap markets.

The context for these government efforts was the structural marginalization of migrants under the *hukou* (household registration) system. The ways in which the complex of regulations related to *hukou* affected the lives and work of migrant recyclers in the 1990s were too multifaceted and variable to present comprehensively,[10] but a snapshot of the situation in the summer of 2000 provides an impression. At that time a rural migrant needed four types of identification to work in Beijing legally: a national identity card; a temporary residence permit (about 200 RMB); a work permit (also 200 RMB); and a health card. Each document was provided by different offices. But mere possession of these was hardly enough to work as a recycling entrepreneur. Licenses for three-wheel carts were frequently denied migrants, while truck and car licenses were available only to Beijing residents. Migrants could not lease land, so any recycling market was either unregistered or leased under a Beijing resident's name. The metal trade, which was under government oversight, banned migrants from obtaining such permits. Even buying and using a cell phone was more expensive at that time for migrants than for Beijing residents. And, of course, this does not skim the surface of regulations affecting migrant families, such as differential access to health care and education—in the year 2000, schools organized by migrant communities had no legal status.

Municipal efforts to eliminate informal recyclers from Beijing in the 1990s must be seen against this backdrop of the secondary citizenship held by people from the excluded caste which, of course, includes most migrants. Police harassment, though probably unsystematic, was pervasive. A survey we conducted among recyclers in 2010 found that fourteen out of twenty-nine respondents who had worked as recyclers in Beijing in the 1990s had been detained and deported under the Custody and Repatriation procedure at least once. Some were apprehended because they lacked papers or a bike-cart license, but many said police did not care if they had papers or not, they were still detained. Abuse, including beatings, during detention was fairly common. Indeed, the Custody and Repatriation procedure was notorious for such abuse and only finally ended after the beating to death of the young college graduate Sun Zhigang in Guangdong in 2003. Those who managed to avoid deportation and abuse generally did so by paying bribes. Hiding from authorities was a common daily experience—one recycling couple told a story (which they found hilarious in hindsight) of hiding the wife's mother under bales of Styrofoam when authorities came by because she didn't have her papers on her.

Such harassment, while mainly a form of petty corruption, was premised on the assumption that migrant recyclers had no legal right to be in the city. An offhand comment by Wang Weiping (a Beijing government representative frequently described in the Chinese media as the country's leading authority on the informal waste sector) in his oft-cited 1999 report on informal recyclers that "we all know, the majority of crimes in Beijing are caused by migrants" is typical of government and state media reports at the time.[11] Migrant recyclers, particularly the prototypical itinerant collectors on their three-wheel bike carts, were incessantly described as noisy, dirty, disruptive, and cheating residents with fake scales; one Haidian government report even referred to them as "population pollution" (*renkou wuran*).[12]

In contrast to such amorphous expressions of hostility, campaigns to ban informal scrap markets were clearly deliberate actions by district governments to uproot the sector. Circular 17 of the Chaoyang District Urban Renewal Office in 1997 titled "On the Elimination of Independent Markets and a Pilot of State-Run Recycling Markets" is exemplary. The report begins with an assessment of Chaoyang's latest crackdown on migrant markets:

> Since 1997 our district . . . has eliminated over 100 recycling stands and rubbish markets, making a great improvement to our district's environment. But [this] did not cause petty recyclers to naturally die off. Instead, in places like Dongfeng village and Mazidian you no longer see a slew of independent recycling traders, but these petty hawkers have adopted the tactic of "retreat from the streets, enter the villages; retreat from the streets, enter the households" and are renting peasant yards to do their trade, creating one more cause of pollution and unsafety. Though these new stalls are smaller in scale, they are more numerous than they were before the clean-up.[13]

While most authorities chalked these tactics up to the criminal tendencies stereotypical of migrants, researchers Tang Can and Feng Xiaoshuang, coauthors of the *China Perspectives* article on Henan Village, realized the situation was more complex. Many peri-urban village residents on the outskirts of Beijing had discovered that it was quite profitable to rent housing and yard space to migrant recyclers. Some made half their income from such rents; those who stopped working altogether and lived on rents were said to "eat roof tiles" (*chi wapian*). In some villages almost every resident had entered into this new income stream, and the researchers found that villagers were helping protect recyclers from local authorities and the police:

> In many peri-urban villages we found the same situation where news of a surprise inspection by the local government traveled like wildfire before it could be implemented. We repeatedly saw and heard about situations like: . . . [local landlords] turning a blind eye to their [migrant tenants] stowing away what was obviously government property banned for private sale, such as whole drums of military-use electric cable and sacks of new steel piping and plumbing fixtures. Moreover, landlords rented to tenants lacking temporary housing permits; they hid tenants' illegal or prohibited goods from inspectors; helped tenants steal electricity; allowed their names to be used so migrants could get truck and three-wheel cart licenses; assisted migrants in making connections for their illegal business activities . . . and in all sorts of ways turn a blind eye, tolerating or sheltering migrants' unlawful activities.[14]

Feng and Tang argued that Beijing villagers realized that if migrant recyclers profited, they did too; their common interests, based on market transactions, led to collusion that ignored or violated government policies and laws. While some of these laws, such as those against theft, seem unassailable, others—that licenses only be made available to Beijing residents or government approved enterprises—were clearly discriminatory. The laws and regulations increased the social and economic costs migrant recyclers shouldered, but they clearly did not stop them from accessing housing, trucks, yards, and permits. At least in the marginal spaces and economies of migrant recycling, the market forces in the 1990s seemed too powerful for authorities or policies to contain.

To give China's municipal authorities credit, by the early 2000s they had come to the conclusion that eliminating the informal recycling sector was beyond them. Beginning in 2003, the requirement that recycling markets be administratively approved was cancelled,[15] meaning that informal recycling markets no longer faced the constant threat of crackdowns.[16] Several peri-urban village governments quickly approved larger, paved, and planned markets hosting scores of stalls for migrant traders. The village of Dongxiaokou in Changping District (about twenty-five kilometers or fifteen miles from the city center) became famous as a center for recycling, with some markets hosting up to one hundred stalls, but similar markets could be found in Daxing, Fengtai, and Chaoyang. Combined with the end of the Custody and Repatriation process and more relaxed *hukou* restrictions, since 2003 it would seem that the Beijing government has taken a live-and-let-live attitude toward the informal recycling sector. But a closer look reveals persistent antagonism and disenfranchisement.

Though authorities have stopped their daily assault on informal recyclers and their markets, municipal administrators have not ceded the sector entirely. Municipal recycling and sanitation companies have continued to invest in attempts to wrest the recycling sector from the hands of informal migrants. Here it is important to note a phenomenon fairly unique to China: its municipal sanitation and recycling systems are completely separate bureaucracies. This peculiar division of responsibilities has a clear historical explanation. Back in the 1950s, when these bureaucracies were formed, China's urban waste stream was almost entirely composed of food wastes and coal ash (for heating), with the portion of recyclable materials useful to industrial production typically around 2 percent. Recycling and reuse were therefore of little relevance to sanitation. Rather than arising out of a waste management bureaucracy, China's state-managed recycling network grew out of bureaus that handled small businesses, handicrafts, and industries. The separation between sanitation and recycling persisted throughout the Mao era and in fact still exists today—municipal waste management in China in the present still lacks any mandate or accountability over urban recycling. Thus, when postconsumer waste emerged as a major sector in the 1990s and the Gongxiaoshe's recycling network evaporated, the recycling sector was administratively up for grabs.

As a result, over the last fifteen years in Beijing both the sanitation and the recycling bureaucracies have received subsidies to pursue two completely separate and uncoordinated programs to handle recycling, but neither have been charged with responsibility or accountability for the sector. On the sanitation side, since 2000, the Beijing government has spent hundreds of millions of yuan[17] on repeatedly failing "pilot programs" attempting to implement community-based source separation.[18] Meanwhile, the city's district level recycling bureaus have also received subsidies to experiment with schemes like fee-based registration of informal collectors and online apps for "authorized" recycling services. As just one example, the company Tiantianjie (that grew out of the Chongwen District's recycling department) received four million yuan in 2007 to create a recycling network (including eighteen neighborhood collection points, uniforms for collectors, trucks with company logos, etc.) that resulted in collecting only ten tons of material per month (consider that a single successful informal collector with one three-wheel cart can collect four tons in a month).[19]

What has been the point of keeping these district recycling companies and municipal source-separation programs on such expensive life-support for over a decade when they contribute nothing to recycling the city's wastes? I would argue that the state has found a way to have its cake and eat it too. The "cake" it has is an exceptionally efficient recycling system, run and managed by informal migrants entirely free of charge; moreover the city contributes next to nothing to the subsistence needs of these outsiders. Formal municipal recycling systems require massive and costly infrastructures—barrels, trucks, processing yards, education campaigns, thousands of employees. The city not only saves enormous sums every year by letting migrants do all this work, it also saves about 25 to 35 percent of its waste collection and landfill costs due to the diversion of trash into recycling.

But the state also gets to "eat" that cake: by refusing to formalize the system, it shunts economic risk and blame for failures onto the migrants. This becomes most obvious during important urban events such as major party congresses or the 2008 Olympics. At such times migrant recyclers' carts and trucks are banned from the city, scrap markets are closed or, as happened during the 2008 Olympics (much like in the 1990s), summarily bulldozed. The subsidies frittered away on the district companies should be understood as the cost of disavowing that the informal system actually is the recycling system. The Beijing government could not see itself, nor be seen by others, as modern and effective if it were to admit that it really has no formal recycling system. Even more dangerous would be to actually grant legitimacy to an entirely informal, self-organized network of hundreds of thousands of migrant workers who, as members of the lower "caste," are seen as not "of the city." The array of failed government recycling programs and subsidized offices is a small price to pay when compared with such options. These half-baked programs are a necessary fig leaf to cover an embarrassing reality: Beijing (and every other city in China as well) has no effective formal recycling system. Meanwhile, the informal sector does the work and makes the profits, but it, and its millions of migrants, remain fundamentally illegitimate, without a chance to break through the barriers that exclude them.

SURFING THE TSUNAMI OF REAL ESTATE PRICES

Few cities so graphically manifest a systematic pattern of urban development as Beijing with its ring roads expanding from its center like ripples. And it is almost uncanny, though not surprising, how the geography of informal recycling in Beijing has shadowed this expansion, so much so that, in addition to Beijing's six ring roads, it is common these days to refer to Beijing's "garbage seventh ring" (*laji qi huan*). Since they first emerged, Beijing's informal recycling markets have amassed at the peri-urban edge of the city's construction, and they have followed and marked that ever-widening edge ever since. The economic logic for this is obvious and a win-win for peri-urban villagers and recyclers alike. For peri-urban communities, recycling markets are an ideal transitional investment: cheap, easy to build, hosting a dynamic cash economy and yielding nearly instantaneous rents. Recyclers, for their part, want the cheapest site that is as convenient as possible to the scrap-rich urban center.

On the other hand, as one can see in any city in the world, recycling is not valuable or profitable enough to command real estate once development has pushed land prices past a certain level. Scrap yards cannot pay rents that compete with more profitable land uses and are generally not welcomed by middle-class communities or retailers. The geography of Beijing's recycling sector tracks this market logic. Over the last twenty years recycling markets have been essentially temporary, built in a few months, thriving for a few years, and then demolished for more profitable development. Migrant recyclers who have been in the trade since the 1990s have moved on average a half-dozen times in that period, steadily outward, human mile-markers recording the ever-widening waves of land speculation and investment.

The ramifications of this pattern on recyclers' lives and livelihoods is predictable. Back in the 1990s and early 2000s, when markets were located near the third and then the fourth ring roads, three-wheel bike carts were the preferred form of transport. Today, trucks dominate (though bike carts, particularly motorized ones, still have a role in local collection). The cramped, unsanitary, and oft-described "primitive" nature of migrant recycler shantytown life is strongly attributable to the fact that these towns are fundamentally transitory—no one looks upon the conditions they are living in as permanent, and anyone who invested their money to improve these conditions would be throwing it away. Likewise, it would be foolish to invest too much in community institutions like a migrant elementary school if your community will likely be uprooted before your child graduates. Of course the Beijing municipal and local governments have no reason to provide services to such transient "outsiders" either.

Migrant recyclers have become used to this cycle. Typically, migrant community leaders (the most successful traders) take on the role of securing a new site for those who wish to follow them—and of course these leaders put up the capital for building these markets and then collect a cut on stall rents. In the transition, significant amounts of capital are sacrificed by everyone linked to the demolished market. Sometimes the injustice of a forced removal rankles and costs more dearly than other demolitions, such as when a market of over seventy stalls in Zuigongcun was forced to close in the crackdown that preceded the 2008 Olympics. The market bosses had been told they needed to close only temporarily, but then the police held them until they signed an agreement to have the yard bulldozed.

This process reflects a market logic common across informal sectors throughout the world—gray market entrepreneurs (though they are at the pinnacle of the sector and have the most agency of all their co-practitioners) have no access to insurance or legal protections and so bear these risks. But just as importantly, this processes reveals a municipal government practice of self-enrichment through deliberate inaction. In my fieldwork, starting around 2004, both informal entrepreneurs and district administrators repeatedly told me they were waiting for the city government to designate sites where permanent recycling markets and processing centers would be built, complaining that until that happened creating a stable recycling infrastructure in Beijing was impossible.

For years, rumors held that such a proclamation was just around the corner, and this was not just back-alley news; for just one example, a 2006 article in the journal *Urban Management and Technology* claimed a "special plan for Beijing municipal resource recycling implementation" that designated the locations for such markets was in its final drafting stages.[20] But no such plan ever materialized. Recycling markets, while indispensable to any sustainable planning effort, were simply not profitable enough—local governments were unwilling to sacrifice the potential for much higher rents. The rumors finally ended in 2015 when the Beijing government forbade the building of any "low-profit" businesses within the city; recycling markets were included on the official list of forbidden businesses.[21] Such an order underlined and contributed to impediments against entry that those in the sector, at whatever level, had to face.

In sum, since the 1990s recycling in Beijing and in most of China's cities has been handled by an informal migrant network that has: 1) provided a highly efficient recycling infrastructure at no cost to municipal governments, saving them billions on such services while diverting 20 to 35 percent of waste away from disposal (thereby also saving millions in disposal costs); 2) reaped considerable profits to sustain millions of households through their work; 3) provided billions of tons of material inputs for Chinese industry; and 4) provided small cash to countless millions of urban residents in exchange for their scrap. Yet up until now, Beijing's municipal government has not even been willing to accept the loss on return on the investment required to set aside a few tracts of land for the permanent stationing of recycling facilities.

CONCLUSION: THE FUTURE OF CHINA'S WASTE MANAGEMENT—INCINERATION

A central theme of this volume involves analyzing the role of the state in contributing to China's rich-poor gap. In the informal waste sector, we find that while the market has been beyond the control of regulators, governmental behavior has had an unmistakable part to play in its development: millions of poor migrants struggle in unfavorable and unhealthy environments to raise their incomes (relative to rural opportunities) by collecting the wastes of urban consumers and real estate development, even while a subset—if tiny—of these migrants have successfully managed to enter the urban middle class. But a key point of the story is that municipal governments have enriched themselves in a variety of ways by, on the one hand, ceding responsibility for the sector (and thereby saving billions in recycling infrastructure and management) while on the other funneling millions in subsidies to formal companies that, up to now, have dabbled futilely in the sector. Moreover, these administrations have succeeded in sealing down the obstacles that keep the overwhelming majority of the labor in this sector outside the mainstream pale.

Despite shifts in policy and urban economic geography, nonetheless, the informal sector in this field has, overall, been remarkably successful and persistent, but there is no guarantee that it will remain so. Hence, I will conclude with a brief look at a dramatic shift in China's urban waste management today that might (or might not) have dire consequences for the country's three to five million migrant recyclers: incineration.

Sustainability and waste management have become headline priorities under Xi Jinping, and trash incineration is being promoted as a pillar industry of the thirteenth 5-Year Plan, set to run from 2016 to 2020.[22] China built over 100 incinerators between 2010–2015, bringing the number in operation to over 220 with a capacity of 2.3 million tons a day, and the thirteenth plan is slated to grow that to 4 million tons by 2020. Beijing alone is installing three new incinerators to begin operation by 2017, the biggest of which, Lujiashan, cost 2.1 billion yuan. Incineration or "waste-to-energy" plants are being touted as a key piece of China's green urban future. There are many reasons one could have to be critical of this greenwashing investment strategy.

- Incinerators are expensive to construct and, once built, have to operate for twenty to thirty years to realize return on investment. In other words, incinerators demand to be fed garbage for decades to come, so the thirteenth 5-Year Plan is putting China on a path of needing to produce huge flows of trash for decades, this at a time when the leading sustainable cities in the world today are going down the opposite path: Portland, San Francisco, and other cities have reached 60 percent diversion already, while all of Germany is aiming for 90 percent waste diversion by 2020.
- Approximately 60 percent of urban China's household waste is food waste. Food waste has a very high water content and therefore a low calorific value, far too low to burn without supplementing a fuel. In China this usually means coal.

- If you do not burn garbage at a high enough temperature, you end up emitting a lot of toxins, most notably dioxins, some of the most carcinogenic compounds known to science.
- China's incinerator management lacks transparency, and studies that have been undertaken show that almost all of them regularly pollute well beyond the regulatory limit.[23]

There are a number of ironies one might expound upon here: the pretense of giving renewable energy credits to incinerators that actually require 20 to 70 percent coal to burn and the touting of an infrastructure that demands unstaunched waste flows as "sustainable."

But for our purposes, at issue is how the enormous investment in incineration marks a continuation and intensification of the government's exploitative neglect of the informal waste sector. The most obvious continuity involves the state (yet again, though now on a massive national scale) directing investments and subsidies for waste management, not to the millions currently doing the sorting and recycling work but to a select set of state-affiliated companies. Moreover, incineration is glaringly at cross-purposes with recycling in the Chinese context. Given China's high-water-content urban waste, the main way to raise its calorific value is to increase the amount of burnable content, namely paper and plastic, two key recyclables. Incineration creates a financial incentive for urban sanitation departments to appropriate control over recyclable materials, and the dubious assertion that incinerators deliver "renewable" energy green-washes this as a move toward sustainability.

Of course, it is doubtful that pro-incineration regulations alone will strangle the informal recycling sector; as long as the markets for recycled paper, plastic, and metals remain robust, migrant recycling networks—with decades of accumulated expertise and a culture of hard work—will likely persist. However, should a protracted manufacturing downturn drive the prices of recycled materials so low that recycling becomes less profitable, the state's incineration push might also drive recyclers out of the sector.

Most recently the government has shown that it will not wait idly for the invisible hand of the market to push urban waste management from recycling to incineration; indeed, the government has demonstrated, with the violent evictions and massive wave of neighborhood demolitions at the close of 2017, that it is perfectly content to use a highly visible iron fist to push migrants from Beijing, unquestionably exhibiting the limits of trash collectors' agency. This has already proven a tragic and costly loss for thousands of migrant recyclers and likely for China's environment as well.

NOTES

1. Roland Linzner and Stefan Salhofer, "Municipal Solid Waste Recycling and the Significance of Informal Sector in Urban China," *Waste Management & Research* 32, no. 9 (2014): 896–907.

2. Unless otherwise noted, descriptions of the informal sector are based on eighteen months of accumulated fieldwork, interviews, and surveys from summer 2000 to winter 2010.

3. Benjamin Steuer, Stefan Salhofer, Roland Linzner, and Florian Part, "Is China's Waste Management Legislation Successful? Evidence from Urban Chinese Waste Management Practices," presentation, 4th International Conference on Industrial and Hazardous Waste Management, Crete, Greece, September 2–5, 2014.

4. Linzner and Salhofer, "Municipal Solid Waste Recycling," 900.

5. Y. Hou, "Searching for an Effective Plan for the Development of the Scrap Recycling Sector in the Capital" (Beijing: Municipal Scrap Metal Recycling Office, 1999).

6. Weiping Wang, "Survey Report on Problems Related to Beijing's Garbage, Resource Recycling and Related Enterprises" (Beijing: Urban Waste Management Office, 1999).

7. Dorothy J. Solinger, *Contesting Citizenship in Urban China: Peasant Migrants, the State, and the Logic of the Market* (Berkeley: University of California Press, 1999), 234–38.

8. Jean-Philippe Béja, Michel Bonnin, Xiaoshuang Feng, and Tang Can, "How Social Strata Come to be Formed: Social Differentiation Among the Migrant Peasants of Henan Village in Peking, Part 2," *China Perspectives* 24 (July–Aug 1999): 45.

9. Béja et al., "How Social Strata," 36.

10. See Solinger, *Contesting Citizenship in Urban China.*

11. Wang, "Survey Report on Problems," 7.

12. Anonymous, "Regarding a Plan for the Development of Implementing Reform in Haidian District's Recycling Sector" (Beijing: 1999), 7. It is interesting to compare the phrase "population pollution" (人口污染) with one that became infamous in 2017, "low-value population" (低端人口).

13. Chaoyang District Urban Renewal Office, "Circular 17: On the Elimination of Independent Markets and a Pilot of State-run Recycling Markets" (Beijing, 1997), 1.

14. Tang Can and Xiaoshuang Feng, "Beware the Social: Migrants and Peri-Urban Village Unity of Interests," *China National Conditions and Strength* 3 (1993): 27.

15. State Council of the PRC, "Decision to Cancel the First List of Projects Requiring Government Approval" (2002), retrieved at http://www.gov.cn/gongbao/content/2002/content_61829.htm.

16. Xin Tong and Dongyan Tao, "The Rise and Fall of a 'Waste City' in the Construction of an 'Urban Circular Economic System': The Changing Landscape of Waste in Beijing," *Resources, Conservation and Recycling* 107 (2016): 10–17.

17. For example, 400 million yuan was slated in 2011 for a program for 1,200 Beijing neighborhoods. "1,200 Communities in Beijing Pilot Trash Sorting, Rewarding Reduction at the Source," *Beijing Evening News* (Beijing), August 23, 2011.

18. "Source separation" describes how recycling is typically handled by most municipal programs, with households being made responsible for sorting different kinds of waste (organic, recyclable, garbage, etc.) into different containers for city pickup. A 2012 NGO study of the sixty communities involved in a pilot sorting program found that only 24 percent of residents were able to accurately describe how to sort their waste and only 1 percent of kitchen wastes were actually being properly sorted. Yalin Yuan and Mitsuyasu Yabe, "A Research Report on Garbage Separation of Pilot Communities in Beijing in 2012," Friends of Nature (2013).

19. Companies in Haidian and Chaoyang Districts turned short-term profits by opening their own recycling markets that rented out stalls to migrant traders, essentially becoming landlords to the informal sector. But these markets, no different from those capitalized by informal entrepreneurs, have had a short life span in Beijing's real-estate market (see the next section of this paper).

20. Anonymous, "Beijing Resource Recycling to Plan Dedicated Markets," *Urban Management and Technology* 8, no. 4 (2006): 183.

21. Beijing People's Government General Office, "Catalog of Banned and Restricted New Construction Projects for Beijing Municipality: Capital Government Law (2015), no. 42," retrieved at http://images.mofcom.gov.cn/www/201601/20160113152837770.pdf.

22. Zhe Liu, "Trash Incineration: A Pillar Industry of the 13th 5-Year Plan," *China Construction News*, May 29, 2015, retrieved at http://www.chinajsb.cn/bz/content/2015-05/29/content_159696.htm.

23. Qie Jianrong, "Environmental Protection Organizations Survey: 27 Incinerators Over 25 Days Exceed Regulatory Limits 2,533 Times," *Legal System Daily*, January 10, 2017.

Part III

The Upper Reaches of the Urban Rich

SIX

China's Party Kings

Shanghai Club Cultures and Status Consumption, 1920s–2010s

Andrew David Field and James Farrer

In March 2016, according to Chinese and Western media sources, the son of China's wealthiest businessman spent 2.5 million RMB, or around 400,000 USD, on a night of partying at the aptly named "King of Party" (*Ke ge zhi wang*) nightclub in Beijing. These reports include photos of Wang Sicong partying with his friends and images of the actual receipts for his big night on the town.[1] Spending that amount of money on a night of drunken fun staggers the imagination. This extravagant outing serves as an indicator of how far removed the lives of China's wealthiest people are from those of the common people or *laobaixing,* portraying in the most graphic of ways the polarization that stamps Chinese society. While no other nightclub bill of note has come close to that record, the *fuerdai*—sons and daughters of China's nouveaux riches millionaires and billionaires—are now reported to spend tens of thousands of RMB on a night of clubbing, especially, though certainly not exclusively, in the city of Shanghai where they are most highly concentrated.

As scholars of Chinese history and urban sociology, we spent much of our early careers researching and writing about nightlife cultures and spaces in the former treaty port (1843–1943) and current global metropolis of Shanghai.[2] Based on this earlier research and recent follow-up interviews with key producers of nightlife culture in Shanghai,[3] this chapter extends our understanding of Shanghai's nightlife culture, demonstrating how the emergence of the big-spending *fuerdai* represents but the latest, though most extreme, phase in the development of night clubs into urban stages for status consumption in China. We also posit that club owners, managers, and liquor companies are now networked into larger organizations and associations that are engaged in what urban sociologist David Grazian describes as the "hustle" of urban nightlife: the commercial tactics these actors employ to maximize their profits by taking advantage of the desire of super-rich elites in China to display their status through public consumption.[4] While the champagne-drinking *fuerdai* are a recent phenomenon, many of their practices are deeply rooted in the glamorized and mythologized history of Shanghai as a nightlife metropolis.

As ethnographers of nightlife, we became intimately familiar with both the universalized and localized rituals of clubbing that enable customers to playfully explore their nocturnal personalities, seek out sensual pleasures, and showcase their economic, cultural, sexual, and social capital within the "action environment" of a public entertainment space.[5] Grounded in a brief overview of the legendary heyday of Shanghai as a nightlife city in the 1920–1930s, and concentrating on the past three decades of "reform and opening," our contribution to this volume paints a portrait of people at the extreme upper pole of urban society while analyzing how nightclub business models have changed over the past three decades to focus increasingly on their needs and desires.

We trace the current clubbing industry from a social dance hall model in the 1980s, in which nearly every customer counted equally both economically and socially, to a lounge bar model of the 1990s, in which some types of customers paid much more than others, to the "king in his castle" model today, in which clubbing spaces are structured entirely around a tiny group of big spenders (mostly though not exclusively male), while hundreds of other patrons and employees are but bit players in a show centered on filling up these VIP spaces.

These trends represent local urban history in Shanghai. But the rise of the privileged VIP club space also provides a window onto the leisure lives of what could be termed the upper caste, revealing how social class distinction is now expressed, performed, and celebrated in urban China. Our overview of changing clubbing spaces reveals the concrete spatial practices through which this caste of hyper-rich urban Chinese has actively created social boundaries that insulate it from the mobility strategies of other urbanites. Whereas two decades ago, Shanghai dance clubs served as relatively free-flowing zones of interaction among clubbers from different backgrounds—youth, foreigners, sex workers, and others—the new VIP clubs severely limit interactions across social divides, effectively cutting away the sexual and social agency once possessed by less (and un-) privileged players in nightlife scenes.

SOCIAL DISTINCTION IN SHANGHAI NIGHTLIFE IN THE 1920s–1930s

Shanghai was the first modern city in China to develop a culture of nightlife that would have been familiar to people in major Western metropolises.[6] Prior to the 1920s, nightlife was a very different experience for Chinese and Westerners inhabiting the semicolonial treaty port city. For the Westerners, private clubs organized by national, class, and common interest affiliations dominated the social life of the city, and grand balls were the highlights of the social calendar.[7]

For the Chinese, the city's courtesan culture with its elaborate rituals, music halls and houses, and its customs of courtship, mating, and pleasure was the nearest equivalent to Western "nightlife." Between the late Qing and early Republican eras, this culture was taken to grand new heights under the relatively laissez-faire regulatory environment of Shanghai's two foreign settlements.[8] As in other cities around the world, from Paris to New York, Chinese courtesan culture revolved around the young women who served as social and sexual companions to their male clients. Male access to beautiful women—what Ashley Mears calls "girl capital" in the contemporary clubbing scene—has been a feature of male-oriented nightlife status since its early days, including in Shanghai.[9]

During the "jazz age" 1920s, a new phase in the city's cultural history was underway. Chinese and Western spheres of nighttime entertainment were coming together in the space of the ballroom, nightclub, dance hall, or cabaret, and the courtesans of Shanghai were beginning to give way to more novel roles for women and even more modern forms of entertainment, most notably dance and film. The global trend of dancing the Charleston, foxtrot, and rumba to the tunes of a live jazz orchestra caught on in the city like wildfire, starting with Westerners, eventually infecting the elite Chinese society, but then quickly also embedding itself in the sphere of the city's middle-class popular culture. By the 1930s, dozens of cabarets, nightclubs, and other dance establishments operated in the city, catering to thousands upon thousands of night owls with itchy feet.

At first, being able to dance well was a source of distinction in and of itself, since up to the late 1920s these dances were virtually unknown in Chinese society. Yet after the dancing trend took off in a big way in 1928, elite Chinese looked for other forms of distinction, building and patronizing exclusive ballrooms that most members of society could not afford to set foot in, let alone frequent. There, they would book and occupy exclusive tables either near the dance floor or else in semiprivate rooms. In these sites they would consume copious amounts of whiskey and champagne, building up huge debts in the form of "chits," which were paid off monthly.[10]

One of the keys to the success of the dance industry in Shanghai was the adaptation to suit Chinese society of the Western institution of the taxi-dance hall.[11] As in great American cities like New York and Chicago,[12] most dance halls in Shanghai employed dozens if not hundreds of women nightly to serve as dancing and drinking companions for unaccompanied men. Like the courtesans who preceded them, these women, known simply in Chinese as *wunü* or "dancing girls," whom we shall refer to as "dance hostesses," were young, usually ranging in age from sixteen to twenty-one years old.[13] Many of these women were recruited from the nearby hinterlands to serve in the city's dance halls.[14] Within the growing sphere of taxi-dance halls and in the media realm of newspapers and magazines devoted to the city's dance culture, distinction came in the form of competitions to declare the top hostesses through an annual citywide event known as the "dance empress" (*Wu guo huang hou*) contest, in which men "voted" by donating money to a charitable cause in the name of their favorite hostess. Those men with intimate access to the "dance empress" were expressing their dominant status among the city's business elites and gangland bosses, and that status was dutifully promoted in the tabloid press.[15]

As the culture of the taxi-dance hall spread throughout Shanghai and thousands of Chinese women came to serve this role of hostess, the city's more elite nightclubs, cabarets, and ballrooms looked for ways to distinguish themselves from the more run-of-the-mill establishments that offered paid company. One important form of distinction was the architecture and design of the ballroom itself. Since the early 1920s, the city's elite hotels, such as the Astor House, Majestic, and Cathay, had been vying to build and operate the fanciest and finest ballrooms and clubs in town.[16]

By the early 1930s, a new trend of building stand-alone dance palaces was underway. Chief among these was the Paramount Ballroom, financed by Chinese bankers, built by a Chinese architect, and opened for business in December 1933. With its ultra-modern, intricate design, meant to comfortably hold as many as a thousand guests while also catering to much smaller numbers on any given weekday evening, the ballroom proved hugely successful, attracting many of the city's financial and political elites. In addition to the main dance floor, it featured a cozy bar, two semiprivate banquet halls where business leaders and gang bosses dined, and an upper dance floor built on thick glass lit up underneath by colored lights.[17] As we shall discuss later in this chapter, the intricately thought-out design of the Paramount presaged in some ways that of Park 97, the most successful nightclub in Shanghai in the early 2000s.

This elaborate and sophisticated nightlife culture continued to flourish into the war years of the late 1930s and 1940s, when that region of China was under invasion and occupation by the Japanese Empire, and lasted despite the Chinese Nationalist government's attempts to shut it down upon their return to power in the late 1940s. It was only after the Communist Revolution of 1949 and the building of a new socialist society that the multitiered nightlife industry of Shanghai met its demise—at least, until its revival starting in the 1980s.[18]

EARLY-REFORM ERA NIGHTLIFE: CLUBBING WITHOUT CLASS

Between the late 1950s and the Cultural Revolution era of the 1960s and early 1970s, social or partnered dancing became a forbidden pastime in Shanghai and elsewhere in China, and was only practiced behind closed doors and dark curtains. In the 1980s, under the new "reform and opening" (*gaige kaifang*) campaign launched by Deng Xiaoping, social dancing reemerged into the light of day as a popular pastime, but it did so under very different socioeconomic circumstances than those that had prevailed in Republican era China. Under the Communist Party leadership and through campaigns culminating with the Cultural Revolution, social and economic distinctions had largely been eradicated in Shanghai, and even in the 1980s Shanghai society was relatively egalitarian and homogeneous compared to the mix of glamour and poverty of the 1920s and 1930s. Despite the advent of a market economy, social life, including leisure, was still organized around socialist work units or *danwei*. The relatively austere social dance hall culture of the 1980s reflected the low level of social stratification, the socialist organization of the economy, and the essentially working-class ethos of the population. Thus, people of various social ranks could find their spare-time pleasure in the same venue.

The dozens of social dance halls that appeared in neighborhoods across the city in the early 1980s were generally simple, sometimes makeshift establishments featuring portable stereos for producing dance music and selling thermoses of tea to male and female customers who paid a few *mao* for the privilege of frequenting these sites. Many of the halls were situated in work unit or community spaces such as cafeterias and cultural centers. They operated in a legal gray zone, since commercial dance halls were not officially allowed until 1986.[19] Dancers showed off their skills and style on the dance floor but, notably, as compared with the present, not through consumption. Customers sat at tables surrounding a large dance floor, drinking green tea, and conversing with each other while eying potential dance partners. Couples three-stepped, jitterbugged, or slow-danced around the "dance pool," and the design of the clubs did not create either zones of distinction or of exclusivity. Given the low cost of a night at a dance hall, women attended the establishments as paying customers and as social equals to men.

By the late 1980s, fancier social dance halls emerged. Many featured live bands, and some even occupied famous venues from the Republican era. But the culture of social dance remained a working-class one, or what could be seen as the common culture of the "salaried classes" (*gongxin jieceng*) throughout the 1990s. By the late 1990s, this was increasingly regarded as a middle-aged practice as well, an intimate space in the city for working-class, married men and women to fraternize with each other and covertly indulge in extramarital relations, a growing trend in the city during that period.[20] But in the eyes of restless urban youths in the 1990s, these neighborhood dance halls were becoming passé.

This largely forgotten period in Shanghai's nightlife history is important not only because of its broad popularity but also for what it shows about how the spatial organization of leisure supports, or does not support, the display of social distinctions. Of course, people competed for attention—sexual and otherwise—but the dance hall itself was organized neither around the price of seating nor even with respect to the types of beverages consumed. The business model in which everyone paid for a ticket put dancers from all social classes on the same level, literally and figuratively. This would all change as polarity among the populace set in and Shanghai once again became a city built by and for the big spenders.

THE RETURN OF THE BIG SPENDERS: KARAOKE CLUBS AND DANCE CLUBS IN THE 1990s AND 2000s

Beginning in the late 1980s, inspired by trends abroad, the city saw the introduction of newer forms of nighttime entertainment culture. These styles of clubbing arose hand in hand with the proliferation of new forms of cultural and social distinction that came with China's evolving class structure. While social dance halls catering to the city's working-class society continued to flourish well into the late 1990s, discos, bars, and clubs began to spread as well, catering increasingly to the city's young white-collar workers especially, and to a growing international population of visitors and settlers from abroad.

Whether attached to dance clubs or restaurants, or standing alone as independent entities, karaoke halls or KTVs became the places where the biggest spenders tended to go in the 1990s.[21] These establishments had been popular in Japan and also in Taiwan and South Korea since the 1980s, and they were brought over to China with the influx of businessmen from these "Asian tiger" societies, which had experienced their own "economic miracles" since the 1970s and were now eager to develop business ties and factories in China. Combining the cost of renting a private room with a big sofa or lounge space and a large-screen TV for singing karaoke, and the expense of a few bottles of fancy imported liquor and the money spent on *xiaojie* or club hostesses, male customers could spend several thousand RMB easily on a night of KTV fun. As Anne Allison has argued in the case of 1980s Tokyo hostess clubs, and as Tiantian Zheng, John Osburg, and others have shown in the case of Chinese KTVs, these spaces were constructed more as intimate masculine social bonding sites for small groups of men to cement their friendships and business and political ties with each other while enjoying paid female company, rather than as "see and be seen" spots for society people to mix and mingle in the company of strangers.[22]

In its design, the typical KTV hostess club looked and functioned similarly to a hotel, with multiple floors of private rooms that customers could rent by the hour or for the evening. Service attendants provided the customers with food and drinks, usually fruit plates and other snacks. Upon entering the private room, the group of male customers would await the arrival of the "mama," often a former KTV hostess herself, who would solicit clients' requests and bring a selection of hostesses for them to choose. Sometimes the hostesses would even line up by height, and it was typical for them to announce their province or place of origin. The main function of the KTV club space was to provide private rooms for groups of male customers to party with their intimate circles of friends and associates, where they could consume copious amounts of alcohol and engage in behaviors that would not have been acceptable in a more public setting. It was common in Shanghai, for example, for men holding birthday or wedding parties—that is, a Chinese version of the "stag party" prior to the wedding for one's male friends—to hold them in KTV hostess clubs.[23] Business associates met in KTVs to cement their relations, much as they did in other cities in China, and as Osburg notes, they often did so by engaging in "illicit" forms of sexual behavior with the hostesses, which created a bond of mutual secrecy for the men.

If nightlife can be said to be on a continuum from public to private, the hostess club existed on the private and illicit end. The thrill for their patrons consisted not only of spending money and enjoying luxury but also of a deliberate flouting of everyday social norms, particularly regarding sexual propriety. At a time in the 1990s when university students were still being taught to preserve their virginity, KTV clubs allowed raucous displays of shared debauchery. Men bonded with each other over the hypersexualization of hostesses, taking digital photos of their breasts, bottoms, and other sexual body parts (most of the time clothed but not always), and sometimes posting these images on the emerging internet. Sexual play of various sorts played a big role in these clubs, yet arguably the main goal of attending KTV clubs was for men to enjoy each other's company and to drink—often to excess. The choice drink was whiskey, and the leading brand was Chivas.[24]

The hostess clubs represented a form of hidden, even illicit, status consumption within a closed circle of familiar faces. Dance clubs, which emerged at the same time, allowed a more public, unpredictable, and heterogeneous stage for status display. The social functions of these two types of nightlife overlap but also differ. Both create solidarity among elites—especially among men,[25] generally involving the status accrued from the patronage of younger attractive women as a form of male-centered "girl capital."[26] Dance clubs, however, were much more a site of performance in front of strangers. They also served as sexual fields in which embodied sexual capital could matter as much as the social, economic, and cultural capital that actors brought with them from their "daytime" social lives. These were venues in which women as customers also participated in the rituals of sexual play, sexual performance, and social one-upmanship, not simply as paid accomplices, servers, and sex workers (as was largely the case in the hostess bars and KTV rooms described previously).[27] The dance club was thus a more porous arena for sexual and social play.

Catering to the revival of Shanghai's love for dancing, already evident in the social dance craze of the 1980s, discos with computerized lighting and advanced sound systems were opened in the city beginning in the early 1990s. Rather than promoting social or partnered dancing, these discos encouraged more individualized styles of dancing, though in the early days most dancers got their cues from the DJs.[28] The popular discos of the early 1990s, such as New York New York near the Bund, the Galaxy and Casablanca in Hongqiao, or J.J.'s Disco on Yan'an Road, featured cavernous dance spaces that attracted huge crowds numbering in the hundreds. Unless you were the DJ, who was often the subject of mass adoration, it was rather difficult to distinguish yourself from the sweaty masses in these large, cavernous halls. Among the young customers, the actual expenses were often limited to the price of admission so that the growing social differences among the patrons were not yet in evidence.

Operated essentially along the business model of the older dance hall, such places represented an intermediate development between the older social dance hall and the table service clubbing model described below that was soon to appear. In contrast to the social dance halls, these clubs attracted a wide spectrum of customers from the newly upwardly mobile classes, including foreigners, returnees, entrepreneurs, and white-collar workers. Indeed, the elite customers in these clubs tended to be those who booked one of the adjacent karaoke rooms, venturing out into the larger public spaces to participate briefly in the relative democracy of the dance floor. In the 1990s, some high-end dance clubs became a side business to the more profitable semiprivate KTV rooms with which they shared a common venue.[29]

Dance clubs, however, would change radically in their design and business model over the ensuing two decades, on the one hand taking advantage of the changing market of the newly rich and, at the same time, giving such people a social stage on which to celebrate their newfound elite status. One of the first, and most successful, nightclubs to exploit the growing desire of Shanghai residents to "see and be seen" in more public, open venues was Park 97.

Opened in 1997, the year that Hong Kong was officially "handed over" to China, this club was first financed and operated by a group of Hong Kong–based expatriates who had run clubs in the Lan Kwai Fong nightlife district in Hong Kong. They joined together with some partners based in Shanghai, including a Shanghainese returnee from the USA named Tony Zhang.[30] Tony exploited his local connections with police and government agents to enable the club's founders to build the club inside a famous park in the former French Concession. Fronted by a beautiful rose garden, the posh and elegant design of the club harkened back to fancy nightclubs of the 1930s, but its design was more contemporary than retro.[31]

Almost immediately after opening its doors in 1997, Park 97 began to attract wealthy customers, mainly foreigners (both Westerners and Asians) and overseas Chinese, who enjoyed the elegance, the cuisine, and the music. At first, it was designed more as a fine dining and drinking space. Yet in contrast to many other elite clubs in town, Park 97 did not offer paid female company for the male clientele. As Tony Zhang explained during an interview conducted in 2003:

> You know Westerners, when they look at Asia they are full of curiosity because there's a very sexy connotation to it, and Shanghai, the name itself also. One thing that impressed people coming back from overseas is "wow look at here the girls are really gorgeous and beautiful", they want to find a place to meet these gorgeous girls. So here we're not typical of those hostess bars or KTV—that's coming more from Korean or Japanese or Taiwan cultures, where you offer ladies for people, but we don't do that. Basically, here, this is a platform, we provide freedom of choices, where everybody can come in and have drinks, and then mingle and socialize with each other.

Although Park 97 attracted men and women from the "beautiful young" set of Chinese and foreigners, the rise of other clubs in Shanghai put intense pressure on the club to keep up with the clubbing trends. With its low-key restaurant-lounge atmosphere, Park 97 was losing customers to other clubs in other neighborhoods, such as the rowdy bar street of Maoming South Road, which offered more active nightlife establishments that included dancing. As Tony explained in 2003:

> Park 97 has evolved in experience as the market evolved. In the beginning, we wanted to make it sort of the high fashion place where people can hang out, you know just sort of have drinks and casual conversations. But that really didn't last long, where we [found] the customers started to leave in the early hours because they needed something more stimulating. So, after one or two years, we realized we needed to have a new dimension added to the place where people can have choices, not only just have drinks and talk but maybe they have something more exciting, so that's how the disco club came into our sight. In the year 2000, when the Lan Kwai Fong group entered the partnership, it spearheaded the project. So, we opened the first club called California Club. And it works, it really made the life come back to the Park again, so I say this is our second life in the past seven years' history.

Thus, by 2001, Park 97 had taken on a new identity as a dance club with a ground floor hall featuring a dance floor surrounding a large circular bar, dubbed the California Club. There, with crowds pressing in nearly every night and long waiting lines extending into the park grounds on the weekends, it was one of the most profitable pieces of nighttime real estate in the city. In a follow-up interview we held with Tony Zhang in 2016, he recalled that the club was attracting all sorts of big spenders, with an average bill around 1,000 to 1,500 USD per table, a fantastic sum of money for the average Chinese consumer in those days. Other informants involved in the industry claimed that the club was pulling in as much as 200,000 to 300,000 RMB per night on average, and much more on weekends. Most of the money was being generated by the tables.

Thomas Yeung, a Hong Konger who served as the floor manager of Park 97 in those days, was one of the keys to the club's financial success. Over the years, he carefully cultivated a long list of elite customers for whom he personally booked tables and VIP lounge spaces. He was known for filling the place up nightly with models, celebrities, and other glamorous people, who in turn attracted other big spenders. During his follow-up interview with us in 2016, Tony Zhang confirmed the importance of Thomas Yeung to the club's success, and recalled that many celebrities who came to Shanghai from abroad would spend at least one night at Park 97 during its heyday.

These guests included famous American, Hong Kong, Korean, and Taiwanese pop stars as well as A-list Hollywood film stars. Chinese officials mingled with them and with big corporate CEOs and dot-com company founders. According to Tony, when President Clinton visited the city in 1998, secretary of state Madeleine Albright had lunch there, while the Clintons' daughter Chelsea spent a whole evening at Park 97 with her entourage of secret service agents in tow. Tony claims that Bill Clinton himself was slated to go there too, but he decided not to do so once it was discovered that the voluptuous female figure painting on one of the club's walls bore a striking resemblance to Monica Lewinsky. Meanwhile, Park 97 also distinguished itself by attracting A-list international DJs to perform, such as Paul Oakenfold, who played to a huge crowd of revelers in the club's heyday in 2004.[32]

In the opinion of Tony Zhang, Park 97 had a great and lasting impact, not only on China's clubbing industry but also on other industries as well. It helped to introduce new forms of fashionability into the Shanghai scene and also to train a new generation of cadres in high-end service establishments in China. In his 2003 interview he told us:

> So, first we look at the impact on the younger generations. In the beginning people had no ideas about what's really fashionable or what is good music and so this is something we really want to enforce. We

> want to create a platform where people can come in and really make a statement, you know, like in fashion, because like everywhere in the world, a club is a place for people to see and be seen. So here, you [encounter] people dressed up in different fashions, so they think, this is where the trends are. Also, we were able to bring in the first-class music, so we had a lot of international DJs coming here from Europe and America introducing the latest music trends, so you know, people really enjoy being at the cutting edge of this kind of nightlife scene. Another important point is that we were able to educate a big group of people involved in this industry, because even if we just open for seven years, wherever I go, to five-star hotels, high end restaurants, and nightclubs, I see a lot of our former staff.

Unwittingly, the club's huge success also helped to set up the conditions for its eventual downfall. In 2003, Tony Zhang claimed that the club was already a big influence on the rise of club cultures all over China:

> This idea [of an elite nightclub] came from outside, but now we are much more integrated than seven years ago with the local society. I think this idea is going to happen not only in Shanghai—we have business people coming from everywhere, even from Guangdong, Zhejiang, where the moneys are, they all came in here to study this model, customers too took a lot of pictures, they were wondering why we are able to make so much money, so they want to bring this culture back to their home. And a lot of people believe this kind of club will work back in their hometown, and I love to see that. I think five or ten years from now, you'll see this kind of trend probably happening everywhere in China. So, we were able to bring this culture in and plant it and [watch] it becoming something much bigger, you know.

But by the mid-2000s, other clubs in Shanghai began to eclipse Park 97, eventually leading to its takeover by a leading rival. One of those clubs was Bar Rouge; with its rooftop location on the Bund overlooking the Huangpu River and the spectacular skyline of Pudong, this became one of the top clubs in town and a must-see for international travelers to the city.[33] Another was Muse, a tony club in the Jing'an District that employed top-flight designers to create a unique clubbing space for elite customers.[34]

One of the investors in Muse was Hong Kong starlet Carina Lau (Liu Jialing), and the upstairs area of the club was known enticingly as "Carina's bedroom." Muse also employed other tactics that were becoming standards in the industry, such as hiring attractive young men and women to just sit in the club and consume drinks, so that on any given night the place seemed to be popular, even if most of the "customers" were only hired hands. Then, in a coup de grâce, Muse succeeded in poaching Thomas Yeung from Park 97, along with his long list of contacts from the city's glamorous world of nightlifers. Muse went on to establish other venues in town, and eventually its club chain bought up Park 97, turning it into Muse at Park 97, and adding a shark tank as one of the club's features.

With their eyes on this market, aspiring "VIP clubs" took the idea of the exclusive ownership of nightlife space to new extremes. At Club Linx on Huaihai Road, staffers aimed to book 90 percent of the tables in advance, mostly to Chinese high rollers with their young dates (or "PR girls" arranged by the clubs). Where the dance floor would have been in Shanghai clubs past, in Club Linx there was a VIP area on hydraulic pumps that raised the big spenders above the floor so that other clubbers could watch them in envy as their "champagne trains" came chugging in, while they advertised the unapproachable orbit they occupied. Like medieval European kings dining in public, Linx's VIPs wanted to be admired for having their fun. Dancing was relegated to floor shows by professionals.[35] "Once a customer orders above a certain amount we do a show," Linx general manager Kyle Sun explained to a journalist. "For this champagne train, the minimum order is six [bottles]—a regular Dom Pérignon costs 3,180 yuan ($500). The most premium brand is Ace of Spades, which costs 9,000 yuan ($1,450), and if people order it we have the most beautiful showgirls serving it, plus a train to the table."[36] This kind of distinction delineated a realm that was surely notably beyond the reach of most other customers.

"The game has completely changed," confirmed Tony Zhang, the cofounder of the now legendary Park 97 club in Shanghai during our interview with him in Shanghai in September 2016. Figures of how much the new Mainland customers spend on a night of clubbing vary of course by club and by customer. Insiders claim that at clubs like M1NT or Linx, a group of six people can easily spend 12,000 RMB (around $2,000) in an evening; at the bigger tables they are spending upwards of 30,000 RMB (close to $5,000) on an average night—far and above what VIP tables at Park 97 earned during its heyday in the earlier years of the new millennium.[37]

The rise and fall of dancing as Shanghai's favorite nocturnal pastime is a story we have told in somewhat greater detail elsewhere.[38] Two closely interrelated things were happening: the increasing importance of wealthy customers and the changing designs of clubbing spaces. First, a new and mobile super-wealthy elite was emerging in Shanghai whose members were looking for places to enjoy their money. In response to this, nightlife entrepreneurs in the 1990s initially built large fancy discos with adjacent karaoke rooms to give these people a place to play. These were glittery spectacles but, in retrospect, they were comparatively "democratic" spaces in which the nouveaux riches rubbed shoulders (literally) with a wide range of urban youth and transnational interlopers. Shanghai clubs up until and including spaces like the California Club in Park 97 in the early 2000s still remained relatively open spaces of social friction and competition.

The second new development came with the rise of VIP clubbing in the 2000s. At this point the business model and the spatial organization of clubs were altered. No longer dance halls (selling tickets), they essentially became bars (selling alcohol). Tables replaced dance floors, and rich patrons now are able to safely dominate the social space of the clubs with no annoying interruptions from foreigners, freelance sex workers, or other lower-class interlopers. In comparison to the free-flowing contact zones of the earlier discos, the contemporary VIP club is culturally speaking a "safe space" catering only to young *fuerdai*.

From a strategic action perspective, we might define "agency" in nightlife as the possibility of capital conversions, or the chance for clubbers with sexual and cultural capital to convert those resources to social and economic capital, whether through seduction on the dance floor or by means of sociability at the bar. The closed spaces of VIP clubbing therefore restricted the agency of the merely sexy or exotic (for example, youth and foreigners) by limiting access to prime clubbing spaces to those with huge sums of money and their guests. This exclusion seems deliberate, in that it protects the top elite men and women from sexual and social competition. This pattern of social blockage is even more overt in the private party spaces we discuss below.[39]

KING OF PARTY: PRIVATE CLUB ROOMS AND TROPHY CHAMPAGNE

The ratcheting up of the anti-corruption campaign under Xi Jinping that began in 2013 has meant that extravagant public consumption is, at least for now, potentially dangerous for those with government connections, which includes many *fuerdai*. Newer, more private clubbing venues have emerged to meet the paradoxical need for discreet ways of showing off. When we met Thomas Yeung in October 2016 for an interview that had been facilitated by Tony Zhang, he was managing the new club, King of Party. Located in midtown Shanghai, this club was then offering a combination of KTV club-like privacy along with the sleek elegance of a VIP lounge club or disco, as well as high-end service from a cadre of well-trained staff. When asked how the industry had changed over the past fifteen years or so, Yeung replied:

> It's changed a lot. Completely different . . . I found a lot of my regular people that dance in [clubs] disappeared. And [now there are] so many young kids that I never saw before the past eight or ten years. So, then I find out what is going on. This kind of kids, they just graduate from overseas, they get back in town, or from the other cities nearby to Shanghai—Ningbo, Guangzhou, Nanjing, Suzhou—they all concentrate in the Shanghai metropolis you know. . . . So, then . . . they started building up their kind of lifestyle, you know, champagne culture. And

> after some time, I find I need to create some not only just, you know, music and dancing club, that kind of business. . . . I decided I should design a kind of private place, like here. [For the customer,] "you won't see me. I spend a lot of money but physically you don't know I'm here."[40]

In the mid-2010s, as Thomas observes, while many wealthy mainland Chinese club-goers still preferred to display their wealth through extravagant binges in the public space of a nightclub, others were increasingly choosing to frequent more private sites in order to show off their spending abilities to a more select group of friends and associates. Until around 2010, this was generally done in the venue of the KTV, which has always been a male-dominated consumption space.

Over the past few years, while KTVs continued to operate in the city, their numbers rapidly diminished owing to a number of factors, including their decreasing popularity among wealthy Chinese and the major crackdown on corruption that the Xi Jinping regime has launched in China. Since KTVs were originally a favored haunt that government officials used to build their relations with each other and with businessmen, as the work of John Osburg reveals, they were an obvious casualty of the anti-corruption crackdown.

Meanwhile, the *fuerdai*, who were generally much more highly educated than their nouveaux riches parents, were increasingly less interested in partying with the relatively uneducated KTV hostesses, and favored the company of women who tended to be better educated, were themselves from wealthier backgrounds, and understood (or set) trends in fashion, the arts, and other high-culture subjects.

While the KTV hostess clubs became passé among younger single men, it was mainly just older married men who continued to patronize them to some extent. Such overt practices of gendered sexual patronage could still be seen as late as 2017. However, the shift in the status of these women within the clubbing world can be understood as yet another way in which members of the Chinese wealthy caste are sealing themselves off from the upwardly (and often vainly) striving poorer strata, in this case the KTV hostesses, who are usually rural-to-urban migrants.

Moreover, the privacy of a KTV-style club was still valued by some wealthy Chinese customers by then, men who did not wish to show off their wealth or their spending habits to a crowd of anonymous people. Also, since the age of the internet and social media accelerated in the 2010s with the rise of smartphone technology and platforms like Weibo and WeChat, people in China became even more conscious of their public identities and tended to seek privacy. Many wealthy people or their sons and daughters were now celebrity figures in the Chinese media, and it was not in their interest to have strangers take photos or videos of their drunken antics with their smartphones.

Clubbing entrepreneurs came up with various solutions to this new desire to be out of the limelight. One of them was King of Party (*Ke ge zhi wang*), a KTV-style club in essence, but with some key differences to the typical KTV clubs. This establishment is located on the fifth and sixth floors of a building on the corner of Xizang and Huaihai Roads, in a premier retail and entertainment section of the city. Thomas Yeung, the former floor manager of Park 97 and Muse, started working there in 2014, and in November 2016 he offered us a tour of the place. Like a typical KTV, the club features halls full of private rooms of various styles and price ranges. There are attractive young women hired by the club standing around in the halls, dancing or playing pool, who presumably can be enticed into the rooms by male customers.

But the outfit does not function as a typical hostess club. Instead, most of the customers are mixed-sex groups of young men and women. The biggest difference from most KTV clubs is that King of Party offers a huge private room, which is the size and style of a not-so-modest private apartment, complete with a kitchen, dining room, and living room. This room can be rented out for a minimum fee of 20,000 RMB, but those who rent it tend to spend much more than that on a typical party. Bills range from 50,000 or 60,000 to 150,000 RMB for a night of partying. This large chamber allows people to hold a grand private party within the club, one that is fully catered by the wait staff and which can involve potentially dozens if not hundreds of guests over a long night of fun. Beijing also has a King of Party, and that is the establishment and most likely the room in which Wang Sicong, China's most notorious *fuerdai*, held his now legendary party in 2016 that racked up a bill of 2.5 million RMB.

One telling trend in clubbing consumption in the past decade has been the rising popularity of consuming champagne. Overall, the champagne industry began to grow enormously in mainland China after about 2010, with the number of imported bottles breaking the million mark in 2011, and reaching over 1.6 million by 2014.

However, this figure represents only 1 percent of all grape wine consumption in China.[41] Indeed, one wine importer pointedly said over dinner in winter 2015, "Chinese people really don't like the taste of champagne." It is sour, cold, and fizzy, qualities that are not generally appreciated in China. Indeed, champagne is primarily a prestige drink and 80 percent of sales are in hotels, nightclubs, restaurants, or KTV clubs.[42] While this rapid growth tapered off somewhat after the anti-corruption crackdown began in earnest in 2014, by all accounts and by our own observations, champagne bottles have become the most conspicuous form of consumption in the club scene in Shanghai and elsewhere in China.

It is common to see buckets or even tubs full of champagne bottles on ice served by teams of waiters to VIP tables, with colored sparklers alit atop the buckets to show them off to the public eye. Champagne bottles are on display in stacks and pyramids in most clubs. Moët & Chandon is the entry-level brand, and the price climbs rapidly with other brands, culminating in the Armand de Brignac or "Ace of Spades" brand—so called because of the Ace of Spades logo on each bottle. Produced by Champagne Cattier and acquired in 2014 by mega-rapper Jay-Z—three years after his notorious champagne binge involving heavy purchases of the label's bottles—this is the premier luxury champagne brand worldwide.

In the big room of King of Party, bottles of "Ace of Spades" are arranged conspicuously on the tables. These can sell for up to 20,000 RMB per bottle or for much more for the large bottles, such as the 10-magnum or 15-liter Brut Gold Midas, which has to be brought in by at least a pair of hefty waiters. Costing around 100,000 USD, this bottle has been dubbed by some as the "ultimate nightlife trophy" and has been conspicuously consumed by people such as Dallas Mavericks owner Mark Cuban after his team won the NBA championship in 2011.[43] Only the wealthiest *fuerdai* in China, such as Wang Sicong, can afford to consume such stuff.

According to a sales executive from the champagne industry whom we interviewed in November 2016, the world of the nightclub in Shanghai and elsewhere in China has become saturated with champagne, which replaced whiskey as the club drink of choice after about 2010.[44] Working hand in hand with the distributors, clubs have come to the realization that they can generate far higher profits through champagne sales—particularly though certainly not exclusively the high-end brands such as Armand de Brignac—than from sales of whiskey, cognac, vodka, or other hard liquors, no matter how well-branded and packaged they may be.

Shanghai was the trendsetter in this nationwide champagne binge, and other cities quickly followed. Even the low-end brand, Moët, can be sold to customers for as much as two-and-a-half times the original cost of around 450 RMB, and people might order as many as one hundred bottles in one night, earning a 20 percent discount on the markup price. "In one outlet in Shanghai alone—the club M2—we sold more than 10,000 bottles per month," an informant told us.[45] The entire Shanghai club market sells around 25,000 bottles per month, while Western lounge bars and hotel bars sell another 5,000.

Again, consumption is largely driven by the *fuerdai*. Most of them are children of men who made their fortunes in the real estate business since the 1990s, and are earning a steady cash income by renting out as many as one hundred apartments. With a stable cash income and an unlimited expense account, it is not difficult for the *fuerdai* to spend 40,000 or 50,000 RMB in just one night of partying. Our informant estimates that over five hundred people from all over China who have come to Shanghai to party are spending this much money almost every night of the week. Besides what they spend in only an evening, many of the *fuerdai* go out clubbing two or three times per week. A typical night on the town may involve dinner at a fancy restaurant on the Bund, followed by partying at a popular nightclub, and then an after-party at an exclusive place like the Nest (also located on the Bund near the Peninsula Hotel). While other cities such as Beijing and Guangzhou have a small concentration of such clubs, the number of clubs and that of *fuerdai* spending money in Shanghai's VIP club scene is far greater than in any other city in China, suggesting a strong connection with the century-long legacy of Shanghai as an international nightlife metropolis.

Most of these clubs are now owned by the syndicate known as Noah's Ark. According to one informant, sales executives working in them can earn a monthly salary of 200,000 RMB, which is far more than what even corporate CEOs can take in at many companies. These people command an army of salespeople—usually more than one hundred—who make the phone calls and keep the tables and VIP lounge areas occupied nightly, while also encouraging their clients to spend as much as possible.[46] Though some partygoers share the bill, most *fuerdai* prefer to pay for their friends in order to show off their wealth while creating reciprocal bonds with their clubbing companions. Women are usually among the nonpaying guests.

Besides the exorbitant prices, other barriers to entry keep out all but the super-wealthy, such as social capital, a critical component of elite privilege. A phalanx of gatekeepers at fancy Shanghai clubs like Linx, Muse, and Myst makes sure that only the truly appropriate kinds of people gain access to the most exclusive spaces. At the King of Party club in Shanghai, Thomas Yeung taps his own extensive social network to ensure that the right people are given privileged access to the biggest, fanciest room in the club. Sometimes these are people who can even afford to buy their own private jets.[47]

Even for VIP clubbers, there are still risks, such as being exposed in risqué situations on social media. Given its somewhat stigmatized status as an extravagant, wasteful, unhealthy, and even immoral activity, clubbing is not necessarily even very popular among all wealthy young people. But it is one stage upon which some elites perform class culture while still seeking a thrill.

THE CHANGING SHAPE OF CLUBBING CONSUMPTION

Our story starts in the early twentieth century with the invention of the modern nightclub in Shanghai, especially the taxi-dance hall. While these venues evoked the courtesan houses in their commodification of female companionship, they differed among themselves in many key respects. One was their relatively public nature. These early sites were places where, for the price of a ticket, anyone could experience the unique thrills of urban nightlife. Though open, they were, however, stratified spaces. The fancier clubs included private rooms for dignitaries. And while anyone could purchase a dance with a hostess, the star "dance empresses" were not accessible simply for the price of a single ticket. These dance palaces celebrated the lives of the rich and powerful, and the aspirations and fantasies of the middle classes. The elites were at center stage, but everyone else could still be part of the fashionable swirl.

When dance halls reemerged in the 1980s, a much more democratic and socialist ethos prevailed. The degree of social differentiation among the patrons was minimal, and very little of this distinction was achieved through consumption per se. The convertibility of economic capital to social capital was curtailed by the emphasis on dance itself. As massive discotheques opened in the 1990s, the business model remained essentially that of the dance hall, relying on ticket sales. Patrons crowded together on a giant dance floor, creating the potential for mash-ups with people from various social backgrounds. Even the most fashionable club of this period, Park 97, was, in retrospect, a maze of relatively open spaces in which social mixing and social competition were common. Park 97 and other clubs of its era (the late 1990s through the early 2000s) were ethnosexual contact zones among transnational migrants, local Shanghainese, and internal migrants (particularly women) from all over China. Encounters with strangers across ethnic, class, and gender boundaries were fluid and easy, and these were also known as spaces for intercultural romance, particularly between foreign men and Chinese women.[48]

In contrast, the VIP clubbing scenes that have emerged since 2005 are designed for the monied super-elite to enjoy their status and celebrate their wealth in ways that guarantee—without embarrassment or disruptions—the convertibility of economic capital into social, cultural, and sexual capital. At the same time, VIP clubbing *limits* the conversion strategies of social climbers—whether sex workers, ordinary urban youth, foreign students, or others with relatively low incomes—to the marginal spaces of the club. The organization of the club with its VIP seating ensures that unwanted strangers will not appear and that attractive women can be invited and corralled in the rented spaces. Meanwhile, extravagant displays of alcoholic consumption still will have wide audience. The designs of these spaces, though varied, render them essentially "safe spaces" for the *fuerdai* to celebrate their personal charisma and their untouchable status without socially "achieving it" in the space of the club itself.

NOTES

1. "Wang Sicong At It Again, China's Richest Son Blows 2.5 Million RMB at KTV in Single Night," Shanghaiist (website), March 17, 2016; "Son of China's Richest Billionaire Spends $385,000 at a Beijing Karaoke Bar," NextShark, March 17, 2016, retrieved at https://nextshark.com/wang-sicong-beijing-ktv/.

2. Our most significant publications in this field are James Farrer, *Opening Up: Youth Sex Culture and Market Reform in Shanghai* (Chicago: University of Chicago Press, 2002); Andrew David Field, *Shanghai's Dancing World: Cabaret Culture and Urban Politics, 1919–1954* (Hong Kong: Chinese University Press, 2010); and James Farrer and Andrew David Field, *Shanghai Nightscapes: A Nocturnal Biography of a Global City* (Chicago: University of Chicago Press, 2015).

3. Follow-up research includes recorded long-form interviews with a club owner, a liquor company executive, and a club manager in fall 2016 and unrecorded conversations and observations with other clubbing regulars.

4. See David Grazian, *On the Make: The Hustle of Urban Nightlife* (Chicago: University of Chicago Press, 2008).

5. The concept of "action environment" is explored in Lewis Erenberg, *Steppin' Out: New York Nightlife and the Transformation of American Culture, 1890–1930* (Chicago: University of Chicago Press, 1984), 113–42. For an exploration of the concept of different selves, see Erving Goffman, *The Presentation of Self in Everyday Life* (New York: Doubleday, 1959). For a study of nightlife as an expression of cultural capital, see Sarah Thornton, *Club Cultures: Music, Media, and Subcultural Capital* (Hanover, NH: University Press of New England, 1996). For studies of the expression of personal capital through sexuality, see Adam Isaiah Green, "The Social Organization of Desire: The Sexual Fields Approach," *Sociological Theory* 26, no. 1 (March 2008): 25–50; Ashley Mears, "Girls as Elite Distinction: The Appropriation of Bodily Capital," *Poetics* 53 (October 2015): 22–37; Farrer and Field, *Shanghai Nightscapes*, 170.

6. See chapter 2 of Farrer and Field, *Shanghai Nightscapes*, for a concise summary of this era of Shanghai nightlife.

7. The most comprehensive account of Western lifestyles in Shanghai during the 1920s is Nicholas Clifford, *Spoilt Children of Empire: Westerners in Shanghai and the Chinese Revolution of the 1920s* (Hanover, NH: Middlebury College Press, 1991). For a description of the grand balls, see Field, *Shanghai's Dancing World*, 21–29.

8. Authoritative studies of prostitution and courtesan culture in Shanghai are Christian Henriot, *Prostitution and Sexuality in Shanghai: A Social History, 1849–1949* (Cambridge: Cambridge University Press, 2001); Gail Hershatter, *Dangerous Pleasures: Prostitution and Modernity in Twentieth-Century Shanghai* (Berkeley: University of California Press, 1997); and Catherine Vance Yeh, *Shanghai Love: Courtesans, Intellectuals, and Entertainment Culture, 1850–1910* (Seattle: University of Washington Press, 2006).

9. Mears, "Girls as Elite Distinction."

10. See Field, *Shanghai's Dancing World*, chapter 2, for an account of the rise of Chinese "dance madness" (*wukuang*) in 1928. Chits are mentioned on p. 218. Many Western accounts of nightlife from this era in Shanghai also mention the common use of chits. For example, see Whitey Smith, *I Didn't Make a Million* (Manila: Philippine Education Co., 1956), 45–46.

11. In addition to the works of Field and Farrer cited above, see also Ma Jun, *Wuting, Shizheng: Shanghai bainian yule shenghuo de yi ye* [Dance halls, politics: one page in a hundred years of Shanghai entertainment life] (Shanghai: Shanghai Dictionary Publishing Company, 2010).

12. The classic study of taxi-dancers and dance halls in America is Paul Cressey, *The Taxi-Dance Hall: A Sociological Study in Commercialized Recreation and City Life* (Chicago: University of Chicago Press, 1931; rep. 2008).

13. For extensive information on Shanghai's dance hostesses in the 1920s–1930s, see Field, *Shanghai's Dancing World*, 119–153.

14. Field, *Shanghai's Dancing World*, 129. The best account of the recruitment of Shanghai dance hostesses appears in Edna Lee Booker, *News is My Job: A Correspondent in War-torn China* (New York: McMillan, 1940), 25–26.
15. Field, *Shanghai's Dancing World*, 140–46.
16. Field, 30.
17. See Field, 98–111, for detailed accounts of the design and functions of the Paramount and other famed ballrooms from the 1930s. The original article describing the design of the Paramount appears in the architectural magazine *Zhongguo jianzhu* 2, no. 1 (1934).
18. The economic and political history of the cabaret industry in the 1940s and 1950s is analyzed in detail in Field, *Shanghai's Dancing World*.
19. Farrer and Field, *Shanghai Nightscapes*, 47. This section is based on Farrer's fieldwork in ballroom dance halls in Yangpu and Hongkou Districts in the 1990s.
20. James Farrer and Sun Zhongxin, "Extramarital Love in Shanghai," *China Journal* 50 (July 2003): 1–36.
21. James Farrer, "Play and Power in Chinese Nightlife Spaces," *China: An International Journal* 6, no. 1 (2008): 1–17.
22. Anne Allison, *Nightwork: Sexuality, Pleasure, and Corporate Masculinity in a Tokyo Hostess Club* (Chicago: University of Chicago Press, 1994); Tiantian Zheng, *Red Lights: The Lives of Sex Workers in Post-socialist China* (Minneapolis: University of Minnesota Press, 2009); and John Osburg, *Anxious Wealth: Money and Morality Among China's New Rich* (Stanford: Stanford University Press, 2013). For research on nightlife districts devoted to commercial sex, see Pan Suiming, *Shengcun yu tiyan: dui yige hongdengqu de zhuizong kaocha* [Survival and experience: an examination of one red-light district] (Beijing: Zhongguo shehuikexue chubanshe, 2000).
23. While living in Shanghai between the 1990s and 2000s, coauthor Field was invited to several of these sorts of parties by both Chinese and Western male friends who were either getting married or else holding birthday parties.
24. This section is based on fieldwork and interviews with KTV habitués by coauthor Field in the 2000s. Owing to the high cost of attending these clubs, the fieldwork was limited to a few occasions.
25. Osburg, *Anxious Wealth*.
26. Mears, "Girls as Elite Distinction."
27. Farrer, James. "Disco 'Super-Culture': Consuming Foreign Sex in the Chinese Disco: Cosmopolitan Dance Culture and Cosmopolitan Sexual Culture," *Sexualities* 2, no. 2 (1999): 147–65.
28. Farrer and Field, *Shanghai Nightscapes*, 70.
29. Interview with former DJs Ali Wong and Vic Kishinchand, August 30, 2014.
30. Andrew Field, "From D.D.'s to Y.Y. to Park 97 to Muse: Dance Club Spaces and the Construction of Class in Shanghai, 1997–2007," *China: An International Journal* 6, no. 1 (March 2008): 18–43; Farrer and Field, *Shanghai Nightscapes*, 79–88.
31. Interviews with Tony Zhang, December 20, 2003 and September 23, 2016. Also, Farrer and Field made dozens of visits to this club between 1997 and 2007. In 2003, Field captured the club in its heyday on video including extensive interviews with Tony Zhang and DJ Chris Lee.
32. Interview with Tony Zhang, September 23, 2016.
33. Farrer and Field visited all the clubs in this section.
34. See Farrer and Field, *Shanghai Nightscapes*, 88–93.
35. Farrer and Field, *Shanghai Nightscapes*, 97.
36. Jamie Fullerton, "Clubbing with China's Cocky 1 Percenters," *Vice* (July 2, 2014).
37. Interview with Tony Zhang, September 23, 2016.
38. Farrer and Field, *Shanghai Nightscapes*, 1–97.
39. For similar applications of field theory to clubbing, see Green, "The Social Organization of Desire"; Mears, "Girls as Elite Distinction"; Farrer and Field, *Shanghai Nightscapes*, 170.
40. Interview with Thomas Yeung, October 18, 2016.

41. Ruby Gao, "Chinese Wine Market Keeps Falling," *Shanghai Daily*, January 14, 2016.
42. "French Champagne Consumption in China," Marketing China (website), December 18, 2012, retrieved from https://www.marketingtochina.com/french-champagne-consumption-in-china/; "Champagne Market in China," Daxueconsulting (blog), November 24, 2014, retrieved at http://daxueconsulting.com/champagne-market-china/.
43. "How Jay-Z's Armand De Brignac Became the Gold Standard of Champagne," Maxim Media, May 19, 2016, retrieved at https://www.maxim.com/entertainment/armand-de-brignac-champagne-jay-z-2016-5.
44. Anonymous interview, October 2016.
45. Anonymous interview, October 2016.
46. Anonymous interview, October 2016.
47. From a conversation with Thomas Yeung and Tony Zhang, October 2016.
48. James Farrer, "Global Nightscapes in Shanghai as Ethnosexual Contact Zones," *Journal of Ethnic and Migration Studies* 37, no. 5 (2011): 747–64.

SEVEN

Corruption, Anti-Corruption, and the Dynamics of Class Formation in Post-Mao China

John Osburg

How does the party-state fight corruption in a context in which corrupt practices are not only ubiquitous but are more or less institutionalized as the "unwritten rules" (*qianguize*) of the game? What are the meanings and effects of an anti-corruption campaign in a context in which virtually all Party cadres and state officials have engaged in illicit activity of varying degrees? Such questions have come to the fore since the Chinese Communist Party (CCP) launched its largest crackdown on corruption and official ostentation in the post-Mao period (1978–present). Starting in early 2013 with a directive against excessive spending on food and drink by officials, the campaign has brought down tens of thousands of officials from low-ranking "flies" to high-ranking "tigers" (to use the language of the campaign). To date, the largest "tiger" deposed is a former Politburo Standing Committee member, Zhou Yongkang, along with many members of his network, including other prominent officials and businessmen.

Many scholars and observers cynically view anti-corruption drives in China as politically expedient means of purging rivals along with their factional networks. During the Maoist period, the Anti-Rightist Campaign (1957) and several others associated with the Cultural Revolution served to purge rival cliques or simply to remove people whom Mao deemed not sufficiently loyal to himself. Thus, some have assumed that Xi's crusade against corruption, although larger in scale, can ultimately be reduced to factional politics, and that Xi is using the guise of anti-corruption to get rid of political rivals and replace them with officials more personally aligned with him.[1]

Some view his ultimate goal, to consolidate power, as a precursor to implementing reforms, while others point to signs of a cult of personality surrounding Xi to suggest that he may be simply amassing power for its own sake. While political rivals of President Xi Jinping have no doubt been targeted in the campaign, reducing this campaign to a pure cover for factional struggles among the party elite ignores many of its effects, which I explore in this essay.

Rather than trying to piece together bits and pieces of data to attempt to create a coherent picture of elite party politics, a task which many scholars are more qualified to do than I am, this essay situates the recent battle against corruption in a longer history of corruption during the reform period. In particular, I highlight the ways in which corruption, broadly conceived, exacerbated inequalities that had their roots before the reform period but also enabled certain forms of mobility, primarily via entrepreneurs' cultivation of official patronage. I begin with an overview of the political and economic structures in post-Mao China through which corrupt alliances and transactions flow and consider which groups were able to benefit from the opportunities generated by economic reforms. I then move from the macro level to the micro to explore the practices—bribery, entertaining, gift-giving, etc.—through which elite networks were formed and the role they played in the creation and demarcation of new classes in the post-Mao period.

As in many parts of the world, corrupt transactions and relationships in China are built through everyday forms of sociality—banqueting, drinking, gift exchange, and other forms of shared, gendered leisure.[2] What makes the recent anti-corruption crusade unique is that it is not only specific individuals who are being targeted for investigation; more significantly, the very forms of sociality which have enabled the formation of expansive networks comprising government bureaucracies, state-owned enterprises, private companies, and entrepreneurs have been hampered as well. I examine recent changes in the practices of these groups brought on not only by Xi Jinping's anti-corruption drive but also by shifts in elite forms of sociality, leisure, and consumption. My observations are based on the ongoing ethnographic research that I have been conducting with a group of businesspeople in Chengdu since the early 2000s.

Finally, I offer some tentative thoughts on the effects of this campaign on class formation in post-Mao China. Rather than fostering clean and transparent government or market efficiency, I argue that the recent anti-corruption campaign's primary effect has been, whether intended or not, class consolidation. This development has been the result of pruning away those not sufficiently embedded in China's elite networks to be exempted from the purges. I hypothesize that, as China's new rich gradually becomes a class-for-itself, embeddedness in elite networks is increasingly acquired by birth—as in a caste system—rather than cultivated in the nightclub. This marks a transition from the more open field of state-business networks that characterized the 1990s and 2000s.

THE NEW RICH IN POST-MAO CHINA

China's so-called new rich refers to the diverse stratum of entrepreneurs, government officials, professionals, entertainers, and artists who have grown wealthy in the nearly four decades since China began reforming its planned economy. At this point, the "new" rich have been around long enough that much popular attention now focuses on their children—the *fuerdai*, or "second-generation rich," who began to come of age in the early 2000s.

Given the complex ways that class background impacted life chances in Maoist and post-Mao China, new rich backgrounds are diverse. Among this stratum, one can find those who are descendants of families who were elites prior to the 1949 revolution, as well as those from poor peasant backgrounds, a status that conferred political advantages during the Mao years which some were able to translate into economic advantage with the advent of reforms. Despite this diversity in backgrounds, there are still identifiable patterns that track the changing economic and political environment of the reform period.

Given the politically precarious status of engaging in business in the early reform period, when socialist ideology still held sway, many of the first urban entrepreneurs in the early 1980s were those with bad class labels, who had little to lose by taking a chance in private business.[3] These first small-scale entrepreneurs were referred to as *getihu* (independent laborer) to signal their independence from the state-controlled work-unit system. Initially, *getihu* were looked down upon by those still enjoying the final years of security and status associated with the state-run economy.[4]

In rural areas, many of the first wealthy entrepreneurs emerged from successful Township-Village Enterprises (TVEs), which ranged from de facto private businesses to collectively-owned ventures. This first crop of wealthy rural entrepreneurs included former cadres who were able to leverage their managerial and technical skills to develop businesses, but also included former peasant farmers turned entrepreneurs.

Given that many in the first crop of the new rich originated from outside the established urban elite, stereotypes surrounded this group, who were often derogatorily labeled "upstarts" or "parvenus" (*baofahu*, literally "suddenly rich person"). Even the term *getihu* had a derogatory connotation well into the 1990s in northeastern cities.[5] In urban areas, relatively low-status positions in work-units such as purchaser or driver were suddenly rendered valuable by economic reforms, as they enabled both opportunities for moonlighting and for the accumulation of social capital which could lead to further business ventures. During the late 1980s, several popular sayings reflected the sense that in the nascent market economy, income no longer reflected hierarchies of education, talent, or virtue. Examples of these aphorisms included: "Those who hold scalpels earn less than those who hold eel knives" and "those who produce missiles earn less than those who sell tea eggs."[6]

Despite the sense in some areas that business opportunities were upending the established order, reforms presented former and current party and state cadres with new paths to wealth. Some were able to prosper simply due to the managerial experience and social connections they had acquired during the Mao period, which rendered them better positioned to engage in business with the advent of reforms.[7] Other state officials could leverage their administrative power for gains in the emerging market. For example, a common form of corruption in the 1980s involved well-placed officials amassing profits from discrepancies between state-controlled and market prices for certain goods due to the so-called dual-track pricing system, which allowed for market prices to exist alongside officially designated ones for scarce and valuable commodities.

After Deng Xiaoping's southern tour in 1992, which gave the green light to forge ahead with economic reforms, the composition of the new rich began to change, as increasing numbers of well-educated workers, intellectuals, and professionals left the security of their work-units to embark on business ventures, a phenomenon known as "jumping into the sea" (*xiahai*). By the late 1990s the once stigmatized *getihu* had been transformed into the now esteemed figure of the entrepreneur (*qiyejia*). The background of the typical entrepreneur shifted as well, with both higher levels of education and experience in the party-state increasingly the norm.[8]

In 2001, entrepreneurs were formally welcomed to join the Party, giving official sanction to what had become a common practice at the local level. Since that time, in addition to gaining party membership, entrepreneurs have been invited to occupy a growing number of seats in People's Congresses and Chinese People's Political Consultative Congresses (CPPCC) at local, provincial, and national levels. Increasingly, as I describe in the next section, party-state officials and entrepreneurs in informal networks were able to combine their respective advantages to dominate many areas of business.

But despite their official recognition, in the public's view, new rich entrepreneurs have continued to be associated with corruption and immorality.[9] Even those in the public eye who run well-established companies have been subject to rumors about their having secret high-level government backers (*kaoshan*) or are said to have made their initial wealth through corrupt or illegitimate means, a state of affairs sometimes referred to as the "original sin" (*yuanzui*) of China's new rich.[10]

CORRUPTION AND ELITE NETWORKS

Since 2002, I have been conducting ongoing fieldwork with a group of wealthy entrepreneurs in the city of Chengdu in southwest China. The bulk of my fieldwork, from 2002–2006, was spent accompanying these businessmen as they courted clients, partners, and government officials through drinking at banquets, singing in karaoke clubs (KTVs), carousing in nightclubs, and playing mahjong in teahouses. The patron-client relationships between state officials and businesspeople in China are a significant subset of the broader phenomenon of *guanxi*, the web of social connections through which people in greater China exchange favors, from the mundane to the fortune-making.[11]

Notwithstanding the dramatic transformation in China's economy brought by ongoing economic reforms, state agents still largely control access to capital, business licenses, and land. Beyond allowing for state control of key aspects of the economy, in many industries strong ties to the party-state offer one a huge competitive advantage. Well-connected businesspeople are more likely to win government contracts, obtain tax breaks, gain knowledge of insider information, and receive regulatory flexibility; they also can get privileged access to China's most valuable state-controlled commodity, land.[12] In some instances entrepreneurs are able to appropriate state power to punish their competitors and advance their interests, a phenomenon David Wank dubs "local state takeover."[13]

While some scholars predicted increasing antagonism between the emergent class of entrepreneurs and the established political elite, others have clearly shown that the relationship between officials and businessmen is better characterized as "symbiotic" or "symbiotic clientelism": entrepreneurs obtain protection and many benefits that enhance their business success, while state agents both generate revenue for local government agencies and garner illicit income for themselves through bribes or kickbacks that often dwarf their official salaries.[14]

By distributing favors, privileges, contracts, and protection, officials are also able to build their own networks of entrepreneurs to accomplish various projects, from enhancing their own personal status and pleasure to achieving state-driven goals of economic development. To give an illustration: an entrepreneur from my study managed to use his connections to government bureaus in charge of urban planning—connections he maintained through lavish dinners and gifts—to obtain lucrative contracts that enabled him to demolish neighborhoods marked for redevelopment. He also served as middleman between real estate entrepreneurs looking for insider access to state-controlled land and local officials.

Scholars often divide corruption in post-Mao China into two forms, corresponding to two different periods in China's economic reforms.[15] For example, in an early assessment of the effects of corruption during the reform period, Rocca distinguished between "creative" forms of corruption that enabled the empowerment and mobility of new social classes (such as the emerging entrepreneurs) and "predatory" forms, which primarily served to maintain the power of the communist bureaucracy.[16]

In the early reform period (1978–1992), corruption, in the form of illicit ties and transactions between entrepreneurs and state officials, has been viewed by most scholars as serving to grease the wheels of a communist bureaucracy still reluctant to sanction capitalist activity, both for reasons of ideology and political survival. During this time, *guanxi* ties cultivated through dinners and gift exchange served to create relationships of trust in a context in which most private business was legally gray and politically suspect at best.[17] While government officials and the officially connected personally benefited in that era, the spoils of rapid growth tended to reach not just nouveaux riches entrepreneurs but non-elite groups as well, largely through the investment and employment that resulted from official deal-making. This was especially the case in rural areas with successful collectively-owned enterprises or in places where collectively-owned land was leased to foreign-invested factories.[18]

Most scholars see a shift in the forms and social effects of corruption as reforms deepened after 1992, however. Corruption at that point shifted to something more akin to "predation," which tended to reinforce and even magnify existing inequalities.[19] This behavior involved classic forms of rent-seeking, with officials demanding ever-larger bribes, dinners, and sexual entertainment for access to state-controlled resources or in exchange for preferential patronage. Some entrepreneurs who made their fortunes in the early reform period cultivated even deeper ties with state officials in these subsequent years, enabling them to commandeer state power to their advantage. For example, the Fujianese tycoon, Lai Changxing, started off in manufacturing in the 1980s but, relying on his strong official connections, shifted to smuggling in the early nineties. Through a mixture of bribes and lavish entertaining, Lai was able to co-opt the entire customs administration and a good portion of the provincial government of Fujian, and his appropriation of state power enabled him to run a multi-billion-dollar smuggling operation that lasted until he fled to Canada in 1999.[20]

The early 1990s also marked the beginning of a massive transfer of collective or state-owned land, assets, and companies into private hands. While this process formally resembled "privatization," in reality rarely did such transfers conform to how economists envision this process. Writing in the late-1990s, the Chinese economist He Qinglian described this activity as follows:

> The fact is that what has emerged in China is a system for distributing resources that is rooted in neither a purely planned nor market-based economy. Instead rent-seeking activities that lead to the acquisition of capital and other forms of wealth rely on a highly elaborate and informal network or web of social connections rooted in regional loyalties, family relationships, friendships, and old school ties, and the like. . . . Informal networks of social relationships are, in short, a major resource, in that they are the key mechanism for mobilizing and directing the flow of wealth.[21]

Many officials, along with their friends and families, were able to obtain ownership or shares in these assets cheaply through backdoor means, sometimes referred to as "insider privatization." Managers of state-owned enterprises (SOEs) often employed complex techniques of asset stripping, in which they made deals that benefited private firms owned by family and friends but often bankrupted the SOEs they controlled.[22] In the process, workers were typically cheated out of their shares in collectives and TVEs.[23]

Starting in this period, some family members of high-ranking party and state officials amassed huge fortunes by serving as brokers for access to state-controlled land and assets, either receiving bribes or shares in newly formed or newly publicly traded companies (often through byzantine holding company structures and offshore accounts) in return.[24] Many times the official shareholders were not the officials themselves but their family members.[25] Beginning in the early 2000s, the officially connected were able to acquire windfall profits through the timely acquisition of shares in companies prior to their public offerings in foreign and domestic stock markets.[26]

In some cases these shares were gifted to elite-linked family members or sold cheaply to these individuals by companies hoping to speed up the arduous process of becoming a listed company or, simply, to curry favor with political elites.[27] Other family members of the CCP leadership capitalized on their positions by serving as middlemen in deals between SOEs and multinational companies. For example, Jiang Mianheng, the son of Jiang Zemin, brokered deals involving Microsoft, Nokia, and DreamWorks.[28] Global investment banks working in China also commonly hired (and some still employ) family members of high-ranking cadres to gain access to deals, a practice known as a "relationship hire" in the banking industry.[29]

Despite ever-increasing levels of predatory corruption, from 1992 to 2008, China's economy underwent a historically unprecedented expansion, sustaining double-digit rates of growth nearly every year. This combination of high levels of predatory corruption along with high levels of economic growth defies the logic of conventional models that presume that predatory corruption is a drag on economic growth.[30] Wedeman dubs this the "double paradox" of Chinese corruption.[31]

The "double paradox" of corruption in China—high levels of corruption and high growth—appears somewhat less paradoxical when one takes into account some specific characteristics of China's state capitalist system. In some respects, China has had two interrelated and overlapping economies or two "engines" of growth, one dependent on exports, the other on state-controlled investment. The first of these has been driven by the private sector, dominated by often foreign-invested export-oriented manufacturing, which is concentrated in the southern coastal region. The other primary driver of growth is state-directed infrastructure and real estate investment: building office towers, airports, roads, high-speed rail networks, and subways.

This state-directed investment has generated considerable wealth for officials and well-connected entrepreneurs and has been a prime enabler of corruption. Obtaining contracts to undertake these massive projects is incredibly lucrative, but it requires a mix of bribes and connections (see the next section). Frequently the initial winner of the contract then goes on to sell it to someone else. Sometimes contracts are sold multiple times before they finally reach the subcontractor who actually performs the job, and who finally must complete the job with a budget significantly smaller than the amount allotted by the initial contract if he is to turn a profit.[32]

Subcontracting practices such as these, along with truncated or nonexistent bidding, have been reported to be widespread in public works projects and, prior to the arrest of the minister of railways, Liu Zhijun, in 2011, particularly common in railway construction.[33] This corrupt subcontracting system is in many ways responsible for an epidemic of what Chinese citizens refer to as "tofu dregs construction" (*doufazha gongcheng*): shoddily built roads, bridges, and buildings that prematurely deteriorate or dramatically collapse. Due to the various cuts and kickbacks taken by officials and contractors, subcontractors frequently employ low-skilled workers, cut corners, or substitute low quality materials to recoup their costs. The most famous instance of "tofu dregs construction" was the substandard schools that crumbled during the 2008 Wenchuan earthquake.

Since the beginning of economic reforms, state officials and entrepreneurs have largely operated in symbiotic networks of mutual dependence and benefit resulting in corrupt practices that follow the "unwritten rules" of business and development.[34] This has been demonstrated in several anti-corruption cases in which the prosecution of a single official often brings down a whole network of interlinked officials and businesspeople.

In the midst of Xi's anti-corruption campaign, the Taiwanese phrase "white gloves" (*baishoutao*) has gained popularity in the PRC to refer to the businessperson who is the primary source of an official's illicit income and the principal beneficiary of the official's patronage.[35] During the 2013 trial of Bo Xilai, for example, the real estate entrepreneur Xu

Ming was revealed to have purchased a villa for Bo in France, and to have financed many of Bo's son's expenses in exchange for protection and insider access to deals.[36]

Officials caught in anti-corruption investigations often defend themselves by claiming that they couldn't advance their careers and further economic growth in their regions without accepting bribes from entrepreneurs, giving kickbacks to their superiors, and doing favors for their own kin and *guanxi* networks.[37] In fact, some observers have pointed to a growing "bureaucratic paralysis" as a result of the recent anti-corruption campaign.[38] That is, officials fear embarking on new projects or initiatives because of the attention they might attract. Many have opted for the safest route of lying low and doing nothing, which some observers fear will further dampen China's currently sputtering economy.

CULTIVATING STATE-BUSINESS NETWORKS

The networks of entrepreneurs and officials with whom I conducted my research were deeply financially and socially intertwined. They were shareholders in each other's companies and purchased each other's products and services. They exchanged information, offered advice, provided both material and nonmaterial assistance, and served as intermediaries in bringing together business partners, introducing clients, and soliciting patrons in the government. New business opportunities often united people from very different backgrounds—urban officials with rural entrepreneurs, gangster bosses with the state security apparatus.

But despite their diverse backgrounds, the entrepreneurs and government officials I knew aspired to a similar masculine "boss-patron" ideal—a dispenser of favors and opportunities, someone who can command the assistance of powerful individuals with just a phone call (or, as is more common these days, a WeChat message). I have argued that participation in these networks as both patron and client has been fundamental to post-Mao ideologies of masculinity, in which career and financial success have served as the dominant measure of a man's worth.[39]

The networks they built and came to rely upon had (and continue to exert) a profound effect on their business ventures, interpersonal ethics, and consumption habits. Although some of these networks are based on preexisting ties of kinship, colleagueship, and native place, the bulk of the relationships that make up these networks were forged and maintained through ritualized leisure typically referred to as *yingchou*—experiences of shared pleasure in venues catering to the desires of elite men. One moderately successful businessman whom I came to know quite well estimated (in 2008) that he spent 2 to 3 million RMB a year in one particular nightclub entertaining business associates and friends, and given that his bill often exceeded 10,000 RMB in a single evening, I believe his estimate.

These networks were primarily composed of men, drawing upon idioms of kinship, and were forged through highly gendered practices, such as drinking at banquets, carousing in nightclubs, and joining in group visits to brothels and saunas. Among the entrepreneurs with whom I worked, business relationships were often couched in rhetorics of male solidarity, brotherhood, paternalism, mutual aid, and *yiqi* (honor or a sense of obligation in personal relationships).

Patrons and well-connected bosses were frequently referred to as "big brothers" (*dage*), and their status depended on fulfilling paternalist obligations and providing for the well-being of the other members of their networks. They were expected to put their brotherly relationships above all other commitments, sharing their success and using positions of power to the advantage of other members of their network. While the alliances I observed in my research were oriented toward profit and career advancement, internally they were governed by a moral economy of distribution, in which patrons accrued status by dispensing opportunities to dependents in their networks.[40]

In a context in which relatives of China's political elite are granted insider access by birth, the businessmen with whom I worked competed and labored to develop their own privileged relationships by courting government officials. My research subjects and I spent most nights and many afternoons in entertainment venues fostering business ties or maintaining existing ones. I argue that we should view these techniques of embedding as a form of emotional labor.[41]

While such interactions tend to be casually dismissed as "male bonding" or "networking" in the West or as supplements to the "real work" of business, the businessmen I knew viewed these techniques not as peripheral to but as *the* work of business. They employed various performative techniques—invoking kinship idioms, engaging in subtle forms of flattery, group karaoke singing and trips to brothels, introductions to mistresses, etc.—to "condition" the subjective states of their clients, partners, or official patrons.[42] In these contexts, actors employed cultural notions of brotherhood or *yiqi*, at times sincerely, at other times in highly calculated, instrumental ways. Sometimes these techniques generated their intended performative effects; other times they failed.

My informants viewed these techniques of conditioning as necessary for two reasons. The first of these was the ubiquity of bribery. Because anyone can offer a bribe or a kickback, cash and luxury gifts by themselves were not particularly effective in forging ties: as commodities their value was transparent and comparable with other commodities. One ran the risk that someone else's bribe would be higher or that another's gift would be legibly more valuable. Thus, my informants attempted to marshal these objects to generate *incommensurable* ties rooted in affective, embodied memories.

The second reason that necessitated this conditioning was that many of my businessman informants were competing against those who were already embedded in elite networks through kin ties: the children, spouses, and relatives of government officials who were at a distinct advantage in almost all areas of business. My informants could only hope that, through their courtship techniques, they could go (in the words of one entrepreneur) "from acquaintances to friends and from friends to 'iron-clad brothers'" (*cong renshi dao penyou; cong pengyou dao tiegemen'r*) and thus create their own fictive kinship networks which (ideally) linked up with those of the elite.

FAMILY BACKGROUND AND THE "SECOND-GENERATION RICH": EMERGING DISTINCTIONS AMONG THE ELITE

In 2010, 2013, and 2014, I returned to China to meet up with entrepreneurs I had met ten years earlier. In the past, the businessmen I knew would often cite *guanxi* ties as the foundation of their success, claiming that the right relationship could compensate for deficiencies in their ability and experience. They expressed faith in the notion that a well-placed connection would ensure success and often boasted of their abilities to court ties with powerful officials.

But something has changed. In my more recent visits with entrepreneurs, my informants depicted *guanxi* as a less pervasive force than it had been in the past. The feeling of being a part of a seemingly open-ended realm of deal-making and network-building in which, through the right combination of charisma and alcohol tolerance, seemingly anyone could amass a fortune had been replaced by a sense of being constrained by a new set of political, economic, and social realities.

Those I interviewed often complained that despite their efforts to cultivate powerful ties to protect their businesses and facilitate their expansion, the growth of their ventures was ultimately limited by those with already established *guanxi*. These businesspeople now contrasted their own *guanxi*—ties formed through many years of liver-destroying effort—with that possessed by the close friends and relatives of the political elite, which they referred to as *beijing* (literally, "background").

One successful salesman of computer network hardware, whom I had met in the early 2000s when he was still a university student, summarized this sentiment. Despite being from a poor village outside of Chengdu, he had tested into a key high school in his county and then attended one of the top universities in Sichuan. By his late twenties, he owned a centrally located apartment in Chengdu, a BMW 5 series, and had traveled abroad several times. When I pointed out how well he had done, he expressed frustration:

> I've done ok, but there's still so much I want to do. Look at my parents; they continue to live in a small apartment back in my hometown. I want to buy them an apartment in Chengdu. I want to do more to help out my friends and family, but there's only so much that I can do. I have lots of ideas, but [since] I don't have *beijing* (strong family connections), there's no way for me to realize these hopes.

He described his line of work as relatively "healthy" (*jiankang*), in that he didn't have to provide many kickbacks, and the entertaining of his clients, while mandatory and time-consuming, was not excessive in his estimation. However, since many of his clients were SOEs, universities, and other government units, he expressed considerable frustration about how the superior connections of his competitors undermined his ability to compete. He gave an example of how a successful bid from his company was suddenly rejected before he could sign the sales contract in favor of that of a different company. He interpreted this chain of events as follows: "Some *lingdao* [leader] must've decided that the contract needed to go to that company. No doubt because of someone's *guanxi*. Everyone knows that company's products are worse in quality, and their prices are more expensive."

While *guanxi* continues to be important, the ways in which it is cultivated and employed have undergone key changes in the past decade or so, the most significant of these being the decline of the entertaining practices described above. This decline is due to a number of factors, most notably the changing class dynamics of the elite, which I describe below. The first factor in this transformation, however, is more mundane: a growing aversion to the mental and physical toll of excessive eating and drinking. As they approached their late forties and early fifties, many of my informants' bodies just couldn't tolerate the constant drinking associated with *yingchou*. Some had even developed chronic illnesses or drug and alcohol addictions. Even those who had managed to avoid serious health problems had grown tired of the time investment required by business-related entertaining.[43]

A second issue in this drop-off of entertaining was that, many of my interviewees complained, their endless social obligations to business associates, government officials, and other members of their social networks prevented them from pursuing their own business and leisure interests. Several of them griped that successful, wealthy individuals in particular are forced to "live for others" (*weibeiren shenghuo*) rather than for themselves. In order to avoid their oppressive entertaining obligations, some of my more successful informants had retreated from their social networks in the only socially acceptable way: by emigrating to Australia, Canada, or the United States.[44]

Several of my interviewees, tired of constant entertaining, wished that they could just give a bribe or a kickback to cement a deal. But, exemplifying the recent shifts in the formation of *guanxi*, my informants stressed that these days possessing *guanxi* has become the precondition for giving a bribe in the first place. Some related, for instance, that those who, in addition to money, can offer the trust, familiarity, and durability that accompanies established *guanxi* are at a distinct advantage over those who seek to forge new ties through dinners and gifts.

However, beyond growing mentally and physically exhausted by many years of *yingchou* and frustrated by its growing ineffectiveness, my recent visits in Chengdu revealed a major shift in the practices and venues associated with *guanxi* brought on by the rise of the second-generation rich and the closing of elite circles. My previous (2002–2006) research revealed a fair amount of uniformity in techniques of *guanxi* cultivation. While establishments varied considerably in their price and extravagance, the practices and idioms that accompanied this entertaining were part of a trans-class and trans-regional masculine culture of entertaining. Its basic forms and etiquette were familiar to peasant farmers and high-ranking officials alike.[45] Through such techniques businessmen (and, in some instances, businesswomen) of humble means were able to cultivate the protection of some of China's most powerful high-ranking officials.[46]

However, as China's first-generation rich has given rise to the second generation, new practices and venues for *guanxi* cultivation have emerged that are just not accessible to those not "in the know." Private clubs that charge exorbitant membership fees and require extensive background checks have emerged as the favored entertaining places among the wealthy. These clubs ensure that those who frequent them are from similar socioeconomic backgrounds. Golf clubs and auto clubs, which require wealth, social ties, and forms of cultural capital to enter, have also become significant venues for networking but only with other members of what is now the established elite.

Moreover, as many of China's first-generation rich emigrate or spend considerable time overseas, some elite *guanxi* building has moved outside China's borders. And as growing numbers of China's second-generation rich study abroad, their connections are more likely to be forged (with classmates possessing a similar socioeconomic background) in a college dorm in Sydney than in a karaoke club in Chengdu. In other words, elite *guanxi* cultivation is starting to diverge from the shared forms of the 1990s and early 2000s as the lines separating China's emerging social classes become more well-defined. One could view this movement as the incipient forging of a kind of caste system at the very top.

While the first generation of successful post-Mao entrepreneurs often benefited from already-existing *guanxi* from school and work ties, many also built expansive *guanxiwang* (networks of *guanxi*) from scratch as their businesses expanded. Now, the second-generation rich and their official counterparts (*guan'erdai* and *taizidang* or *hong'erdai*) increasingly benefit from *guanxi* inherited by their parents. For them, *guanxi* is less something that is achieved, experienced, and embodied in actual relationships. Rather, *guanxi* has turned into a resource that functions as a pure form of social capital that can be exchanged for jobs, business opportunities, and official positions. Popular representations of the *fuerdai* emphasize how their social circles are not just, as in the past, tightly knit, but now are essentially closed.[47]

On a recent trip to China, I was introduced to the son of a local official, who, I was hoping, would help introduce me to wealthy followers of Tibetan Buddhism for a new research project. It turned out, unfortunately, that he didn't know many Buddhists. But he was eager to introduce me to his coterie of young, wealthy friends. When we first met, I had casually mentioned to him that my mother works for a city government office in the United States. Later, when he took me out to a wine bar to meet some of his *fuerdai* friends, I was surprised to be introduced to the group as an "American *guan'erdai*" (offspring of a government official).

From my experiences with this group, it quickly became apparent that family background is now scrutinized in a way that was nonexistent in the 1990s, when by default the wealthy were all "nouveaux riches." This now-inherited *guanxi*, coupled with the rise of new *guanxi* cultivation practices, especially those happening behind the doors of private clubs and in overseas enclaves, will serve to enhance the benefits already enjoyed by China's second-generation rich. One could note that, while the agency of this select generation among the rich has become unlimited (presuming they are not caught at corruption), aspirants to this segment have seen their opportunities for upward mobility decline.

ANTI-CORRUPTION AS CLASS/CASTE CONSOLIDATION?

When I returned to Chengdu in the summer of 2014, many of the entertaining practices I had observed on previous trips were in dramatic decline due to the anti-corruption campaign launched by Xi Jinping in 2013. Xi's attempts to curb official ostentation and excess, exemplified by the "four dishes and a soup" policy for official meals, had made government officials terrified of accepting dinner invitations and gifts from entrepreneurs. Many of the nightlife establishments I had frequented with my informant-friends in the past had closed or scaled down their operations significantly. The most popular restaurant chain for courting clients and officials, which at its peak had six successful branches, was reduced to just one venue, and its owner was said to be hiding out in Australia.

Also noticeably absent were the luxury cars with government, military, and police license plates that exempted their owners from most parking and traffic regulations. While some of these officially licensed cars had been purchased by government and police units for use by high-level officials, many others were private cars whose owners had obtained these special license plates through backdoor government connections. Virtually all visible symbols of official excess and corruption were now gone from public view.

Several of my informants who in the past had been able to rely on government-controlled contracts and insider access for the bulk of their business were now financially struggling. One businessman, Mr. Wei, who had made his fortune with contracts to demolish old neighborhoods of Chengdu that were marked to be replaced by new high-rises, serves as a good illustration of the dramatic effects of Xi's campaign. At dinner one evening, he recounted to me how officials began returning gifts and payments he had previously made to them as the crackdown got underway. He pondered what to do with his growing collection of gently used luxury watches given back to him by officials. He casually mentioned that he himself had been detained by anti-corruption investigators (*jiwei*) twice in the previous six months but claimed that he refused to provide them with any information. While in the past he was out entertaining at least five nights a week, he was now spending his evenings at home and had even taken up Western-style cooking as a hobby, posting sad photos of sandwiches and pasta dishes on WeChat. As a result of his financial struggles, he fired his chauffeur and started taking the subway. However, embarrassed by his business problems and hoping to keep up the appearance of success, he frequently claimed to his friends that he had merely given his driver the night off and insisted that he only rode the subway out of practicality, citing the bad traffic in Chengdu.

Unable to cultivate and maintain relationships with officials, as of 2015 at least, businessmen like Mr. Wei saw themselves as increasingly closed off from elite networks. They complained that only those with the most durable form of *guanxi—beijing* (kinship ties to the political elite, not to mention the political elite themselves)—could still prosper in the current climate. He did emphasize that the anti-corruption drive had been successful in stopping the flow of bribes to officials, which he viewed as ultimately good for China. But he pointed out that the campaign has been completely ineffective at curbing the privileges of those (and their families) at the extreme political apex. In fact, he claimed, the campaign has made business opportunities easier than ever for them to acquire, since they can effectively monopolize state-controlled deals and industries. Due to the kin ties they've acquired through birth or marriage, those situated at or near the very top don't need to engage in emotional labor, banquets, and gift exchange to generate *guanxi* ties; their family backgrounds ensure access to deals as well as protection. Even once relatively well-connected and successful entrepreneurs like Mr. Wei have been effectively shut out from the spoils of state-controlled growth.

Furthermore, several observers have pointed out that among the "tigers" investigated in the anti-corruption campaign, none (as of late 2016) have been members of the so-called second-generation red (*hong'erdai*), the children of founding and early members of the Communist Party and the People's Republic, also referred to as "princelings" (*taizidang*). Unlike "commoner" (*pingmin*) officials from humble backgrounds, who have had to trade favors and get their hands dirty to advance their careers, princelings can simply rely upon their family name to amass wealth and win promotions.[48]

Ordinary Chinese have picked up on this caste-like unfolding. Thus, it is not uncommon to hear people frequently refer to the ruling elites and their families as "nobility" (*guizu*); indeed, this term is becoming an increasingly apt characterization of the kin-based nature of power in China. The market reforms of the 1980s and 1990s, a time of social openness, enabled dramatic upward mobility for a small minority. Many individuals were able to cultivate ties to the political elite (at local, provincial, or national levels) through what are today considered "corrupt" practices.

One consequence of the anti-corruption campaign, whether intended or not, is that entrepreneurs of humble origin can no longer cultivate (or buy) their way into the system. If the anti-corruption campaign were somehow to bring about more transparency and fairer competition, this would be a positive outcome. However, if the grumblings of the businessmen of Chengdu are to be taken seriously (not to mention the seeming immunity of princelings in the anti-corruption campaign), this campaign has instead yielded a context in which family background has become an even more significant determinant of economic success and political survival than in the past.

Given these developments, I hypothesize that both the anti-corruption campaign and the rise of second-generation wealth and officialdom will render *guanxi* networks more rigid and closed over the coming years and more likely to be the product of family background than of wining and dining. Corruption—conceived of as insider access to the state-controlled economy—rather than diminishing will persist within a more closed system compared to that of prior decades, rather like a caste. With advantages increasingly conferred based upon birth into a family with *beijing*, or even by simply being born into the *fuerdai* class, perhaps in the future the meaning of the Chinese term *guizu* will narrow, signifying not just a wealthy elite but a caste very closely resembling an actual aristocracy.

NOTES

1. For examples see Kerry Brown, "Will Xi's Anti-corruption Campaign Become an Outright Political Purge?," *Diplomat*, April 7, 2015, https://thediplomat.com/2015/04/will-xis-anti-corruption-campaign-become-an-outright-purge/; Murong Xuecun, "Xi's

Selective Punishment," *New York Times*, January 15, 2016, https://www.nytimes.com/2015/01/17/opinion/murong-xuecun-xis-selective-punishment.html.

2. Jennifer Hasty, "The Pleasures of Corruption: Desire and Discipline in Ghanaian Political Culture," *Cultural Anthropology* 20, no. 2 (May 2005): 271–301; J. P. Olivier de Sardan, "A Moral Economy of Corruption in Africa?," *Journal of African Studies* 37, no. 1 (March 1999): 25–52; John Osburg, *Anxious Wealth: Money and Morality Among China's New Rich* (Stanford: Stanford University Press, 2013).

3. Thomas Gold, "Guerilla Interviewing Among the *Getihu*," in *Unofficial China: Popular Culture and Thought in the People's Republic*, ed. P. Link et al. (Boulder, CO: Westview Press, 1989), 175–92.

4. Carolyn Hsu, *Creating Market Socialism: How Ordinary People Are Shaping Class and Status in China* (Durham, NC: Duke University Press, 2007), 18–20.

5. Hsu, *Creating Market Socialism*.

6. Dingxin Zhao, *The Power of Tiananmen: State-Society Relations and the 1989 Beijing Student Movement* (Chicago: University of Chicago Press, 2001), 82.

7. Anita Chan, Richard Madsen, and Jonathan Unger, *Chen Village: Revolution to Globalization*, 3rd ed. (Berkeley: University of California Press, 2009), 313–5.

8. David Goodman, *Class in Contemporary China* (Malden, MA: Polity Press, 2014), 79.

9. Xiaowei Zang, "Market Transition, Wealth, and Status Claims," in *The New Rich in China: Future Rulers, Present Lives*, ed. David S. G. Goodman (New York: Routledge, 2008); Osburg, *Anxious Wealth*.

10. Zang, "Market Transition, Wealth, and Status Claims," 56.

11. Mayfair Mei-hui Yang, *Gifts, Favors, and Banquets: The Art of Social Relationships in China* (Ithaca, NY: Cornell University Press, 1994); Mayfair Mei-hui Yang, "The Resilience of *Guanxi* and Its New Deployments: A Critique of Some New *Guanxi* Scholarship," *China Quarterly* 170 (June 2002): 459–76; Yunxiang Yan, *The Flow of Gifts: Reciprocity and Social Networks in a Chinese Village* (Stanford: Stanford University Press, 1996); Yunxiang Yan, *Private Life Under Socialism: Love, Intimacy, and Family Change in a Chinese Village* (Stanford: Stanford University Press, 2002); Thomas Gold, Doug Guthrie, and David Wank, eds., *Social Connections in China: Institutions, Culture, and the Changing Nature of Guanxi* (New York: Cambridge University Press, 2002).

12. Alan Smart, "Gifts, Bribes, and Guanxi: A Reconsideration of Bourdieu's Social Capital," *Cultural Anthropology* 8, no. 3 (1993): 388–408; Frank Pieke, "Bureaucracy, Friends, and Money: The Growth of Capital Socialism in China," *Comparative Studies in Society and History* 37, no. 3 (1995): 494–518; David Wank, *Commodifying Communism: Business, Trust, and Politics in a Chinese City* (New York: Cambridge University Press, 1999); Xin Liu, *The Otherness of Self: A Genealogy of the Self in Contemporary China* (Ann Arbor: University of Michigan Press, 2002); Jaesok Kim, *Chinese Labor in a Korean Factory: Class, Ethnicity, and Productivity on the Shop Floor in Globalizing China* (Stanford: Stanford University Press, 2013).

13. David Wank, "Local State Takeover as Multiple Rent Seeking in Private Business," in *Rent Seeking in China*, ed. T. W. Ngo & Y. Wu (New York: Routledge, 2009), 79–97.

14. Dorothy J. Solinger, "Urban Entrepreneurs and the State: The Merger of State and Society," in *State and Society in China: The Consequences of Reform*, ed. Arthur L. Rosenbaum (Boulder, CO: Westview Press, 1992), 129; Wank, *Commodifying Communism*, 11.

15. Jean-Louis Rocca, "Corruption and Its Shadow: An Anthropological View of Corruption in China," *China Quarterly* 130 (June 1992): 402–16; Yan Sun, *Corruption and Market in Contemporary China* (Ithaca, NY: Cornell University Press, 2004); Alan Smart, "The Strength of Property Rights, Prospects for the Disadvantaged, and Constraints on the Actions of the Politically Powerful in Hong Kong and China," in *Marginalization in Urban China: Comparative Perspectives*, ed. Fulong Wu and Chris Webster (London: Palgrave Macmillan, 2010), 90–111.

16. Rocca, "Corruption and Its Shadow," 403–4. This distinction between "creative" and "predatory" forms of corruption is somewhat difficult to uphold diachronically, however. Networks which helped enable business activities to emerge in the early reform period in many cases evolved into "predatory," monopolistic, vested interests that dominated portions of the economy in subsequent decades.

17. Wank, *Commodifying Communism.*

18. However, in booming areas such as the Pearl River Delta, locals with land rights or shares in collective enterprises benefited far more than the migrant workers who composed the vast majority of the workforce in this area but lacked (and continue to lack) access to basic social services. Chan, Madsen, and Unger, *Chen Village*; Kaxton Siu, "Continuity and Change in the Everyday Lives of Chinese Migrant Factory Workers," *China Journal* 74 (July 2015): 43–65.

19. Sun, *Corruption and Market*; Minxin Pei, *China's Trapped Transition: The Limits of Developmental Autocracy* (Cambridge, MA: Harvard University Press, 2006); Andrew Wedeman, *Double Paradox: Rapid Growth and Rising Corruption in China* (Ithaca, NY: Cornell University Press, 2012).

20. Wank, "Local State Takeover"; Oliver August, *Inside the Red Mansion: On the Trail of China's Most Wanted Man* (New York: Houghton Mifflin, 2007).

21. Qinglian He, "The Origins of Rent-Seeking Behavior in the Chinese Economy," *Chinese Economy* 34, no. 2 (2001): 49–72.

22. Xueliang Ding, "The Illicit Asset Stripping of Chinese State Firms," *China Journal* 43 (2000): 1–28.

23. See Wendong Fan, *My 20 Years with a State Enterprise* (Hong Kong: Globalization Monitor, 2011) for a detailed account of this process at one state-owned factory.

24. For example, during the 2014 corruption investigation of Zhou Yongkang, the *South China Morning Post* linked Zhou and his family to thirty-seven different companies, many registered in North America. See Keira Lu Huang and Laura Zhou, "How Much Wealth Had Zhou Yongkang's Family Amassed Before the Former Security Tsar's Fall?," *South China Morning Post*, August 8, 2014, http://www.scmp.com/news/china/article/1568634/keeping-it-family. The release of the so-called "Panama Papers" from the law firm Mossack Fonseca, which specialized in arranging secretive holding companies, also included the names of several senior officials' family members. Michael Forsythe, "Panama Papers Tie More of China's Elite to Secret Accounts," *New York Times*, April 6, 2016, https://www.nytimes.com/2016/04/07/world/asia/china-panama-papers.html?_r=0.

25. David Barboza and Sharon LaFraniere, "'Princelings' in China Use Family Ties to Gain Riches," *New York Times*, May 17, 2012, http://www.nytimes.com/2012/05/18/world/asia/china-princelings-using-family-ties-to-gain-riches.html.

26. See the example of then-premier Wen Jiabao's family fortune documented in Barboza and LaFraniere, "'Princelings.'" Companies controlled by Wen's relatives invested in Ping An Insurance before its public offering, earning billions.

27. Arthur R. Kroeber, *China's Economy: What Everyone Needs to Know* (Oxford: Oxford University Press, 2016), 204.

28. Barboza and LaFraniere, "'Princelings.'"

29. John Garnaut, "Macquarie's Getting Well Connected in China," *Sydney Morning Herald*, October 2, 2010, http://www.smh.com.au/business/macquaries-getting-well-connected-in-china-20101001-1616u.html. JPMorgan Chase, for example, instituted a "sons and daughters" hiring program for children of China's leaders. This program prompted an investigation by the SEC into violations of the Foreign Corrupt Practices Act in 2013. See Jessica Silver-Greenberg and Ben Protess, "JPMorgan Hiring Put China's Elite on an Easy Track," *New York Times*, August 29, 2013, https://dealbook.nytimes.com/2013/08/29/jpmorgan-hiring-put-chinas-elite-on-an-easy-track/.

30. Wedeman, *Double Paradox.*

31. Wedeman.

32. See Osnos for a vivid illustration of this contracting system at work in the rail ministry. Evan Osnos, "Boss Rail," *New Yorker* (October 22, 2012).

33. Osnos, "Boss Rail."

34. Solinger, "Urban Entrepreneurs"; Wank, *Commodifying Communism.*

35. Xiangwei Wang, "Corruption Trials Expose the Roles of the 'White Gloves' Who Manage the Ill-Gotten Gains," *South China Morning Post*, September 9, 2013, http://www.scmp.com/news/china/article/1306529/corruption-trials-expose-roles-white-gloves-who-manage-ill-gotten-gains.

36. Wang, "Corruption Trials." Similar examples of entrepreneurs acting as "white gloves" for officials include Ding Shumiao, who managed bribes for and supplied mistresses to Liu Zhijun, the former minister of railways, and the Sichuan businessman Wu Bing, who was closely tied to Zhou Yongkang's family.

37. See, for example, the detailed confession of the corrupt official Li Zhen in Yunhua Qiao, *Diyu Menqian: Yu Li Zhen Xing Qian Duihua Shilu* [At the Gates of Hell: A Record of Conversations with Li Zhen Before His Execution] (Beijing: Xinhua Chubanshe, 2004).

38. Daniel Bell, "China's Corruption Clampdown Risks Policy Paralysis," *Financial Times*, May 30, 2017, https://www.ft.com/content/293d3b2a-2f1c-11e7-9555-23ef563ecf9a; Pei, *China's Trapped Transition.*

39. Osburg, *Anxious Wealth.*

40. See Osburg, *Anxious Wealth*, chapter 3.

41. Arlie R. Hochschild, *The Managed Heart: Commercialization of Human Feeling* (Berkeley: University of California Press, 1983).

42. Jane Schneider and Peter Schneider, *Reversible Destiny: Mafia, Antimafia, and the Struggle for Palermo* (Berkeley: University of California Press, 2003), 118. I borrow the term "condition" from Jane and Peter Schneider's description of the Sicilian mafia. The Schneiders describe how the Sicilian mafia strove to create "many stranded relationships of intertwined interest and affect" that transcend "quid pro quo exchanges." Schneider and Schneider, *Reversible Destiny*. This nicely captures the key element of *yingchou*: one doesn't simply want to create a relationship of indebtedness in one's guest but rather to render one's relationship "thick" and imbued with affect. See also Everett Zhang, "Goudui and the State: Constructing Entrepreneurial Masculinity in Two Cosmopolitan Areas of Post-socialist China," in *Gendered Modernities: Ethnographic Perspectives*, ed. D. L. Hodgson (New York: Palgrave, 2001), 235–66.

43. In southeastern coastal areas in particular, these practices are being stripped down to shorter and less elaborate encounters and becoming more transactional. Prices are quoted more openly and readily, and in cases in which bribes or kickbacks are necessary, these are broached more directly, with less of the etiquette and "tact" that accompanied these transactions in the past. See Smart, "Gifts, Bribes, and Guanxi."

44. See Liu-Farrer for an analysis of emigration among China's new rich. Garcia Liu-Farrer, "Migration as Class-based Consumption: The Emigration of the Rich in Contemporary China," *China Quarterly* 226 (2016): 499–518.

45. For example, Lai Changxing, the smuggling tycoon mentioned previously, famously built a private club known as the Red Mansion (*Honglou*) where he entertained government officials with banquets, karaoke, and an on-site brothel. See August, *Inside the Red Mansion*. In Sichuan, where I conducted my research, the gangster-businessman Liu Han, the son of a teacher and a street vendor, built a multi-billion-dollar mining and energy conglomerate due to ties he cultivated with Zhou Bin, the son of Zhou Yongkang, a member of the Politburo Standing Committee. The downfall of Zhou Yongkang in the recent anti-corruption campaign brought down Liu Han as well, who was executed in 2015.

46. See Osburg, *Anxious Wealth*, chapter 5, for a discussion of how women entrepreneurs navigate the masculine entertaining practices and spaces associated with business.

47. One can see the influence of *fuerdai* consumption practices in the changing configuration of high-end nightclubs in China. The dance floors and public spaces where one can mingle with others have gradually shrunk (or disappeared entirely) since the

mid-2000s. Most high-end nightclubs now consist of clusters of tables in which groups of wealthy clubgoers conspicuously order expensive champagne and spend the evening staring at their mobile phones.

48. Some princelings themselves have even publicly stated that they are less corrupt due to the tradition (referred to by one princeling as the "red gene" (*hongse jiyin*)) they inherited from their parents of "frugality" and "placing the people and the nation above all." Quoted in Geremie R. Barmé, "Tyger! Tyger! A Fearful Symmetry," *China Story* (October 16, 2014), https://www.thechinastory.org/2014/10/tyger-tyger-a-fearful-symmetry/. Xi Jinping, himself a member of the red second generation, has been rumored to refer to party elites who are not direct descendants of revolutionary martyrs or founding party members as "shopkeepers' sons" who aren't entitled to rule the PRC. Lily Kuo and Naomi Rovnick, "The New Chinese Leadership: A Guide to China's Men in Black," *Quartz*, November 15, 2012, https://qz.com/27918/chinas-new-leadership-a-guide-to-chinas-men-in-black/.

Urban Polarities

Inequality, Social Mobility, and the Role of the State

David S. G. Goodman

As Wang Feng points out earlier in this volume, the paradox of the rapid economic growth of the People's Republic of China (PRC) over the last four decades is that it has reduced global inequality while increasing inequality dramatically within the country itself. The portrayal of the PRC as one of the most unequal countries in the world is now a well-established theme in writings of all kinds. Often this description emphasizes rural development and rural-urban differences. That perspective is not without considerable justice given that for some time about half of all income inequality has been accounted for by the rural-urban divide.[1]

The contribution of this volume is that it focuses on the more neglected inequality within urban China, and particularly on its extremes. In the process it also moves the discussion away from the bald statistics of income inequality to consider the wider understandings of inequality, the limits to and barriers against upward social mobility, and the role of the state in creating and maintaining stratification. Its central themes are that state policies in the reform era have resulted in the creation of two castes: one extremely wealthy; the other, equally extreme, living in poverty. Government-sponsored unemployment (aka economic readjustment) and state-delivered changes in asset ownership (including, significantly, housing), aided and abetted by China's entry to the World Trade Organization (WTO), have significantly polarized urban China and created family-based separate social structures of wealth, status, and power.

The portrait of urban China that emerges is often not comfortable. There are the obvious images of polarization in wealth, power, and status. In terms of wealth, at one extreme there is not just the existence of exclusive clubs for the possibility of a very rich young man (or rather, more accurately, a young man with a rich father) being able to pay 2.5 million yuan RMB for a night's entertainment (Field and Farrer in chapter 6) but also the description of the country's 200-plus billionaires who together are worth more than Australia's entire gross domestic product. At the other are those who do not even qualify for the compensatory *dibao*

Minimum Livelihood Guarantee provided for people below the official poverty line, which varies with specific localities (Solinger in chapter 3).

In terms of political clout, Li Zhang's description of the relative success (and failure) of different housing communities to defend their homes and their wider environment is telling. The upper-middle-class inhabitants of Riverside Garden in Kunming were able to use their political connections to good effect when the sanctity of their new housing development was threatened. In contrast, the far poorer and considerably more politically unconnected living at the center of old Kunming were essentially powerless as redevelopment swept them aside. The most they could hope for was an occasional act of resistance where one resident held out for a short while before being relocated.

In terms of status, at one extreme there is that section of the elite who can remain untouched by accusations of corruption, while other lesser mortals, albeit still among the privileged and in the elite, bear the brunt of the political campaign (Osburg in chapter 7). At the other extreme are the migrant workers in the cities, very necessary to the running of society and the economy but universally despised by their host society, the majority of whom have little, if any, hope of transcending their current station in life (Cho, Goldstein in chapters 4 and 5).

At the same time, urban China is not a particularly clear concept; instead, it is one that suffers somewhat from boundary maintenance.[2] Urbanization has proceeded apace in the last few decades in two different ways: one is by the administrative expansion of cities to include peri-urban rural areas; the other is through development of new residential, commercial, and industrial urban areas.[3] One result is that while the majority of the population now lives in urban administrative jurisdictions (cities) formally, the majority of the population is still designated as having rural residence.

Paradoxically, the boundaries of urban China are further complicated by the maintenance of the system of household registration. This extremely complex system classifies and divides the entire population according to a range of criteria, some of which carry significant benefits, including access to health and educational services. Starting from the 1950s, household registration was introduced to delineate state support and benefits to different categories of households, and eventually to create population movement control. A major difference has ever since existed between the state benefits provided to urban and rural residents, and there remains a significant gap in entitlements. With changes over the last few decades people can move elsewhere but they may not have access to health and education services without being compelled to pay far beyond their means. Individuals have the right to full civil rights only in the location where their mother was born.[4]

One result is that there are two different working classes, both located in urban China, but only one is regarded (within China) in most ways as being *of* urban China. The first is the former industrial working class, now considerably smaller than was the case before the restructuring of the state sector of the economy set many of them adrift, yet with the rights and benefits of urban life.[5] The second are the migrant workers: former peasants with rural residence who come to urban areas seeking work. Construction, light industry, and the retail sector are significantly dominated by this more recent (post-1980) migrant working class, largely living and working in the cities but barred from full participation.[6] Only rarely have migrant workers gained urban status, and only recently are they (sometimes) included in any calculation of the urban population, and then most usually not in full.

All this is to reinforce the message that urban China is also both complex and necessarily varied. Socioeconomic conditions are dramatically different East to West, North to South. An income of 5,000 RMB a month in Lanzhou, the capital of Gansu Province in northwest China, can lead to a comfortable lifestyle; in Suzhou, in southern Jiangsu Province at the heart of the lower Yangtze Delta, such an income can barely support an independent lifestyle. International economic penetration of local economies is not even across the country any more than is local government's domination of economic development.[7] These complexities then perhaps make it worthwhile to explore the dimensions of inequality, social mobility, and the role of the state in stratification a little further, not least to aid future research. The frequently encountered claim that the well-to-do versus poverty-stricken division of the population is simply one between urban and rural areas, therefore, misses a great deal of real importance.

INEQUALITY

Wang Feng in his chapter in this volume highlights the need to see beyond the statistics on income inequality to understand the impact and consequences of inequality in general. Consumption, as he points out, is another equally important measure. And one might add, the differences in real disposable income, which can be quite significant when regional differences are brought into the calculations, are also not insignificant. From that perspective the calculus of inequality becomes quite complex. It is relatively easy to hypothesize that there will be places where incomes are on average higher but so too is the cost of everyday expenditure. And there are places where incomes are relatively lower, as is the cost of living. Equally, though, there are places where incomes are relatively high and everyday expenditure leaves more real disposable income, and other locations where incomes are (by national average standards) low but everyday living expenses are high. The problem for analysis will come in that while data for income are relatively easily accessible, those for consumption are not.

Certainly, there is generally, when dealing with the issue of inequality in China, an almost obsessive interest in income inequality and in the level of the Gini coefficient of income (in)equality. This index is based on the Lorenz curve, where 0 is perfect equality and 1 is perfect inequality. Since the effective end of state socialism in China, the coefficient has risen from about 0.30 in 1978 to somewhere (according to different calculations) between 0.46 and 0.61 in recent years, though there is evidence it has begun to decline from its heights, as Wang Feng details earlier in this volume.[8] Perhaps defensively the PRC National Bureau of Statistics stopped publishing changes in the Gini coefficient between 2000 and 2013, admitting later this was because of concerns for social stability.[9]

Immeasurability is in many ways the key to understanding the conceptualization of equality in the PRC and certainly its importance in public discourse. In Chinese there is a word for equal (*pingdeng*) which can be used as an adjective. But when it is used strictly as an abstract noun, it brooks no negative: Equality is a spectrum, so there is no inequality, just degrees of equality. When the Chinese Communist Party (CCP) wants to criticize the rank egalitarianism of the Cultural Revolution, it talks about equality using that term. Otherwise, when the Party is being more positive about the need for future change, it talks about equality of opportunity (*gongping*), equity of treatment or fairness. So it was at the Eighteenth CCP Congress in November 2012 when a whole session was devoted to the discussion of a future greater equality in terms of three equalities: of rights, of opportunity, and of rules.

Generally in the scholarly literature the target is on income inequality, in part because of its more ready accessibility as a metric compared to wealth, which in some ways it has become a proxy for. Yet of course the two are different and, especially in terms of the intergenerational transfer of economic inequality, wealth is considerably more important. Again, as Wang Feng points out, this is where housing becomes important since, in China as elsewhere, many people's wealth is tied up in their residential property.

China has extremely high levels of home ownership, or mortgaged ownership, yet there are significant variations in different types of housing and not just between urban and rural areas. The reassignment of state sector housing at the end of the twentieth century has been a major source of wealth inequality. Those with employment within the party-state—whether in CCP institutions or government offices, state-owned enterprises, education, or health activities—have gained dramatically. In the words of Beibei Tang's analysis of the contemporary middle class in China, particularly, but not exclusively, because of this housing redistribution, "the privileged access to the socialist state's distribution practices has contributed more to the emergence of prestigious middle class lifestyle than has the accumulation of wealth."[10] House ownership may be generally high but the better quality housing has gone to those who previously occupied that housing and were given the opportunity to move to ownership.

Taking this issue further, as Tang and others have argued, a crucial source of inequality is occupation "within system" (*tizhinei*) as opposed to extra-system. The system in question is the party-state, its administrative, economic, and social organization interests. Though the state sector of the economy is no longer the majority employer and by far contains the least productive parts of the entire economy, it remains the source of considerable social and economic privilege, along with government offices, the CCP's organization, the educational and health services, for its leaders and managers in particular. The iron rice bowl—the guarantee of a job with income, housing, and welfare for life—may have been smashed for the ordinary workforce with the development of economic reform, but this is not the case for those in leadership and management positions in the party-state. Indeed, it is far from far-fetched to argue that those within the system are the social base of the contemporary elite, whose real disposable income has increased exponentially with the developments of the Reform Era.[11]

These comments point to the interdependence of wealth, power, and status, and by extension to the importance of inequalities in power and status as well as of wealth. Inequalities in political power certainly are not least by reason of the political hierarchy, but it is uncertain whether they have changed fundamentally with the transformations of the last four decades or not. Perhaps the most significant alteration is that the rising force of economic entrepreneurs and activists has been incorporated into the operating system of the party-state.[12] The relationship between the CCP and the state administration remains one in which, unsurprisingly, the former retains the upper hand at national and provincial levels,[13] while at more local levels the picture is more varied, with in some places the development of a more corporate model of local governance obtains.[14]

Inequalities in social status would certainly seem to have increased with economic growth. The last twenty years in particular have seen the development of the public discourse of *suzhi*. This is a word that means "quality," but which has been adopted to talk of human or social quality, and even then the attention is put on very specific social qualities. An individual has *suzhi* by virtue of living an upper- or middle-class lifestyle, by being educated, and by consuming appropriately. Not to have *suzhi* is a mark of distaste offered by the rich and particularly the newly enriched middle classes toward the subordinate classes, and especially the migrant peasant workers who are not "people like us."[15] Despite their role in construction and manufacturing, as well as the service industry, migrant peasant workers are seen as a potential threat to urban middle-class lifestyles. Thus, the use of the term to mark individuals often serves to cement them into places within the social hierarchy, making mobility out of such spaces prohibitively difficult.

Moreover, in addition to essentially class-based inequalities, it would seem that other social inequalities have also increased with the changes of the last four decades, most notably gender inequalities. Fewer women now serve in CCP leadership positions than before, and the elements of positive discrimination that characterized the era of state socialism have been replaced by what Wang Zheng has described as the establishment of a capitalist male-dominated hierarchy of authority.[16]

SOCIAL MOBILITY

Most recent research on social change in China suggests, as does this volume, that upward social mobility is very low, despite expectations to the contrary. The expectation comes from a widespread belief among scholars of modernization that a growing economy will provide opportunities for upward social mobility. This becomes reinforced in particular by the expansion of educational opportunities in China over the last two decades, especially in higher education, where student numbers have increased dramatically from some two million undergraduates in 1998 (when expansion started) to about twenty-five million in 2016. To quote researchers at the Chinese Academy of Social Sciences (CASS) Institute of Sociology:

> The expansion of college enrolment has enabled millions of students to enjoy opportunities for higher education, the opportunities for social mobility have gradually increased and each year the several millions of college graduates directly create a reserve force for the expansion of the middle class characterized by high academic qualifications.[17]

The spread of higher education capacity has also been heralded as providing opportunities for many of those previously excluded or underrepresented in higher education places. The wished-for goal of social engineering in the expansion of higher education is clear:

> a potentially massive middle class is being created through higher education expansion. The expansion allows the new middle class to come from all sectors of the society, broader in scale than ever before and potentially affecting every family and community in China.[18]

Unfortunately the evidence is that these hopes for greater social inclusion have not been realized. On the contrary: higher education expansion has benefited only the already privileged. As Teresa Wright has pointed out, higher education provides the main path to good jobs. Secondary schools provide the access to higher education, and so parents attempt to position themselves through housing and in other ways to ensure their children can attend a school that has a good track record of university entrance.

But as it happens, almost all such schools are located in the neighborhoods of the already wealthy and educated. Even so, admission often also entails payments to the school by parents to ensure their children can enroll.[19] Wright concludes:

> Since the early 1990s in China, more university students have come from financially privileged families who have benefited from economic reform. Fewer qualified students from average and low-income homes have been admitted, and fewer have had the financial capacity to enroll.[20]

The paradox is then clear; to have the opportunity to become middle class in the future, not to mention ever to climb the highest rungs of the ladder, one must come from at least a middle-class background in the first place.

This discussion of higher education and social engineering echoes findings from other research specifically about social mobility. As in other countries, so too in China, there is a high rate of children following a parent (usually the father) into professions such as medicine, law, the military, and even government service.[21] A study from Peking University and the National Bureau of Statistics showed that there is near certainty that a daughter will enter her father's occupation, and a 74 percent certainty that a son will do the same.[22] Hiroshi Sato and Li Shi in their survey of households found that "a class-specific, education-oriented family culture has been shaped as a mixture of, first, family cultural capital inherited from the pre-Maoist era and surfacing again in the post-reform era, and, second, the intergenerational cultural rebound against class-based discrimination."[23]

This image of low if any social mobility is in keeping with comparative research beyond the PRC, but including China, which suggests that generally social mobility is much lower than theorists of modernization have long expounded. One recent piece of research suggested that in most countries the rate of transfer of intergenerational privilege was about 73 percent (that is to say that 73 percent of the population had their level of status, wealth, and political position predetermined by their parents' status, wealth, and political position). In China, according to that study the equivalent rate was even higher (in the first decade of the twenty-first century), at about 84 percent.[24]

On the other hand, and leaving aside exceptions such as world-famous entrepreneurs who have come from humble origins to strut the world stage, there remain some reasons for not accepting an overly rigid account of China's urban social stratification. The first is almost technical. Much of the research (in China and elsewhere) that concludes that there is a high degree of intergenerational transfer of privilege is concerned with studies of the elite. Elite continuation and maintenance of its position is well understood as reproducing itself and taking on only a limited number of new members in every generation and then in a very controlled way. This information reinforces the choice as made in this volume to borrow the term "caste." But how the elite behave is unlikely to be the case for the remaining 95 percent (or more) of the population.

A second reason for interrogating a rigid account of social stratification is the obvious growth in China's intermediate or middle classes in recent decades. The intermediate classes are those who hold their position in society by virtue of their skills, knowledge, and experience (as opposed to their capital, labor, or inherited wealth.) Even as a state socialist political economy, the PRC had a middle class that provided service to the state and to economic enterprises (albeit state-owned), although it was considerably smaller than is now the case and much more limited in its areas of activities. With economic growth and development have come new occupations and professions (most obviously lawyers and financial market workers) and a massive expansion and professionalization of other already established occupations (accountants, business managers, teachers, researchers.)

The size of the middle class in China is notoriously difficult to estimate, with exaggeration a commonplace occurrence. A rough estimate though can be achieved by looking at data produced by the CASS Institute of Sociology to indicate the percentage of the working population engaged in work as professional and technical personnel, or as office workers. According to this source, in 1978, 4.8 percent of the working population might have been considered middle class (3.5 percent were professional and technical staff and 1.3 percent office workers). By 2006, this segment had grown to 13.3 percent (6.3 professional and technical staff, and 7.0 percent office workers).[25]

The third reason for skepticism about an overly rigid account of urban social stratification is the movement of migrant peasant workers into the cities and towns. In 2013 it was estimated that there were some 263 million migrant peasant workers.[26] Not all migrant workers by any means work in towns and cities, and amongst those who do, many are certainly not made to feel that they would be welcome to stay permanently. Nonetheless, scholars believe that some 125 million migrant workers have now settled in urban China for periods of six months or more.[27] Already second-generation "migrant workers" have grown up in cities and towns who have never journeyed back on a regular basis to their parents' rural hometown. Moreover, there are also small towns around the country where migrant peasant workers have been both encouraged to settle and absorbed into urban China.[28]

THE ROLE OF THE STATE

Solinger opens this volume with a discussion of the crucial role of the state in ensuring through the evolution of its development strategy both of the extremes of wealth and poverty found in today's urban China, and the wider polarization of city society. At its greatest extent this has resulted in 0.1 percent of the urban population having a net worth in excess of 10 million USD, while approximately 4 percent of the urban population are counted as living below the level of poverty at which they could receive the Minimum Livelihood Guarantee.

Starting with the decisions of the party-state at the Third Plenum of the Eleventh Central Committee of the CCP at the end of 1978, she outlines how it has been state strategy rather than the market which has driven change at every step. Back in 1978 the policy of opening-up allowed government planning to incentivize new areas of economic activity on a number of repeated occasions. In particular the most important milestones were the introduction of property rights reform in the mid-1990s, the preparation and implementation of China's accession to the WTO, and the restructuring of state-owned enterprises that started at the end of the twentieth century and which made some 60 million workers or so redundant.

The role of the party-state in this way has been as the setter of ideology and strategy; this has been a strategy which has clearly been the major determinant of the polarities that characterize urban China. At the same time, other perspectives on the state may also highlight how it has shaped China's urban stratification and particularly its polarization. One is the role of state administration, through both its actions and, equally as important, its inaction. The other is the posture of the state as a process dominated by a group or groups to serve their own economic and social interests.

The role of the state understood as state administration has also played a critical part in constructing urban China's polarization, especially in the implementation of the post-1978 development strategy, both overall and at each particular stage. At the same time, though, especially at the local level, state administration has taken off in new directions that were not and may still not be part of the recipe entailed in the development strategy.

Perhaps the strongest evidence of this is the emergence of corporatist local governments that essentially run not just their local authority but also the economy under that authority's jurisdiction. In this capacity they operate the economy as either an economic enterprise or as a network of local economic activities, with short-term economic results very much to the fore. Though this was first observed as a rural phenomenon,[29] city governance later developed identically.[30] In this volume, Goldstein's chapter on the actions of local authorities in chasing away migrant workers and their informal waste collection sites, and their suppression of recycling activities, provides ample evidence of the state administration having additional agendas of this kind that clearly reinforce polarization.

At the same time state administration also furthers polarization through its inaction. State administration often does not provide anywhere near adequate "safety nets" or levels of welfare support to ameliorate conditions for those affected by the actions it is taking to reform and restructure the economy. As Solinger's studies of those urban workers with urban household registrations receiving Minimum Livelihood Guarantee or *dibao* (both in this volume and elsewhere) bear ample witness, state administration does not always act and even when it does it provides support too little too late.[31] The situation for migrant peasant workers in the towns and cities (who are at least more usually employed) is necessarily different, though as Cho's investigation of the Foxconn workforce in this volume illustrates, state support is essentially nonexistent. Moreover, migrant workers in towns and cities usually have little or no state support for ensuring healthcare and education for their families.[32]

Finally, there is the role of the state as process for ensuring privilege. The key question here is that of identifying the privileged: In whose economic and social interests has the state come to operate during the last four decades? There has been considerable debate on this matter for some time. At one extreme there is the work of Victor Nee, who has argued for almost thirty years that economic entrepreneurs will replace cadres in local decision-making. Under state socialism, cadres redistributed goods and services for primarily political rather than economic reasons. His argument has been that with reform, redistribution will be replaced as a method of resource allocation by the operation of the market. By 2012 Nee claimed that the market had replaced redistributed power; political capital does not any longer lead to economic success.[33]

Others have contended that the impact of market forces has been more muted, with the influence of the party-state and its participants either continuing to determine or at least remaining dominant in local economic development. Some have even described the emerging political economy as one more characterized by crony capitalism than determined by the operation of the market. Bruce Dickson, for example, has asserted that there is now "a system of interaction between economic and political elites that is based on patrimonial ties and in which success in business is due more to personal contacts in the official bureaucracy than to entrepreneurial skill or merit."[34]

As Li Chunling has noted, the PRC may have capitalists but it is not a political economy run for the benefit of capitalists, or at least not for their benefit as capitalists.[35] This is also clearly one of the conclusions to be drawn from Osburg's chapter in this volume: The ruling class may include the very rich and those who wield political power, but it is an even more limited network of family ties that describes the influence of the even more significant ruling elite. Research by others has highlighted the importance of family not only as of now but over time. In many localities, the same families have dominated the local political economy not just in the reform era but since before 1949, regardless of the apparent political vicissitudes the PRC has experienced.[36] State actions have clearly polarized China's urban society, as this volume has argued. At the same time, there are powerful narrow economic interests at work that have equally as clearly contributed to the creation of one caste and the exclusion of the other, as this book has also demonstrated.

NOTES

1. Jiandong Chen et al., "The Trend of the Gini Coefficient of China" (Working Paper #109, Brooks World Poverty Institute, University of Manchester, Manchester, UK, 2010); Li Shi, Luo Chuliang, and Terry Sicular, "Overview: Income Inequality and Poverty in China, 2002–2007" (Working Paper #2011–10, CIBC Working Paper Series, Department of Economics, University of Western Ontario, London, Ontario, Canada, 2012).

2. Kam Wing Chan, *Cities with Invisible Walls: Reinterpreting Urbanization in Post–1949 China* (Hong Kong: Oxford University Press, 1994).

3. You-tien Hsing, *The Great Urban Transformation: Politics of Land and Property in China* (Oxford: Oxford University Press, 2009).

4. Dorothy J. Solinger, *Contesting Citizenship in Urban China: Peasant Migrants, the State, and the Logic of the Market* (Berkeley: University of California Press, 1999); Kam Wing Chan, "The Chinese Hukou System at 50," *Economic Geography and Economics* 50, no. 2 (2009): 197–221.

5. Dorothy J. Solinger, "*Dibaohu* in Distress: The Meagre Minimum Livelihood Guarantee System in Wuhan," in *China's Changing Welfare Mix: Local Perspectives*, ed. Beatriz Carrillo and Jane Duckett (Abingdon: Routledge, 2011), 36–63; Solinger, "The New Urban Underclass and Its Consciousness: Is It a Class?," *Journal of Contemporary China* 21, no. 78 (2012): 1011–29.

6. Pun Ngai, *Made in China: Women Factory Workers in a Global Workplace* (Durham, NC: Duke University Press, 2005); Eileen Otis, "Labor of Luxury: Gender and Generational Inequality in a Beijing Hotel," in *Creating Wealth and Poverty in Post-Socialist China*, ed. Deborah Davis and Wang Feng (Stanford: Stanford University Press, 2009), 54–68; Pun Ngai and Lu Huilin, "A Culture of Violence: The Labour Subcontracting System and Collective Action by Construction Workers in Post-Socialist China," *China Journal* 64 (July 2010): 143–58.

7. Victor Nee and Sonja Opper, *Capitalism from Below: Markets and Institutional Change in China* (Cambridge, MA: Harvard University Press, 2012); Tony Saich and Biliang Hu, *Chinese Village, Global Market: New Collectives and Rural Development* (New York: Palgrave Macmillan, 2012); David S. G. Goodman, "The Changing Face of China's Local Elite: Elite Advantage and Path Dependence in Business Communities," *Chinese Political Science Review* (October 2017), https://doi.org/10.1007/s41111-017-0083-x.

8. David S. G. Goodman, *Class in Contemporary China* (Cambridge: Polity Press, 2014), 3.

9. Xinhua [New China News Agency in English], "Gini Coefficient Release Highlights China's Resolve to Bridge Wealth Gap," January 21, 2013.

10. Beibei Tang, *China's Housing Middle Class* (Abingdon: Routledge, 2017), 17.

11. Ying Miao, *Being Middle Class in China: Identity, Attitudes and Behaviour* (Abingdon: Routledge, 2016); David S. G. Goodman, "Locating China's Middle Classes: Social Intermediaries and the Party-State," *Journal of Contemporary China* 25, no. 97 (January 2016): 1–17.
12. Minglu Chen, "Local Governance," in *Handbook of the Politics of China*, ed. David S. G. Goodman (Cheltenham: Edward Elgar, 2015), 104–16.
13. Yan Xu and Dali L. Yang, "The Central Government," in Goodman, *Handbook*, 76–94.
14. Nan Lin and Chih-Jou Jay Chen, "Local Elites as Officials and Owners: Shareholding and Property Rights in Daqiuzhuang," in *Property Rights and Economic Reform in China*, ed. Jean Oi and Andrew Walder (Stanford: Stanford University Press, 1999), 145–70.
15. Andrew Kipnis, "Suzhi: A Keyword Approach," *China Quarterly* 186 (2006): 295–313; Ann Anagnost, "From 'Class' to 'Social Strata': Grasping the Social Totality in Reform-Era China," *Third World Quarterly* 29, no. 3 (2008): 497–519.
16. Wang Zheng, "From Xianglin's Wife to the Iron Girls: The Politics of Gender Representation," in Goodman, *Handbook*, 288–309.
17. Hu Jianguo, Li Chunling, and Li Wei, "Social Class Structure," in *Social Structure of Contemporary China*, ed. Lu Xueyi (Singapore: World Scientific Publishing, 2012), 419–20.
18. Lin Jing and Xiaoyan Sun, "Higher Education Expansion and China's Middle Class," in *China's Emerging Middle Class*, ed. Cheng Li (Washington, DC: Brookings Institution, 2010), 222.
19. Ching Kwan Lee, "From Inequality to Inequity: Popular Conceptions of Social (In)justice in Beijing," in Davis and Wang, *Creating Wealth and Poverty*, 220.
20. Teresa Wright, *Accepting Authoritarianism: State-Society Relations in China's Reform Era* (Stanford: Stanford University Press, 2010), 66.
21. Christopher Buckley, "How a Revolution Becomes a Dinner Party: Stratification, Mobility, and the New Rich in Urban China," in *Culture and Privilege in Capitalist Asia*, ed. Michael Pinches (Abingdon: Routledge, 1999), 66.
22. C. H. Gong, A. Leigh, and X. Meng, "Intergenerational Income Mobility in Urban China" (IZA Discussion Paper No. 4811, Institute for the Study of Labor (IZA), Bonn, Germany, March 2010), 16.
23. Hiroshi Sato and Shi Li, "Class Origin, Family Culture, and Intergenerational Correlation of Education in Rural China" (Hi-Stat Discussion Paper Series 007, Hitotsubashi University, Tokyo, Japan, October 2008).
24. Gregory Clark, *The Son Also Rises: Surnames and the History of Social Mobility* (Princeton: Princeton University Press, 2014).
25. Goodman, *Class in Contemporary China*, 60.
26. Xinhua [New China News Agency in English], "Urban Chinese Per Capita Income Grows in 2012," January 18, 2013.
27. Li, Luo, and Sicular, "Overview."
28. Beatriz Carrillo, *Small Town China: Rural Labour and Social Inclusion* (London: Routledge, 2011).
29. Jean C. Oi, "Fiscal Reform and the Economic Foundations of Local State Corporatism," *World Politics* 45, no. 1 (October 1992): 99–126; Oi, "The Role of the Local State in China's Transitional Economy," *China Quarterly* 144 (1995): 1132–49.
30. Jae Ho Chung and Tao-Chiu Lam, eds., *China's Local Administration: Traditions and Changes in the Sub-national Hierarchy* (Abingdon: Routledge, 2010).
31. Dorothy J. Solinger, "Labour Market Reform and the Plight of the Laid-off Proletariat," *China Quarterly* 170 (June 2002): 304–26; Solinger, "The New Crowd of the Dispossessed," in *State and Society in 21st Century China*, ed. Peter Gries and Stanley Rosen (New York: Routledge, 2004), 50–66; Solinger, "Path Dependency Re-examined: Chinese Welfare Policy in the Transition to Unemployment," *Comparative Politics* 38, no. 1 (2005): 83–101; Solinger, "*Dibaohu* in Distress."

32. T. E. Woronov, "Class Consciousness, Service Work: Youth and Class in Nanjing Vocational Secondary Schools," *Journal of Contemporary China* 21 (2012): 779–91.
33. Nee and Opper, *Capitalism from Below*, 255.
34. Bruce Dickson, *Wealth into Power: The Communist Party's Embrace of China's Private Sector* (New York: Cambridge University Press, 2008).
35. Li Chunling, "Sociopolitical Attitude of the Middle Class and the Implications for Political Transition," in *Middle Class China: Identity and Behaviour*, ed. Minglu Chen and David S. G. Goodman (Cheltenham: Edward Elgar, 2013), 12–33.
36. Saich and Hu, *Chinese Village, Global Market*; Lu Peng, "Xin gudian shehui xue zhong de 'a'er jizhi mi': Zhongguo di yi dai zui fuyou siying qiye jia de shehui qiyuan" (The Horatio Alger Myth in Neo-classical Sociology: Origins of the First Generation of Visibly Rich Chinese Private Entrepreneurs) *Xuehai* 3 (2013): 46–61; David S. G. Goodman, "China's Emerging Ruling Class: Power, Wealth, and Status Under Market Socialism," in *Handbook on Class and Social Stratification in China*, ed. Yingjie Guo (Cheltenham: Edward Elgar, 2016), 243–61; Goodman, "The Changing Face."

Selected Bibliography

Cornia, Giovanni Andrea (ed.). *Inequality, Growth, and Poverty in an Era of Liberalization and Globalization*. Oxford: Oxford University Press, 2004.

Davis, Deborah, and Wang Feng. "Poverty and Wealth in Postsocialist China: An Overview." In *Creating Wealth and Poverty in Postsocialist China*, edited by Deborah Davis and Wang Feng, 3–19. Palo Alto: Stanford University Press, 2009.

Hu, Anning, and Jacob Hibel. "Changes in College Attainment and the Economic Returns to a College Degree in Urban China, 2003–2010: Implications for Social Equality." *Social Science Research* 44 (2014): 173–86.

Meng, Xin. "Wealth Accumulation and Distribution in Urban China." *Economic Development and Cultural Change* 55, no. 4 (2007): 761–91.

Nee, Victor. "A Theory of Market Transition: From Redistribution to Markets in State Socialism." *American Sociological Review* 54 (1989): 663–81.

Li, Jun. "Job Mobility in Post-reform Urban China." *Chinese Sociological Review* 45, no. 4 (2013): 81–109.

Li, Lulu, and Zhu Bin. "Patterns of Intergenerational Mobility in Contemporary China." *Chinese Journal of Social Sciences* 5 (2015): 40–58. (in Chinese)

Li Shi, Hiroshi Sato, and Terry Sicular. *Rising Inequality in China: Challenges to a Harmonious Society*. Cambridge: Cambridge University Press, 2013.

Li Shi and Haiyuan Wan. "Evolution of Wealth Inequality in China." *China Economic Journal* 8, no. 3 (2015): 264–87.

Naughton, Barry. "Is China Socialist?" *Journal of Economic Perspectives* 31, no. 1 (2017): 3–24.

Pei, Minxin. *China's Crony Capitalism: The Dynamics of Regime Decay*. Cambridge, MA: Harvard University Press, 2016.

Piketty, Thomas. *Capital in the Twenty-First Century*. Cambridge, MA: Harvard University Press, 2014.

Riskin, Carl, Zhao Renwei, and Li Shi. *China's Retreat from Equality*. Armonk: M. E. Sharpe, 2001.

Shen, Ke, Wang Feng, and Cai Yong. "Benevolent State against Unjust Society? Inequalities in Public Transfers in China." *Chinese Sociological Review*, forthcoming.

Shi, Faqi. "Analysis of the Macro Structure of Income Distribution in China." In *China Faces Inequality: Studies in Income Distribution*, edited by Song Xiaowu, Wang Tianfu, Li Shi, and Wang Feng, 9–34. Beijing: Social Sciences Academic Press of China, 2013.

Tam, Tony, and Jin Jiang. "Divergent Urban-Rural Trends in College Attendance: State Policy Bias and Structural Exclusion in China." *Sociology of Education* 88, no. 2 (2015): 160–80.

Treiman, Donald. "Trends in Educational Attainment in China." *Chinese Sociological Review* 45, no. 3 (2013): 3–25.

Walder, Andrew G. "Social Change in Post-revolution China." *Annual Review of Sociology* 15 (1989): 405–24.

Walder, Andrew G. "Markets and Inequality in Transitional Economies: Toward Testable Theories. *American Journal of Sociology* 101 (1996): 1060–73.

Wang, Feng. "Housing Improvement and Distribution in Urban China: Initial Evidence from China's 2000 Census." *China Review* 3, no. 2 (2003): 121–43.

Wang, Feng. *Boundaries and Categories: Rising Inequality in Post-Socialist Urban China*. Stanford: Stanford University Press, 2008.

Wang, Feng. "The End of 'Growth with Equity'? Economic Growth and Income Inequality in East Asia." *Asia Pacific Issues,* no. 101 (2011). Honolulu: The East West Center.

Whyte, Martin K. "Social Trends in China: The Triumph of Inequality?" In *Modernizing China,* edited by A. Barnett and R. Clough. Boulder: Westview, 1986.

Whyte, Martin K. *One Country, Two Societies: Rural-Urban Inequality in Contemporary China.* Cambridge: Harvard University Press, 2010.

Whyte, Martin K. "Soaring Income Gaps: China in Comparative Perspective." *Daedalus* 142, no. 2 (2014): 39–52.

Whyte, Martin K. "China's Dormant and Active Social Volcanoes." *The China Journal* 75 (2016): 9–37.

Wu, Xiaogang. "Economic Transition, School Expansion and Educational Inequality in China, 1990–2000." *Research in Social Stratification and Mobility* 28 (2010): 91–108.

Wu, Yuxiao. "Social Connections, First Job Seeking, and Occupational Mobility." *Sociological Res*earch 5 (2011): 128–52. (in Chinese)

Wu, Yuxiao. "Educational Tracking and Stratification in China." *Sociological Research* 3, (2013): 179–202. (in Chinese)

Xie Yu and Xiang Zhou. "Income Inequality in Today's China." *Proceedings of the National Academy of Sciences* 111, no. 19 (2014): 6928–33.

Xie Yu and Yongai Jin. "Household Wealth in China." *Chinese Sociological Review* 47, no. 3 (2015): 203–29.

Yang Wenhui and Chen Ling. "Political Capital and Intergenerational Mobility: Evidence from Elite College Admissions in China." *Chinese Journal of Sociology* 2, no. 2 (2016): 194–213.

Yeung, Wei-jun Jean. "Higher Education Expansion and Social Stratification in China." *Chinese Sociological Review* 45, no. 4 (2013): 54–80.

Zhou, Xueguang. "Economic Transformation and Income Inequality in Urban China: Evidence from Panel Data." *American Journal of Sociology* 105, no. 4 (2000): 1135–74.

Index

About the Contributors

Mun Young Cho is associate professor in the Department of Cultural Anthropology at Yonsei University, South Korea. She is the author of *The Specter of "The People": Urban Poverty in Northeast China* (2013). Cho is currently studying the problematic of "the Chinese social," focusing on the landscapes of social governance and social innovation that loom large in Shenzhen. Her article related to this theme is "Unveiling Neoliberal Dynamics: Government Purchase (goumai) of Social Work Services in Shenzhen's Urban Periphery" in *China Quarterly* (May 2017).

James Farrer is professor of sociology and director of the Graduate Program in Global Studies at Sophia University in Tokyo. His research focuses on cities in East Asia, including projects on sexuality, nightlife, expatriate communities, and urban food cultures. He is the author of *Opening Up: Youth Sex Culture and Market Reform in Shanghai* (2002) and *Shanghai Nightscapes: A Nocturnal Biography of a Global City* (with Andrew David Field, 2015), and editor of *Globalization and Asian Cuisines*. He has lived in Asia more than two decades, both in Shanghai and Tokyo.

Andrew David Field is associate dean for undergraduate programs at Duke Kunshan University. He has resided in China since 2007 and has administered and directed educational programs in China for Dartmouth College, CIEE, Boston University, and Hult International Business School. He has published three books: *Shanghai's Dancing World: Cabaret Culture and Urban Politics, 1919–1954* (2010); *Mu Shiying: China's Lost Modernist* (2014); and *Shanghai Nightscapes: A Nocturnal Biography of a Global City* (with James Farrer, 2015). Andrew is also a producer and director of independent documentary films on China.

Joshua Goldstein is associate professor of modern Chinese history at the University of Southern California. His main areas of interest are the histories of waste and recycling in China and the field of discard studies in the context of China and the global economy. His books include *Drama Kings: Players and Publics in the Re-creation of Peking Opera, 1870–1937* (2007); *Everyday Modernity in China* (with Madeleine Yue Dong, 2006); and *Visualizing Modern China: Image, History, and Memory, 1750–Present* (with James A. Cook, Matthew D. Johnson, and Sigrid Schmalzer, 2015).

David S. G. Goodman is professor of China studies at Xi'an Jiaotong-Liverpool University, Suzhou. His research concentrates on social and political change in China at the local level. His most recent publications include *Class in Contemporary China* (2014) and "The Changing Face of China's Local Elite: Elite Advantage and Path Dependence in Business Communities" in the *Chinese Political Science Review* (September 2017).

John Osburg is associate professor of anthropology at the University of Rochester. His research interests include morality, corruption, luxury consumption, gender and sexuality, and spirituality in contemporary China. He is the author of *Anxious Wealth: Money and Morality Among China's New Rich* (2013), which examines the intersection of China's market reforms with the local moral worlds and social networks of entrepreneurs and government officials in southwest China.

Dorothy J. Solinger is professor emerita of political science at the University of California, Irvine. She has authored six books, including *Contesting Citizenship in Urban China: Peasant Migrants, the State, and the Logic of the Market* (1999) and *States' Gains, Labor's Losses: China, France, and Mexico Choose Global Liaisons, 1980–2000* (2009), edited another six, and published nearly one hundred articles and book chapters. She served as chair of the China and Inner Asia Council (CIAC) of the Association for Asian Studies (AAS) on two occasions and has held numerous fellowships. Her current work is on the urban poor and the assistance program for its members.

Wang Feng is professor of sociology at the University of California, Irvine, and professor of sociology and demography at Fudan University in China. His main research interests include global social and demographic changes, comparative population and social history, and social inequality, with a focus on China. His recent work on social inequality in China includes *Boundaries and Categories, Rising Inequality in Post-Socialist Urban China* (2008), *Creating Wealth and Poverty in Postsocialist China* (coedited with Deborah Davis, 2009), and *China Faces Inequality: Studies in Income Distribution* (coedited, 2013).

Li Zhang is professor of anthropology at the University of California, Davis. Her research concerns the cultural, spatial, political, and psychological repercussions of market reforms and postsocialist transformations in China. She is the author of two award-winning books: *Strangers in the City: Reconfigurations of Space, Power, and Social Networks Within China's Floating Population* (2002) and *In Search of Paradise: Middle-Class Living in a Chinese Metropolis* (2010), and coeditor of *Privatizing China, Socialism from*

Afar (2008). Her current project explores an emerging psychological counseling movement and how it reshapes Chinese people's understandings of selfhood, well-being, and governing.

www.ingramcontent.com/pod-product-compliance
Ingram Content Group UK Ltd.
Pitfield, Milton Keynes, MK11 3LW, UK
UKHW012040150926
475560UK00001B/98

9 781538 116470